International and Comparative

The International Labour Organization

The International Labour Organization was founded in 1919 to promote social justice and, thereby, to contribute to universal and lasting peace. Its tripartite structure is unique among agencies affiliated to the United Nations; the ILO's Governing Body includes representatives of government, and of employers' and workers' organizations. These three constituencies are active participants in regional and other meetings sponsored by the ILO, as well as in the International Labour Conference – a world forum which meets annually to discuss social and labour questions.

Over the years the ILO has issued for adoption by Member States a widely respected code of international labour Conventions and Recommendations on freedom of association, employment, social policy, conditions of work, social security, industrial relations and labour administration, among others.

The ILO provides expert advice and technical assistance to Member States through a network of offices and multidisciplinary teams in over 40 countries. This assistance takes the form of labour rights and industrial relations counselling, employment promotion, training in small business development, project management, advice on social security, workplace safety and working conditions, the compiling and dissemination of labour statistics, and workers' education.

International and Comparative Labour Law

Current challenges

Arturo Bronstein

© International Labour Organization 2009

First published 2009 by
PALGRAVE MACMILLAN

ISBN 978-0-230-22822-1   ISBN 978-0-230-30076-7 (eBook)
DOI 10.1007/978-0-230-30076-7

and

International Labour Office
CH-1211 Geneva 22, Switzerland

ISBN 978-92-2-121202-7 paperback

The designations employed in ILO publications, which are in conformity with United Nations practice, and the presentation of material therein do not imply the expression of any opinion whatsoever on the part of the International Labour Office concerning the legal status of any country, area or territory or of its authorities, or concerning the delimitation of its frontiers.

The responsibility for opinions expressed in studies and other contributions rests solely with their authors, and publication does not constitute an endorsement by the International Labour Office of the opinions expressed in them.

Reference to names of firms and commercial products and processes does not imply their endorsement by the International Labour Office, and any failure to mention a particular firm, commercial product or process is not a sign of disapproval.

Palgrave Macmillan in the UK is an imprint of Macmillan Publishers Limited, registered in England, company number 785998 of Houndmills, Basingstoke, Hampshire RG21 6XS. Palgrave Macmillan in the US is a division of St Martin's Press LLC 175 Fifth Avenue, New York, N.Y. 10010.

PALGRAVE MACMILLAN is the global academic imprint of the above companies and has companies and representatives throughout the world. Palgrave® and Macmillan® are registered trademarks in the United States, United Kingdom, Europe and other countries.

This book is printed on paper suitable for recycling and made from fully managed and sustained forest sources. Logging, pulping and manufacturing processes are expected to conform to the environmental regulations of the country of origin.

A catalogue record for this book is available from the British Library.

A catalog record for this book is available from the Library of Congress.

10 9 8 7 6 5 4 3 2 1
18 17 16 15 14 13 12 11 10 09

Contents

Tables

Boxes

Foreword

Some thirty years ago it was common wisdom that labour law was part of an overall system of social justice and therefore deeply embedded in the concept of industrial democracy. At that point we were firmly convinced that economic prosperity would continue, that the state would carry on putting social equity at the top of its list of priorities, that there would always be jobs available for all those who wished to work, and that remuneration for work would increase. Our reasoning took us almost inevitably to the conclusion that labour law was destined to develop almost in a geological manner: changes in labour legislation came about as layers of new and stronger rights were added to existing ones, which we presumed had been definitively acquired for workers and for that reason were irrevocable and non-negotiable.

It hardly seems necessary to add that since then the world has changed a great deal and the evolution of labour law has not followed our expectations. On the contrary, it is undeniable that at the beginning of the twenty-first century labour law finds itself in deep crisis and faces a number of serious challenges.

Despite these difficulties, there are also reasons to feel encouraged. There is increasingly a tendency to defend not only labour law but the social progress that was made overall in the twentieth century. Moreover, in the last three decades, social dialogue, freedom of association and other trade union rights have unquestionably been advanced more than they have suffered setbacks in most regions of the world, and the influence of apartheid on labour law has now disappeared. Progress has also been made in the protection of the fundamental rights of the individual at the workplace as well as in society.

This volume represents an important contribution to the comparative analysis of labour law, providing an international and comparative account of recent developments and a clear overview of the major issues. It also advances ideas for a new dynamic balance to accommodate the evolution of labour law in the twenty-first century and an agenda of possible solutions to current challenges.

Its author, Arturo Bronstein, is Secretary General of the International Society for Labour and Social Security Law and a former Senior Labour Law Policy Adviser with the International Labour Office. The study has relied on papers prepared by Professors Paul Benjamin (South Africa), Sean Cooney (Australia), Mary Cornish (Canada), and Sir Bob Hepple (United Kingdom), to whom the author and the International Labour Office (ILO) express their sincere gratitude.[1] The book has also drawn on a number of important reports that were submitted to the XVIIth and XVIIIth World Congress of Labour and Social Security Law, held respectively in Montevideo (2003) and in Paris (2006), thus continuing a long-standing tradition of collaboration between the ILO and the International Society for Labour and Social Security Law. We also acknowledge with gratitude the authors of these reports.[2]

Giuseppe Casale, Chief, Social Dialogue, Labour Law and Labour
Administration Branch
Professor Kazuo Sugeno, President, International Society for Labour and
Social Security Law

---

1 These contributions were on the following subjects:
- Paul Benjamin, *The challenge of labour law reform in South Africa.*
- Sean Cooney, *Trends in labour law in Asia and the Pacific.*
- Mary Cornish, *Securing sustainable human rights justice for workers.*
- Bob Hepple, *Labour laws in the context of globalization*, with acknowledgement to the author and publisher of Hepple, *Labour laws and global trade* (Oxford, Hart Publishing, 2005), on which this paper is based.
2 In particular, to the authors of the general reports: Professor Fernando Valdés dal Re, *Labour law and the fundamental rights of the workers* (Montevideo, 2003); Professor Lance Compa, *Trade liberalization and labour law* (Paris, 2006); and Professors Raffaele de Luca Tamajo and Adalberto Perulli, *Labour law and decentralization of production* (Paris, 2006).

Table of cases

Table of legislation

International conventions

Argentina

Australia

Belgium

Brazil

Bulgaria

Cambodia

Canada

Chile

Colombia

Costa Rica

Denmark

EC

Finland

France

Namibia

New Zealand

Panama

Poland

Russian Federation

South Africa

Chapter 1

Labour law at a crossroads

Rights are not eternal realities that exist out of space and time. They are social phenomena which must be considered in a particular historical context, and it is within this context that their birth, development and vicissitudes should be analysed. History is made up of the interaction of many forces – social, economic, political, cultural and ideological – to which can be added the often crucial role played by some outstanding leaders and personalities. Any alteration in these forces can and frequently does lead to a change in the law. This book examines some of the key changes that labour law has undergone in the last three decades in the light of overall societal changes, and the challenges it now meets at the beginning of the twenty-first century. Labour law, like more general social regulation, undoubtedly epitomizes one of the greatest social achievements of the twentieth century. However, it comes as no surprise that today it stands at a crossroads.

Labour law's origins and influences

It is generally accepted that, apart from a few albeit important contributions from other regions,[1] the core of the twentieth century's labour law was first elaborated in Western Europe, as a reaction to both the excesses of the Industrial Revolution and the abuse of rights arising out of nineteenth-century civil law. At the heart of labour law is the acknowledgement that strict civil law equality can lead to unacceptable situations when the parties to a contract where labour is traded for wages do not have comparable bargaining strength. Labour law deviates from the basic civil law and Roman law assumption that no party can complain of unfairness in the terms of a contract which it has voluntarily agreed to become a party to. Instead, the goal of labour law is to ensure that no employer can be allowed to impose – and no worker can be obliged to accept – conditions of work which fall below

---

1 For example, labour and social rights were embedded for the first time in the Constitution of Mexico, 1917. It is very likely that this influenced the ILO Constitution of 1919. In Europe it was the Weimar Republic's Constitution (Germany) which first enshrined social and labour rights in 1919.

what is understood to be a decent threshold in a given society at a given time. Thus labour law is not just a means of regulating the exchange between labour and capital as civil or commercial law does with respect to civil or commercial contracts; rather, it is a means (indeed it is the principal means) to operationalize what the International Labour Organization (ILO) nowadays defines as 'decent work', which, in addition to protecting the worker, calls for the respect of democracy in overall labour relations, including at the workplace.

The body of Western European labour law was expanded considerably throughout most of the twentieth century in both quantitative and qualitative terms. While labour law initially aimed at protecting the industrial worker, its scope was rapidly broadened so as to encompass non-industrial work, agricultural work and the civil service. By the second half of the twentieth century, virtually all workers who undertook work or provided services in an employment relationship or under a public law appointment fell under the protection of labour law or a comparable civil service statute. The content of labour law was also enriched. At the very beginning, only a handful of issues such as limits on the hours of work, the employment of women and minors, and industrial accidents and occupational diseases were targeted by state regulation. From the 1930s onwards new issues began to be addressed, including the employment contract, pay and conditions of work, workers' rights at the workplace, and last but not least the organization of workers' representation at the workplace and at industrial and national levels, including the right to industrial action.[2] Both before and shortly after the Second World War, detailed legislation was enacted in many countries with a view to consolidating and strengthening already existing workers' rights.

The cornerstone of this legal construction was the employment contract, which provided the legal foundation for the employment relationship; those workers who performed work or provided services under an employment relationship were protected by labour law, while those who worked outside the scope of an employment relationship were left unprotected. Indeed, in Western Europe as in North America an overwhelming number of the

---

2 Some Western European countries departed from this model. For example, labour regulation in the Nordic countries, especially Denmark, has traditionally relied on collective bargaining rather than on statutory law. Also, in some countries, collective bargaining rights and the right to industrial action can be denied to certain categories of civil servants, like *Beamte* employees in Germany and federal civil servants in the United States. It should also be recalled that unlike individual employment relations, which follow comparable patterns in a great majority of countries, collective labour rights and industrial relations practices tend to vary widely from one country to another.

economically active population worked within an employment relationship so that the majority of workers fell within the scope of labour law or of a comparable civil service statute. As will be discussed later on, one of the greatest challenges of today's labour law stems precisely from the fact that an increasing number of workers perform work or provide services beyond the scope of an employment relationship, and are consequently denied labour law protection.

Western European labour law patterns have been endorsed (or, according to some critics, 'copied and pasted') in other regions of the world such as English-speaking and French-speaking Africa and Latin America, although it is undisputed that in the greater part of these regions wage employment is not the prevailing form of work organization. To a lesser extent, these patterns have also been followed in the law and practice of Japan and many Asian countries. Furthermore, the influence of Western European labour law has been no less noteworthy in international law: while ILO standards ought to reflect universal common wisdom, the formulation of most ILO Conventions and Recommendations has very largely drawn and continues to draw inspiration from Western European law and practice. More recently, European Community law and the European Union Member States have also been influential in the elaboration of ILO standards.[3] By contrast, the United States has built up a quite different set of labour laws and labour relations patterns, which reflect national values and the common law legal tradition.[4] Some elements of the US pattern (for example the concepts of 'bargaining unit', the 'duty to bargain' and 'unfair labour practice') are, however, noteworthy in a few other countries, such as Canada, the Dominican Republic, the Republic of Korea, Panama and the Philippines.

---

3 For example, EC Directive 75/129/EEC on collective redundancies and EC Directive 80/987/EEC on the protection of employees in the event of the insolvency of their employer have deeply influenced, respectively, the ILO Termination of Employment Convention, 1982 (No. 158), and the Protection of Workers' Claims (Employer's Insolvency) Convention, 1992 (No. 173). At the ILO Conference, where ILO standards are elaborated by tripartite consensus, it is widely acknowledged that the EU Member States acting as a regional group (with, however, the frequent abstention of the United Kingdom) often play a decisive role, with many of their proposals reflecting what is held to be common wisdom in the EU.

4 Although the United Kingdom has a common law system, following the country's accession to the European Economic Community (later the European Community and now the European Union) in 1973, British labour and employment law has been very deeply influenced by the legal approaches of continental Europe. Today, statutory regulation is the main source of labour law in the United Kingdom, though it is applied in light of common law interpretative criteria; thus statutory rights are held to work like immunities and exceptions to common law rather than as positive rights.

Sources of labour law

Contemporary labour law draws on different sources, which can be divided into five categories.

Constitutions

First, mention should be made of constitutional provisions that formally state employees' individual and collective labour rights. This approach was initiated in Mexico in 1917: while nineteenth-century political constitutions were committed to protect political rights as well as a number of fundamental individual freedoms such as property rights and freedom of trade, the Mexican Constitution was innovative in that for the first time ever it also enshrined workers' and social rights. Thus the Mexican Constitution initiated what is known as social constitutionalism (*constitucionalismo social* in Spanish), an approach which was later followed in most Latin American countries as well as in many countries in other regions, though generally with less detail. Typically, national constitutions provide for a number of fundamental workers' rights such as freedom of association, including collective bargaining and the right to strike, equal pay and equal treatment of men and women, non-discrimination in employment and occupation on grounds such as colour, race, social origin, religion or political opinion, prohibition of child labour and prohibition of forced labour. Some constitutions add provisions relating to protection against unfair dismissal and limits on the hours of work. However, not all constitutional texts include labour and social provisions, and some countries, such as the United Kingdom, New Zealand and Israel, do not even have a written constitution.

Statutory regulations

A second source is made up of statutory regulations; these take the form of laws, which can be further developed through secondary regulation such as decrees and other regulatory orders. Apart from a few exceptions – most notably Belgium and Denmark (which have traditionally relied strongly on collective bargaining), and until recently Australia and New Zealand (where arbitration awards have for many years been the major source of labour regulation) – statutory regulation in most countries is actually the most important source of labour law. Although statutory regulation as a source of labour law is less prestigious in the United States than collective agreements, it should be borne in mind that less than 15 per cent of the workforce in the United States is at present covered by a collective agreement. It follows that statutory regulation is in practice the most important source of labour law for at least the remaining 85 per cent of the workforce in that country.

Collective agreements

Collective agreements concluded by both sides of industry through negotiation are a third source of labour regulation. While collective agreements are similar to private-law contracts in their form, their effects are quite different from those of civil or commercial contracts under civil law or common law. Indeed, in comparative law and practice there is a wide diversity of collective bargaining patterns. Thus, depending on the country, collective agreements can apply to a given enterprise or an establishment or to a whole industry or a branch of activity. In addition, collective agreements can have regional scope; for example metal trades agreements generally cover a *Land* in Germany or a state in Brazil. Other agreements can have nationwide coverage. For example, the chemical industry in Spain and the textile industries in Mexico both negotiate national agreements. Industry, branch or sectoral bargaining is a key feature in most Western European labour law and industrial relations systems, as it is in Argentina and Brazil, while local bargaining – at the plant, the factory or the company level – is the prevailing pattern when not the exclusive bargaining level in Canada, Japan, the United States, most Latin American countries and many but not all of the countries of Central and Eastern Europe. In a number of other countries the collective bargaining process takes place at different levels (and is referred to as 'multi-level bargaining'); for example, in France and Italy workers can be covered by an agreement applying specifically to their enterprise and at the same time by a higher-level agreement which has been concluded at the industry, the sectoral or the branch level. In addition, inter-professional bargaining is an important negotiation pattern in some countries. In France, for example, a number of social issues, such as unemployment insurance and training, are addressed by inter-professional agreements, which are signed by the workers' and the employers' umbrella organizations. Likewise, a number of Francophone countries in Africa and some States of the former Yugoslavia used to have a general collective agreement that superseded their labour codes. Mention should also be made of inter-professional bargaining at the national level in Belgium, within the framework of the National Council for Labour (Conseil National du Travail), which is a key feature of that country's industrial relations. Agreements concluded within the National Council for Labour have legal effects that are comparable to those of statutory regulation.

The Nordic countries' practice (which also exists in other countries such as Ireland and Spain) of negotiating national-level framework agreements also deserves attention. This practice consists of agreeing upon a common framework for pay negotiations and industrial relations, which are to be further negotiated at the sectoral or company level.

Last but certainly not least, a distinct European Union level of collective bargaining has developed recently, under the form of framework agreements concluded by the European-level workers' and employers' organizations. Some of these agreements, like the Telework Agreement of 2002 and the Agreement on Harassment and Violence at Work, concluded in 2007, are addressed to the national relevant workers' and employers' organizations, which take up their implementation; yet a number of other framework agreements, like those on parental leave (1996), part-time work (1997), and fixed-term work (1999), have been further endorsed by the European Council, in the form of EC Directives addressed to the Member States for further transposition into national law.

The legal effects of collective agreements also vary depending upon the different national regulatory frameworks and industrial relations practices. Thus, in a number of countries (for example the Scandinavian countries), collective agreements are binding on the parties to the collective bargaining only and their respective members; however, employers who do not belong to an employers' organization can be bound by the collective agreement applicable in their respective branch or industry if they have signed a tie-in agreement (*hängavtal*) with a local trade union. In the Scandinavian countries, only union members are covered by a collective agreement, which has the effect of encouraging workers to unionize and contributes to explaining the high rates of unionization in these countries.

The Nordic practice is, however, in sharp contrast with that of some other countries such as Belgium, France, Germany, Portugal or Spain, where collective agreements can be made applicable to third parties, i.e. non-unionized workers and employers who have not been represented at the bargaining table, provided the agreement has been extended by the administrative authority through a decree of extension. Also, in Argentina or Brazil, a branch-level or an industry-wide agreement will automatically apply to all employers and workers included within its scope of application. In contrast, in the United Kingdom and some other countries which have drawn on the British tradition, collective agreements are not legally binding and cannot be enforced before a court or a tribunal. However, collectively agreed terms and conditions of employment can be transposed into individual letters of appointment, thus creating rights and obligations which can be enforced before a court like any civil law contract.

International law

A fourth source of labour law is made up of international law, such as ILO Conventions, and more recently by European Community law (EC law) in respect to the 27 Members of the European Union. ILO Conventions are binding on the ILO Members only on ratification, and the extent to which they can be used in individual cases depends on the legal system of each country. Ratified ILO Conventions can be directly applicable in individual litigation in a monist system (for example, France, Spain and most Latin American countries), while they need to be further implemented by national law in dualist systems (for example Australia, Canada, Scandinavian countries, the United Kingdom and the United States). By contrast, EC law (EC Regulations and Directives) is binding on all of the EU Member States, for once adopted by the legislative bodies of the European Community it does not need ratification.

Case law

A fifth source of labour law is case law developed by national tribunals and sometimes by international tribunals too, such as the European Court of Justice or the European Court of Human Rights. Case law can have a far-reaching influence in labour–management relations. For example, in Japan, for many years, protection against dismissal was based on case law only, not on statutory regulation. Typically, case law is very important in crucial industrial relations issues such as the right to strike in those countries, such as Germany and Spain, which have refrained from addressing this right in statutory regulation. We can also add, then, that the power of the judiciary to interpret the law can have a potentially significant impact on the effectiveness of labour law. For example, in determining who is an employee, and thus demarcating the actual scope of the law, the courts may give a wider or narrower coverage to labour law.

Finally, some countries have a tradition of establishing terms and conditions of employment through arbitration awards. Until recently this was a distinctive pattern in Australian and New Zealand labour law, but nowadays such industrial awards appear to be no longer used. Arbitration awards still have importance in some countries, as they can be used to settle collective disputes.

We have looked at the broad patterns of influence shaping labour law over time, as well as the five major sources of labour regulation, and the assumption that labour law is or has been very largely Eurocentric can be seen, at least in part, to be accurate. It is therefore important to address some of the factors which in the second part of the twentieth century have strongly determined the expansion and enrichment of labour law in many Western European countries: essentially, economic growth, welfare state policies, labour market conditions, technological and organizational patterns, the international economy and the overall political situation.

The labour law model from 1945 to 1975

The three decades that elapsed between 1945 and 1975 are often known as the Golden Age of Capitalism and frequently referred to in the Francophone world as 'The Thirty Glorious Years' after the famous essay, *Les Trente Glorieuses*, by French economist and sociologist Jean Fourastié.[5] While Fourastié's essay focused on French society, the gist of his analysis can apply in most cases to many other Western European countries. These years were characterized by three decades of unprecedented growth, which were very largely fuelled by post-Second World War reconstruction. A no less important contributory factor to Western European growth was the establishment of the Common Market under the Treaty of Rome in 1957, and the further development and enlargement of the European Economic Community. In addition to enlarging the markets, thus fuelling growth, the Treaty of Rome brought political stability and prospects for long-lasting peace in Europe, which in turn encouraged long-term investment and further growth.

At the time, neo-Keynesianism was the prevailing economic and social ideology. This meant that public policies were committed to strengthening the welfare state and promoting full employment. There was a shortage of workers at that time, something which led many Western European countries to open the door to an influx of migrant workers, and there was a sharp increase in female employment during this period. In addition, economies tended to be industry-based; the industrial paradigm consisted of a large industrial plant employing thousands of workers, all with the same employer; work processes were for the most part labour-intensive, and Fordism was the prevailing organizational pattern.[6] These features also determined the emergence of a strong trade union movement.

Two other elements came to underpin growth and prosperity in this period. First, until the Kippur–Ramadan War of October 1973, Western growth relied on the availability of plentiful and cheap energy. Secondly, international competition was restricted by customs duties and other apparent or disguised obstacles. Moreover, top-level production was restricted mostly to countries that shared comparable labour standards and labour costs, while low-wage and low-productivity countries were mostly raw mate-

---

5 Jean Fourastié, *Les Trente Glorieuses* (Paris, les Editions Fayard, 1979).

6 The adjective *Fordist* refers to a large industrial business engaging in mass production based on job specialization and competencies and pyramidal management (i.e. a hierarchical structure of labour, the separation of product design and manufacture). Fordist enterprises tend to integrate both core and ancillary activities within a unified structure under a single management. It is assumed that most if not all of the workers who work in a Fordist enterprise are in an employment relationship with that enterprise.

rial and bottom-level production providers. The term 'industrialized world' was applied to Japan, North America and Western Europe, while most other countries belonged either to the 'developing world' or to the group of countries behind the Iron Curtain. Thus labour costs did not play a significant role in international trade competition, for there was virtually no competition between high-wage and low-wage countries and, unlike today, offshoring of industries was all but unknown.

This panorama should be completed with some reference to the overall political environment. In the aftermath of the Second World War, most Western European countries (and after Franco's death in 1975, all of them) endorsed political multi-party democracy, which in all cases was accompanied by strong popular participation. This political choice should be assessed in the context of the Cold War environment, which meant that the market economy was not only challenged by the Soviet Union and other communist countries but also confronted internally by national Communist parties, which, in countries such as France or Italy, often relied on strong support from the major trade union confederations. For political democracies, then, it was indispensable to provide evidence that market economies could be both economically efficient and socially advanced. Thus the *social market economy model* was developed, which to a large extent drew on experiences initiated in Bismarck's Germany in the nineteenth century and then were taken further in Nordic democracies before the Second World War. The social market economy implied a trade-off between capital and labour in the form of socially targeted policies in exchange for support for political democracy and the free market model, and such a trade-off was undoubtedly behind many labour-friendly reforms that took place in these years.

It is in this context that labour law found an exceptionally favourable environment in which to flourish. Sustained economic growth, tight labour markets, strong workers' unions, Fordist patterns of work organization, all but harmless international competition, Keynesian policies and political trade-offs all led to successive waves of labour law reform which in most cases strengthened and improved already existing labour rights.

The standard employment relationship

The environment of post-war prosperity led to the consolidation of the 'standard' or 'typical' employment relationship, the key element of which was full-time permanent employment under a contract of employment. A stereotype emerged – namely that of workers performing well-determined tasks in a large production unit, in a subordinate position to the employer or representative of the employer. In return for accepting this subordination, workers expected to spend part or all of their working life in the same enterprise – perhaps even in the same job and performing the same tasks; they enjoyed protection against dismissal, and were unionized. They expected their real wages to increase. Their basic rights were guaranteed by statutory regulation, over which a second layer of rights and entitlements was added through collective bargaining. State-guaranteed social security from cradle to grave completed this picture.

Two further elements completed the stereotype of the post-war worker: (a) this was a male worker, and (b) he was the household's breadwinner. Female employment certainly existed, particularly in clerical positions, the teaching and nursing sectors, and some industries such as textiles which had tradition-ally employed women. However, apart from protection during pregnancy, a prohibition on night work in industry (which was meant to serve as protec-tion for female workers long before it was held to be discrimination) and maternity leave, labour law was a long way from being gender-sensitive. De facto or de jure access to many occupations was barred to women, and pay differentials between men and women were not only acknowledged but socially and legally accepted.

Other forms of employment relationship that deviated from the prevailing pattern did exist, however, but the law generally tried to ignore or restrict them. Typically, labour law provided that a worker was to be taken on under a standard employment relationship unless the employer could establish an objective reason for departing from it, for example when a worker was taken on to perform tasks which were of a limited duration or related to a specified project.[7] In the absence of an objective reason to justify a deviation from the general rule, the deviating patterns of employment were to be treated the same, legally, as a standard employment relationship, that is, they were deemed to be contracts of employment of indefinite duration. Social and political acceptance of this model was so great that in 1982 the ILO Conference had practically no problem in adopting by a two-thirds majority vote the Termination of Employment Convention (No. 158). Convention No. 158 is strongly rooted in the assumption that a contract of employment is agreed upon for an unspecified duration, and that a worker with such a contract should be protected against unfair dismissal.[8] To give some idea how

7 Indeed this is still the rule, but many exceptions are accepted nowadays while previously only a handful of such exceptions were tolerated.
8 As at 30 November 2008 this Convention was in force in 34 countries. Given the relatively low ratification rate it has been suggested that erosion of the standard model of employ-ment protection against dismissal had already begun at the time the Convention was adopted.

times have changed since then, it is worth recalling that in 2006 it was only after tough discussion and with great difficulty that the ILO Conference was able to adopt only a Recommendation on the employment relationship.

Many countries in the world copied these patterns, yet very few, if any, undertook to assess whether their overall economic, social and political parameters were similar to those of Western European countries during these years of post-war prosperity.

Worldwide changes and the emergence of a new work paradigm

The last three decades of the twentieth century and the first of the twenty-first have seen the rise of new economic, social and political realities, which have had a far-reaching effect on developments in labour law. To summarize these in chronological order, they were characterized by the end of the cheap energy era, from 1974 on; the increase in international competition, mainly from South East Asia at the beginning of the 1980s and then from China from the 1990s onwards (to which India should now be added); the digital revolution; the demise of communist regimes and the end of the Cold War; and the globalization process. Each and every one of these phenomena has put conventional labour law (i.e. law that has been developed on the basis of the standard employment relationship) under serious pressure.[9]

The labour flexibility debate and the spread of atypical employment

By the second half of the 1970s, Western European economies had already entered into a phase of stagnation and inflation, commonly referred to as 'stagflation', which was accompanied by rising unemployment. Several factors contributed to this phenomenon, among which the completion of post-war reconstruction, the end of the cheap energy era and tougher international competition were perhaps the most important. In any event, the 'Golden Years of Capitalism' were over, and in this new situation a debate was initiated on the sustainability of the welfare state.[10] During this discussion

---

9 Other important political and societal changes also took place during this period, among them more political democracy, greater popular participation, more human rights awareness and more sensitivity to gender-related issues. The overall favourable impact of these changes on labour law is discussed in Chapter 5.

10 See, for example, Pierre Rosenvallon, *Crise de l'Etat providence* (Paris, Editions du Seuil, 1981).

doubts were cast on real or presumed rigidities of the labour market, and the 'labour flexibility' debate came to the forefront. Some 30 years later, the labour flexibility debate is still underway as most of the labour market reforms have been made on the assumption that the market needs more flexibility than is actually permitted under current labour law. Thus 'flexicurity' (a balance between flexibility for employers and security for employees) has become a hotly debated issue in Western Europe, as reflected in the extract quoted in box 1.1. Flexicurity-oriented labour policies would seem to be encouraged in a recent Green Paper of the European Commission (2006).[11]

Box 1.1 Varieties of flexicurity[12]

There are different national formulas for flexicurity. A first approach is the flexibilization of the whole workforce. This includes the 80 per cent of workers in traditional, permanent work or with 'typical contracts'. There are two main ways of implementing this flexibilization: through new ways of organizing work or through more diverse or flexible working time arrangements. At the same time, this should be complemented with some form of employment security.

The Danish system is a well-known example of such an approach. It combines comparatively relaxed employment protection legislation with a high level of unemployment benefits paid by the government and very active labour market policies (ALMP). The security element of flexicurity is mainly provided by the government, not by the employers. 'Protect workers, not jobs' is the simplified message of the philosophy behind this model. Austrian reforms also focus on that element, with the creation of a severance pay fund which is transferable and not linked to one employer only.

The second approach is the *normalization* of the rights of 'atypical' workers (e.g. fixed-term contracts, temporary contracts or part-time contracts) while retaining the flexibility of these forms of contract.

The Dutch system tries to incorporate this idea by providing more social protection rights for non-standard workers (in particular part-timers but also those on non-permanent contracts) and by improving their entitlements (social security, pension, etc.) to reach levels comparable to those of their

---

11 Commission of the European Communities, *Modernising labour law to meet the challenges of the 21st century*, Green paper (Brussels, 22 November 2006); available online at http://ec.europa.eu. A review of this paper by Joaquín García Murcia has been published in the *International Labour Review* (Geneva, 2007), Vol. 146, No. 1–2, pp. 109–14.

12 European Foundation for the Improvement of Living and Working Conditions, *Varieties of flexicurity: reflections on key elements of flexibility and security, 2007* (Dublin, 2007), background paper; available online at http://www.eurofound.europa.eu.

permanent counterparts in the labour market. Other countries [such as Italy or Spain] have very similar patterns and are considering how to increase the rights for their 'atypical workers'.

Different national approaches have to take account of very different starting points. In particular, the proportion of 'atypical' or non-standard workers varies significantly between Member States. [...] Both the United Kingdom and the Netherlands have high rates of part-time work, particularly amongst working women. Fixed-term contracts are very much in evidence in Spain, representing over 30 per cent of the entire workforce. It is noteworthy, however, that recent major labour market reforms in Spain have attempted to redress some of the disadvantages associated with previous episodes of labour market flexibilization (e.g. excessive labour market segmentation, declining levels of per capita productivity). This has taken the form of new provisions to safeguard and promote the rights of atypical workers and to create incentives for employers to convert atypical to typical contracts.

The choice of a particular form of flexicurity is linked primarily to the historical development of labour markets, collective agreements and the role of the government in these, as well as to basic considerations of public policy in the employment and social protection areas. Policy development depends very much on national traditions as well as on the capacity of individual countries to generate the resources to pay for the chosen solutions.

It is important to recall that a system in place in one country cannot be easily transferred to any other Member State, as policies are embedded in a specific national context. Potential reforms need to take into account the different levels of application (worker, household, enterprise, sector, national) and their interaction.

Nonetheless, an 'open reflection' on an integrated policy is useful. This could lead to a new approach, encompassing the whole set of social policies, including labour market policies and social protection systems in a wider sense.

The labour flexibility debate addressed four real or presumed rigidities in labour law. To begin with, it was argued that protection against unfair dismissal prevented enterprises from adapting staffing levels to their production cycles. The second point was that working time rigidity prevented enterprises from organizing working shifts in keeping with actual needs, especially when these were dependent on unpredictable market fluctuations. The third was that inflexible job classification did not permit enterprises to redeploy workers when and where they were needed. A fourth argument was that minimum wage regulation or, where relevant, sectoral collective bargaining, increased overall labour costs and had a negative impact on competitiveness, in particular when they pushed pay rises above productivity increases. It was further argued that the legislation created a two-tier labour market in that it overprotected those people who were at work but acted as a deterrent for enterprises creating employment so that newcomers could be offered jobs. Thus labour law needed to be flexibilized so as to allow room for employers recruiting staff and organizing the enterprise in a more efficient manner, something which was assumed not to be feasible under existing labour law. The overall social protection system was also called into question; it was argued that apart from being financially unsustainable the benefits on offer were too generous, thus discouraging job-seekers from actively seeking work and making it less likely they would accept any job that was offered to them.

None of these assumptions were free of controversy. However convincing, the arguments of those who urged more labour flexibility were firmly opposed by no less convincing arguments from those who claimed that the apparent 'rigidities' of the labour market actually did not have a significant impact on the overall economic situation, let alone that of the labour market. Other voices drew attention to the positive economic impact of labour regulation, on the grounds, for example, that there were positive cause-and-effect relationships between high wages, labour standards and high productivity. Attention was also drawn to the role played by the labour law in the overall socio-political context, as it provided an element of social fairness which contributed to political stability.

The labour flexibility debate was very largely an ideological one, which more often than not relied on ready-made statements rather than on statistical evidence. However, as the debate continued to run, so unemployment rose to levels unprecedented since the end of the Second World War, becoming a major social and political problem. Leaving aside what so far had largely been an ideological and academic discussion, policy-makers then addressed existing social and labour regulation, in the hope that a new bargain could be worked out, with increased labour flexibility and erosion of workers' rights being traded for job creation. This paved the way for the first wave of labour law reforms in which, for the first time for many years, the law was revised with a view to permitting forms of employment different from the hitherto standard employment relationship. Most Western European countries undertook one or several of these labour market or employment promotion reforms, though the purpose and content of each legislative reform varied from one country to another.

While most of these reforms addressed all of the above-mentioned real or presumed labour market rigidities, those which proved to be the most controversial related to the contract of employment. While the standard pattern of employment (full-time employment with a contract of employment for unlimited duration) was not cast aside, the reforms permitted the use of a wider variety of employment contracts. In a number of countries, rules protecting workers against unfair dismissal were also eased. France, for example, did away with the need for government authorization of collective dismissals while in Italy emphasis was put on the progressive dismantling of the hiring system, which provided for the compulsory intermediation of the public employment service.[13] Several countries also legislated to lengthen the probationary period and to provide for longer periods of employment during which a worker could not claim protection against unfair dismissal; for example, the United Kingdom excluded workers with less than two years of service from the protection afforded under the Employment Protection Act 1975 (later on it shortened this to one year) and Germany revised the Protection Against Dismissals Act 1951 with a view to excluding enterprises with less than 10 workers from the scope of statutory dismissal protection (the threshold was only five workers under previous legislation).

In many other countries, recourse to fixed-term contracts of employment was made easier, though the presumption that a worker is taken on for a contract of employment without limit of time was not reversed. Also, several countries (Belgium, France, Germany, the Netherlands and Japan) acknowledged the existence of triangular arrangements and consequently regulated the hiring or 'dispatching' of workers by temporary work agencies (TWAs), while some others (Spain, Sweden) prohibited that practice (a prohibition which was later lifted). Other emerging patterns of employment which date back to this time, and should be added to the list, include part-time work, on-call work, employment training schemes and some new forms of apprenticeship contracts, internships and home-based work.

---

13 In Italy, a law of 1949 had introduced the Numerical Recruitment rule (*Chiamata Numerica*), a system of hiring whereby the employer was required to submit to the public employment service a list of available jobs, specifying only the number, category and skill levels of the workers needed, so as to permit the office to select the workers to be placed with the employer on the basis of order of precedence. This rule had been set up in the context of the Cold War as it had been alleged that job-seekers known to be communists were discriminated against when they applied for jobs (in particular in some big industrial enterprises in northern Italy). The *Chiamata Numerica* was used to combat discrimination on the grounds of political opinion. Though later becoming more flexible through various reforms, the *Chiamata Numerica* system was not abolished until 1991 when it was no longer needed. Some years later, in Case C–55/96 *Job Centre Coop. Arl.*, the European Court of Justice ruled that state monopoly of placement was contrary to the provisions of the EC Treaty that provided for free competition in the provision of services (Judgment of the Court (Sixth Chamber) of 11 December 1997, [1997] ECR I–7119).

As they diverged from the prevailing patterns, the emerging forms of employment became referred to as 'atypical work', a term which became so popular that it is still used more than three decades later. The term 'precarious work' was also frequently associated with atypical work as all these forms of employment had the effect of weakening workers' rights in comparison with the protection that workers enjoyed under a standard employment relationship. It is little wonder that this terminology was suggested by those who opposed the legal recognition of new emerging patterns of employment. In effect, in a 'battle of the slogans', the use of terms like atypical and precarious would seem to convey negative feelings, as much as the term labour flexibility implies that existing labour law is rigid and therefore should be mistrusted and reviewed, that is, flexibilized.

Yet none of these forms of employment were unknown before the 1970s. Temporary work agencies were already in existence in the 1940s; the well-known agency Manpower was created in 1948. Moreover, part-time work and home-based work had been in existence for a long time. But until the 1970s atypical employment had only a token presence in the overall labour market. What was different from that time onwards was the widening of the slot occupied by atypical work in the labour market. Also new were the State attitudes to these forms of employment. While for many decades the neo-Keynesian State had favoured stable employment, from the mid-1970s and early 1980s it started to have a less negative approach to atypical work. In many cases the State actually promoted atypical employment, for example when an enterprise launched new operations or agreed to take on particularly vulnerable job-seekers.

The spread of atypical work and the support it started to receive from policy-makers and law-makers came as a surprise in trade union circles and among labour law academics, an overwhelmingly majority of whom had taken it for granted that labour law could only be revised with a view to improving already guaranteed workers' rights and conditions of work. Thus, when in 1985 the International Society for Labour and Social Security Law put atypical work on the agenda of its XIth World Congress, most of the academics then attending expressed great concern, and a great majority of them made strong pleas for state intervention to stop the development of atypical employment. Some 20 years later, however, it is undisputed that atypical employment has become a structural element of the overall labour market, even if it takes a minority share of total employment.

Box 1.2 Atypical work in the United States[14]

Atypical workers – temporary workers, on-lease workers, part-time workers, trainees and apprentices and dependent-independent contractors – are a growing portion of the American labour force. In 2005 the Department of Labor classified 16.2 million people – or 12.1 per cent of the workforce – as atypical workers. Of these, there were an estimated 10.2 million independent contractors, 2.5 million on-call workers, 1.2 million temporary help agency workers and 813,000 workers for contract-work companies out of a total workforce of 139 million. In addition, in 2003 the Department of Labor found that there were over 5 million involuntary part-time workers – those who want but do not have regular employment. A survey of firms in all industries and of all sizes conducted by the Upjohn Institute found that 78 per cent of all private firms used some form of flexible staffing arrangements.

International competition

To a large extent both the sustained economic growth and the prosperity of the Golden Age of Capitalism relied on the fact that international trade was not overly affected by competition between high-wage and low-wage countries. On the one hand, well-paid and highly skilled and productive Japanese, North American and Western European workers produced high value-added goods; on the other hand, low skilled and low-paid workers in the developing world supplied raw materials and low value-added production. Customs duties and bureaucratic obstacles to imports[15] completed the protective shield behind which the welfare state distributed wealth, prosperity and protection to both employers and workers.

In the 1980s, however, this situation started to change, with the emergence of the 'newly industrialized' countries, first in South-East Asia and, from the 1990s, China and India. This was coupled with the lifting of customs protection and other non-customs barriers to global trade that came in with the negotiations which eventually paved the way to the establishment of the

---

14 Katherine V.W. Stone, 'Rethinking labour law: Employment protection for boundaryless workers', in Guy Davidov and Brian Langille (eds), *Boundaries and frontiers of labour law: Goals and means in the regulation of work* (Oxford, Hart Publishing, 2006), p. 170.

15 For example, when Asian video-cassette recorders started to invade the French market in the early 1980s, the government ordered that custom formalities be completed in the small provincial city of Poitiers. Because warehouse capacity was limited in Poitiers, it effectively restricted the number of VCRs that could enter the country.

World Trade Organization (WTO) in January 1995 and with it bilateral and multilateral trade agreements. Thus high-wage and low-wage countries started to compete internationally in the same brackets of an increasingly globalized market. International flows of capital, information and other technological innovations as well as new patterns of work organization were also major contributory factors to the delocalization of production, which inevitably affected employment levels in high-wage countries. It was in this context that labour costs and overall labour regulation policies became a critical issue in Japan, North America and Western Europe, as we shall discuss in more detail in Chapter 4.

Technological change and the emergence of post-Fordist organizational patterns

The history of mankind has been punctuated by technological change. At least two significant developments took place in a very short period of time: the first one during the 1970s and the second at the end of the twentieth century. During the 1970s the steel and coal industries in northern countries entered into a long-running process of attrition; at the same time robots arrived to replace workers on assembly lines in the metal trades, while many new technologies were introduced into previously labour-intensive processes. Structural change arising out of these developments led to massive job reductions and resulted in a sharp increase in unemployment.

Yet this was not a worldwide problem as essentially it affected only the old industries in Western Europe. At that point, through negotiation and labour–management consultation, many countries addressed and mitigated the social and economic effects of the introduction of new technologies and the downsizing of some industries. State subsidies, redundancy payment funds and the widespread use of social security and other safety-net mechanisms (such as the Wages Guarantee Fund in many Western European countries or the *Cassa Integrazione Guadagni* in Italy, described in box 1.3) were amongst the tools used to cope with these changes. To a large extent, attention was focused on adjusting labour law to the emerging challenges; yet the basic assumptions on which labour law was based were not affected.

Box 1.3 Wage protection for temporarily laid-off workers: the *Cassa Integrazione Guadagni*[16]

The *Cassa Integrazione Guadagni* was created in 1947, to help enterprises that were forced to lay off workers on a temporary basis, or put workers on short-time working because of temporary economic difficulties. Under this scheme the workers received 80 per cent of their previous wages, up to a maximum level established by law, and their contributions to pension schemes were assumed to have been paid, even if they had not been. Devised originally as a means of temporary income protection for employees, in the expectation that the company and its employees would soon resume normal activity, the wage protection scheme was gradually extended even to cases in which there was no prospect of a return to normal production and work patterns, so that it became a de facto welfare instrument for the management of labour surpluses.

A reform introduced in 1991, however, sought to restore the fund to its original function of providing assistance during purely temporary labour surpluses. It imposed a rigid time limit on eligibility for making up lost pay, and recourse to special availability-for-employment and workforce-reduction procedures in cases where the surplus was structural or there was no prospect of re-employing the surplus employees. This objective was only partially achieved because, as a result of serious economic crisis suffered by Italy from 1992 onwards, the legislator intervened to modify the legal rules governing the fund's operation, and extended the time limit on eligibility for special intervention to make up pay and allowed such eligibility to extend into areas where it had been formerly excluded. In particular, special intervention was made available to commercial enterprises with more than 50 employees, to craft enterprises whose main customers were experiencing serious economic difficulties, to agricultural and stock-rearing cooperatives and to catering and restaurant enterprises.

In contrast, the second technological change, arising out of the irruption of information and communications technologies, has raised a completely different challenge, as it has profoundly affected the entire substance and organization of work. The widespread use of information technologies has generated the need for a response from policy-makers and law-makers, which in the field of labour law has still to be comprehensively developed. Below are some of the issues which have arisen as a result of the introduction of information technology in the workplace.

---

16 Source: European Foundation for the Improvement of Living and Working Conditions, database EMIRE, Italy, *Cassa Integrazione Guadagni (CGI)*.

- The hierarchical, Fordist pattern of work organization is no longer necessary, and is sometimes simply not feasible if the employee is not directly under the employer's supervision, for example, if the employee is a teleworker.
- Tasks are increasingly individualized; it is no longer necessary for all workers to share the same workplace as tasks can be coordinated electronically.
- Decentralization of productive processes and delocalization is made easier. The 'enterprise' becomes a strategic concept rather than a physical unit. Those who take decisions that affect the worker's job, conditions of work and lifestyle are no longer the worker's legal employer.
- It is becoming more difficult to determine what should be meant by 'working time' as the worker continues to perform work-related functions from his or her home, or is required to remain on stand-by on a bleeper or a mobile phone.
- New opportunities are available for the employer to keep an eye on what the worker is actually doing (through the use of pagers, mobile phones, electronic badges, video-cameras, screening of the worker's email and use of internet).
- Workers' personnel data can be gathered, stored and exchanged more easily.
- New illnesses and occupational hazards have arisen, which might be linked to the use of IT.

We will discuss in Chapter 5 how labour law has responded to these questions.

The end of the Cold War

The Cold War environment has had an effect on labour law in several ways. During the Cold War certain countries passed legislation which made members of the Communist Party or even sympathizers of the Soviet Union ineligible for trade union office or excluded them from certain sensitive posts. One example was the Labor–Management Relations Act 1947 (the Taft-Hartley Act) in the United States, under which members of the Communist Party were barred from holding or seeking trade union office.[17] In Germany too, discriminatory dismissals on the grounds of political opinion were made

---

17 Mention could also be made of the US Supreme Court decision in *Black* v. *Cutter Laboratories* (351 US 292 (1956)) which confirmed the validity of a dismissal as a consequence of the application of a collective agreement that had established as a waiver cause the affiliation of workers to the Communist Party.

possible, as civil servants could be dismissed on the sole grounds that they belonged to parties that sought 'to impair or abolish the free democratic basic order or to endanger the existence of the Federal Republic of Germany'. This referred to members of the Communist Party and those of extreme right parties, and could be applied to any job in the civil service.[18] On the other hand, Cold War politics was very probably behind some core ILO Conventions of the 1950s and 1960s, the adoption of which – as of any ILO standard – called for a large consensus between governments, labour and management. Thus the Abolition of Forced Labour Convention, 1957 (No. 105), prohibits the use of forced labour '(a) as a means of political coercion or education or as a punishment for holding or expressing political views or views ideologically opposed to the established political, social or economic system, and (b) as a method of mobilising and using labour for purposes of economic development'; these were practices which were being used widely in the Soviet Union at the time. The Employment Policy Convention, 1964 (No. 122), urged Member States to 'declare and pursue, as a major goal, an active policy designed to promote full, productive and freely chosen employ- ment'. This carefully chosen wording suggested that full employment in the communist world – something which the communists argued was feasible in a socialist economy but not in a market economy – was not necessarily productive, nor was employment always freely chosen.

The Cold War also influenced labour law in a way that was more favourable to workers as both the State and the employers were supposed to be willing to trade social and labour-friendly legislation in return for workers' and unions' political support against communist ideology. To a certain extent this was not really a new departure: it has been argued that the ILO was created in 1919, among other reasons, as a capitalist response to the Bolshevik Revolution of 1917. In any event, the Cold War environment was at the root of the split in 1949 of the World Federation of Trade Unions, from which a large number of non-communist national trade unions seceded to create the

---

18 A representation against Germany was made by the World Federation of Teachers' Unions in 1984, which alleged that German law was in breach of the ILO Discrimination (Employment and Occupation) Convention, 1958 (No. 111); under this Convention political opinion was forbidden grounds for discrimination. In 1985 the ILO Governing Body decided to refer the case to a Commission of Inquiry, which visited Germany in 1986. After having gathered a great deal of evidence, the Commission concluded that there had been a breach of Convention No. 111 by the Government of the Federal Republic of Germany. A comprehensive review of this case has been made in Klaus Samson, 'The "Berufsverbot" problem revisited – views from Geneva and Strasbourg', in *Les normes internationales du travail: un patrimoine pour l'avenir, mélanges en l'honneur de Nicolas Valticos* (Geneva, 2004), pp. 21–46.

International Confederation of Free Trade Unions (ICFTU). Unlike communist unions, which advocated class struggle and the construction of a society based on socialist ownership of the means of production, ICFTU unions endorsed and supported political democracy and market economy, from which they expected a larger share of both political participation and the national income. Indeed, many labour-friendly laws adopted during the Cold War were at the same time supported by the State and not very strongly objected to in business circles. In addition, labour-friendly legislation was economically sustained by overall post-Second World War prosperity.

The end of the Cold War, coupled with the internationally competitive environment of the last few decades, has led to a change in the parameters within which labour law had previously evolved. Two variables upon which labour law had grown during the Golden Age of Capitalism have now disappeared.

Current crises in labour law

Crises in labour law today can roughly be grouped into four different categories: those which relate to the coverage of the law itself; the adaptation of labour law to new technologies and new patterns of work organization; the territorial scope of the law; and challenges to the ideological foundations of labour law.

First, in relative terms, the coverage of labour law tends nowadays to decrease as larger groups of workers perform work or provide services beyond the scope of an employment relationship. This trend is in sharp contrast with the expanding coverage of labour law that had prevailed during most of the twentieth century. One of the characteristics of labour law in the last century was precisely its expansive nature. What is today meant by labour law took its roots from rules that were initially applicable to factory work. Indeed, it is worth recalling that in the first decades of the twentieth century 'industrial law', not 'labour law', was taught in faculties of law. In Britain, for example, the first piece of labour legislation was the Factory Act of 1802.[19]

---

19 The first Factory Act was enacted in 1802: it focused on child labour in cotton and paper mills. Further amendments and enlargements turned the Factory Act into a detailed set of regulations for working conditions in industrial workshops, but did not address the employer–employee relationship, which was dealt with mainly under the Master and Servant Act. (Nowadays under UK labour law, the contract of employment is a common law contract, which statutory law and regulations provide with exceptions and immunities rather than positive rights.) Factory Acts still make up the backbone of labour regulation in countries such as India and Pakistan, whose legal systems have drawn on British traditions.

Consequently the first legislative concerns were focused on limiting the hours of work, the work of minors and women, and workers' compensation in case of industrial accidents and occupational diseases. Nevertheless it did not take long to extend the field of application to non-industrial environments, first to commerce and services and later on to agriculture. Labour laws also had an impact on public administration, in that civil service statutes adapted at least part of the labour law principles to the relationship between the state and its employees. This reached its peak in the 1970s and the 1980s when practically any relationship between a physical person who performed work or provided services in subordination to another person or to a legal entity was presumed to be in an employment relationship if it was in the private sector or in a service relationship in the case of public administration.

So where do we stand today? Everything points to the fact that the scope of labour law has a tendency to attrition. First, one should bear in mind that, whether de facto or de jure, labour law does not apply to the informal economy, which is taking a bigger share in the overall labour market worldwide, thus proportionally reducing the scope of application of labour laws. This trend can be clearly observed in most developing economies: for example, according to ILO research in Latin America, between 1990 and 2003, despite all the economic adjustment and market reform of the 1990s, private investment did not grow sufficiently to create enough formal employment for newcomers to the labour market. It follows that six out of 10 newly employed people were working in the informal economy, which by 2004 represented 63 per cent of the overall employment in the region.[20]

This phenomenon is not, however, limited to developing countries. In industrialized countries too, while salaried employment is still the prevailing pattern, it is no longer as hegemonic as it was in the second half of the twentieth century. Nowadays, autonomous work and other forms of non-subordinated employment – which the Italians call 'parasubordinated' – are undoubtedly increasing everywhere. The explanation of this phenomenon is quite complex; it certainly does not arise from a single cause. However, we will return to this subject in the following chapter, when we address the scope of the employment relationship.

The second category of crisis lies in the adaptation of laws to new technologies and work patterns. While labour law evolved against a background provided first by a Taylorist[21] and later on by a Fordist pattern of work, today it has difficulties in adjusting to new patterns of work organization that are

---

20 ILO, *Labour overview of Latin America and the Caribbean, 2004* (Lima, 2004).
21 Taylorism is a theory of management that analyses and synthesizes workflow processes, particularly in mass production, with a view to improving labour productivity.

emerging, which – for lack of a better term – are called post-Fordist. It should be recalled that within the Fordist model all the production processes, and often their marketing too, were put under a single command. Also, within one company all the employees were in principle subordinated to a single employer. Subordination and dependency were practically synonymous terms and generally interchangeable. While outsourcing and subcontracting were actively practised in some industries or activities, in most others they were rather marginal. Employee status provided the worker with protection and the wisdom of labour-friendly legislation was not under discussion.

Fewer workplaces today resemble this model of a single-employer, single-job site, with full-time jobs which last for a lifetime. Like Fordist enterprises, post-Fordist organizations keep their strategic objectives under a single and unified command. However, Fordist companies also keep all the production and distribution processes under direct control; by contrast, post-Fordist organizations decentralize and contract out most of their production. This phenomenon is known as *productive decentralization*, which encompasses several different definitions; it includes varied practices and has fuelled much discussion in national and international labour law forums.[22] Post-Fordist organizations define the activities and operations which they keep under direct control – their core activities, which are almost always those of greater added value – and contract out non-core activities to other companies. This is not an entirely new phenomenon, as big assembly processes have always relied more or less on parts from external suppliers. What is new, however, is the ever-widening definition of what constitutes non-core activities, which can now encompass entire production processes.

The contracting out of non-core activities can take different forms: some, such as transfers, mergers and takeovers of enterprises (or a part of them), are well known and their legal effects are often addressed by labour law. In contrast, other strategies for decentralization may take the form of arrangements that the law in general and labour law in particular have great difficulty in grasping. Practices like outsourcing, networking and franchising fall within this category. Loans of workers among legally different companies, as well as the supply of labour through temporary work agencies, can also be part of the same strategy. In the same way, increased use is made of civil or commercial contracts for the execution of tasks or the provision of services

---

22 Thus, the subject was addressed in the Xth Spanish Congress of Labour and Social Security Law, Zaragoza, 1999, and in the XVIIIth World Congress of the International Society for Labour and Social Security Law, Paris, 2006. See also Juan Rivero Lamas and Angel Luis de Val Tena (eds), *Descentralización productiva y responsabilidades de la empresa: el 'outsourcing'* (Navarra, Aranzadi, 2003).

which in the Fordist pattern were carried out directly by the main enterprise using its own employees.

In all cases this strategy has a potentially destabilizing impact on the legal protection of workers, whose employment security and conditions of work may depend on the strategic decisions of an entrepreneur who, legally, is no longer their employer or never has been. The notion of *business risk* is implicit in labour law: those who develop an enterprise project harvest its benefits but also assume its risks, including those which arise out of the employment of workers who are subordinated to the enterprise. Yet, following the logic of the productive decentralization argument, a parent company does not assume the risks of the employer in relation to the workers of its subsidiaries or contractors. This is a systemic issue, to which labour law has not so far been able to elaborate a systemic reply.

The third crisis facing labour law today arises out of the weakening of the effectiveness of national law in a globalizing environment. Apart from some exceptions with respect to transnational employment relations, national labour law is applicable only within the political boundaries of a given national State. However, because of technological change, as well as the open-ing up of international trade, movements of capital and technology, and therefore investment, can nowadays 'jump' national borders, whereas laws do not and cannot. On the other hand, it would be naive to deny that labour law places some financial burden on to the shoulders of the employer, and this has obvious importance when the time comes for an investor to decide where to invest. All other factors being equal, moderate labour costs and business-friendly legislation can act as important incentives for investment.

At the same time, tariff barriers and other forms of protectionism tend to be dismantled over time, something which deprives countries not only of revenue but of an important means of protecting both the internal market and the local workers. It follows that, nowadays, a State is no longer entirely free to formulate its own labour and social protection policy, because it cannot improve local levels of social protection without considering the potential implications on the country's competitive position vis-à-vis other states that do not do the same. This cannot but limit the effectiveness of labour law in a purely national context. For that reason, we can talk of a crisis of territoriality, for the economy is worldwide whereas the law is binding only within national boundaries. Unless labour law, like the economy, can become transnationally effective, it will be very difficult to maintain the dynamics that allowed it to offer better protection to more and more workers during most of the last century.

The fourth crisis derives from the overall challenge that neoclassical thought has raised against the welfare state. Neoclassical thought has given birth to neo-liberal and *structural adjustment* policies, which have quite often been demanded by international financial institutions as a pre-condition for the granting or the release of loans. Its cornerstone is faith in the market's capacity for self-regulation; this is why the market is placed above all other values and at the heart of the society's economic, social and political interactions. The assumption is that what is good for the market is also good for society as a whole. Like Adam Smith's invisible hand, the market is capable of generating all the rules it needs to work properly. In neoclassical wisdom, heteronomous regulations are likely to produce malfunctioning, although sometimes this is a necessary evil. From this viewpoint, labour law is itself a necessary evil, and should be limited to the setting up of a threshold of basic rules. Beyond that threshold, labour regulation can only serve to prevent the market from generating growth, employment and wealth, which in time would be fairly distributed. Neoclassical thought is reflected even in its terminology: it refers to labour law as 'labour market regulation', giving the word 'regulation' a negative connotation. Terms such as 'manpower', 'workforce' and 'human resources' are preferred to 'workers'; labour rules are called 'constraints' and labour rights are called 'labour costs'.

There are many reasons to believe that this change of language is not merely semantic. For example, 'labour market regulation' is one of the parameters used by the World Bank's *Doing Business* database to help potential investors to assess and perhaps select the countries in which they might invest. The database provides indicators on the cost of doing business by identifying specific regulations, which it believes enhance or constrain investment, productivity and growth. These indicators relate to a number of topics, including the employment of workers.[23] With respect to labour, the database develops indicators relating to the difficulty of hiring new workers; restrictions on working hours; the difficulty of dismissing a redundant worker; and the cost of dismissal, expressed in weeks of wages. Higher values in the table indicate more rigid regulations while the absence of regulation is represented by 0. Countries with business-friendly labour regulation, or no regulation, are rewarded with a low index while those with labour-friendly regulation get a higher index. Implicitly, this conveys the message that countries with labour-friendly regulation are unattractive for investment. On the contrary, regulation to protect investors or enforce contracts is considered favourably in the

---

23 *Doing Business* provides indicators on the following topics: starting a business, dealing with licences, registering property, getting credit, employing workers, protecting investors, paying taxes, trading across borders, enforcing contracts and closing down a business. The indicators are developed by the Finance and Private Sector Vice Presidency of the World Bank Group.

Doing Business indicators. In short, State regulation is seen as a virtue when it protects business and a sin when it protects workers.

There is a great deal of literature and analysis which either follows this approach or strongly rejects it. Those who challenge this view remind us that neoclassical thought assumes that the market is perfect, and therefore does not acknowledge that monopolies or cartels exist, not to mention more or less hidden subsidies that in practice undermine fair competition. It also assumes that rules are respected by all, that there is neither public nor private corruption, consumers are perfectly informed and credit is made available to all those who intend to initiate or develop a business. It has also been argued that the *Doing Business* database is based on methodological assumptions that are not consistent with reality (see box 1.4).[24] It should also be added that on the basis of research carried out on OECD countries, the ILO did not find evidence that supports the assumption that legislation which protects against unjustified dismissal has had a negative impact on employment;[25] some years ago the OECD came to comparable conclusions with respect to its Member States.[26]

Box 1.4 An ILO view on *Doing Business: The Employing Workers Indicator (EWI)*[27]

In November 2007, the Governing Body of the ILO had a discussion on the EWI of the World Bank's *Doing Business* indicators. The Secretariat prepared a paper noting some of the conceptual and methodological flaws of the indicator as well as its potentially negative implications for policy making. In particular it stated that:

- The EWI is a poor indicator of the investment climate and of labour market performance to promote employment and decent work.

---

24 See in this respect the ICFTU reply to *Doing Business*, available online at http://www.icftu.org. See also Alain Supiot, 'Le droit du travail bradé dans le "marché des normes"', in *Droit Social*, December 2006, and Janine Berg and Sandrine Cazes, 'Policymaking gone awry: The labour market regulations of the World Bank's Doing Business Indicators', in *Comparative Labor Law and Policy Journal*, Summer 2008.

25 Peter Auer and Sandrine Cazes, *Employment stability in an age of flexibility: Evidence from industrialized countries* (Geneva, ILO, 2003).

26 OECD, *Employment Outlook* (Paris, 1999).

27 Excerpts from Document GB 300/4/1, 300th Session of the ILO Governing Body, November 2007, World Bank *Doing Business Report: The Employing Workers Indicator* (document submitted for debate and guidance).

- There are serious methodological and technical limitations with the indicator.
- The design of the indicator and the scoring system suggests that reducing protection to a minimum and maximizing flexibility is always the best option. The EWI does not take into account the need for balance in labour market institutions and policies to ensure that both enterprises and workers have the right combination of security and flexibility to adapt to competition while ensuring an adequate security of income and employment.
- International research does not provide conclusive evidence for the view that labour market regulations are the main cause of informality or that lowering labour market regulations beyond certain points will promote employment and transition to formality.
- The Bank claims that 'it is now possible for an economy to receive the highest score on the ease of employing workers ... and comply with all 187 ILO Conventions'. This claim is misleading. Countries can achieve an EWI high score and face problems in the application of ratified Conventions.
- The *Doing Business* ranking has been used to promote policy reform in developing countries, including via direct or indirect conditionality. While benefits can be derived by reducing the cost of red tape and unnecessary regulations to a minimum, there is a serious problem with promoting reforms of labour law based on the same cost-minimization principles.

In addition, the paper noted that:

- There is little in common between the findings of the *Doing Business* and other investment climate indicators.
- The EWI does not take into account the raison d'être of labour legislation.
- The EWI does not consider the wider economic benefits, or 'positive externalities', of labour market regulations.

On the other hand, the approach whereby labour rules are equated with constraints and additional costs fails to consider those rules which would have positive economic effects. Thus safety and health regulations as well as laws and regulations that encourage training doubtless have beneficial effects on productivity; paid vacations stimulate tourism and leisure industries; maternity leave encourages the workforce to reproduce; and greater job stability confers greater experience on the worker, which is very likely to make him or her more productive.[28] For example, it is commonly accepted that Japanese

---

28 See for example Peter Auer, Janine Berg and Ibrahim Coulibaly, 'Is a stable workforce good for productivity?', in *International Labour Review* (2005), Vol. 144, No. 3.

shūshin koyū (life employment) has created a strong link between Japanese workers and their companies and increased motivation, which would seem to have played a crucial role in the economic success of Japan. In short, rights-based regulation – or, if preferred, 'regulated flexibility' – can also be an important asset for a country developing a comparative advantage in global trade and investment.

Furthermore, there would seem to be some inconsistency in neo-liberal thought, for it advocates free transnational movement of goods and capital, but not of labour, despite the fact that it treats labour like a commodity. Thus US farmers who receive State subsidies can freely export their products to Mexico, but Mexican farmers who are ruined by US subsidized agricultural exports cannot freely emigrate to the United States to sell their labour in the US labour market. Finally, one cannot fail to observe that those arguments which challenge labour law on the grounds that it affects business seem to follow a reasoning which in its substance is not so different from the claims made during the nineteenth century against the abolition of slavery or of child labour in factories.

However, it would seem that very few, if any, of these considerations have been taken into account in a great number of labour market reforms, which have been ideologically inspired by neo-liberal thought and have thus disregarded the positive cause-and-effect relationship between labour law and the economy. The weight of neo-liberal thought in today's policy-making therefore raises a challenge of enormous importance to labour law.

Chapter 2

Who is protected by labour law?

Labour law and the informal economy[1]

Workers in the informal economy are among the weakest and most vulnerable groups of workers. Most of them have a very low income, their jobs are unstable and their conditions of work are precarious. Very rarely are they eligible for health and social security protection. The challenges of the informal economy are manifold, but our focus here is on those posed for labour law.

The following considerations should be taken into account: first, that attempts at working out a legal definition of the informal economy have so far been unsuccessful. This is partly because of the informal economy's heterogeneity and partly because it is an economic reality rather than a legal category. As observed by the Director-General of the ILO, the only certainty about the informal sector is that it exists.[2] However, not only has it not been given legal recognition,[3] it is also much debated whether the informal sector should be legalized or left in a laissez-faire limbo.[4] A great majority – though

---

1 The term 'informal economy' is now preferred to 'informal sector', which was used when the ILO started to address this question in the early 1970s. Three factors explain this change: first, that the workers and enterprises considered to be 'informal' cut across many sectors of economic activity, rather than constituting a sector of their own; secondly, more often than not formal and informal activities are closely linked and interdependent so that it does not make much sense to draw a clear border between what is formal and what is not; and thirdly there is long-standing criticism of the dualistic formal/informal analytical framework for being both oversimplistic and vague; see Ann Trebilcock, 'Using development approaches to address the challenge of the informal economy for labour law', in Guy Davidov and Brian Langille (eds), *Boundaries and frontiers of labour law* (Oxford, Hart Publishing, 2006), pp. 64–5; see also ILO, *Decent Work and the informal economy*, Report VI, International Labour Conference, 90th Session, Geneva, 2002, sixth item on the agenda; available online at http://www.ilo.org, pp. 2–3.

2 ILO, *The dilemma of the informal sector*, Report of the Director-General, International Labour Conference, 78th Session, Geneva, 1991, p. 4.

3 Jean-Michel Servais, 'Secteur informel: un avenir pour le droit du travail', in *Revue de la faculté de droit de Liège* (Liège, 1994), Vol. 3, pp. 661–7.

4 Carlos Maldonado, 'The informal sector: Legalization or laissez-faire?' in *International Labour Review* (Geneva, 1995), Vol. 134, No. 6, pp. 705–28.

not all – of informal economy workers are excluded from the application of labour law, either because they are casual workers or because they are not within an employer–employee relationship. Whether or not they are, legally speaking, employees, most informal economy workers are in fact excluded from the scope of labour law, because law enforcement is minimal or even non-existent in the informal economy.

In order to approach the informal economy from a legal perspective, it is essential first to establish a definition, before proceeding to determine who would be included under that definition. Here one could note that approaches differ widely in developed and developing economies. Thus in most Western European countries the prevailing approach holds that the informal economy is tantamount to an undeclared or clandestine economy. On this basis the application of labour law to the informal economy can be considered essentially a law-enforcement problem to be tackled through measures such as more inspections, more prosecutions and more penalties. However, this would not be a workable approach in most developing countries, where a large majority of people earn their crust in the informal economy. Obviously it would be bizarre, let alone unfair, to argue that all informal workers are illegal workers. The premise in these countries is that the informal economy simply works *beyond* the existing regulations. In short, informal workers are carrying out clandestine, undeclared work in Europe, while in Asia, Africa or Latin America they simply do not exist in legal terms. Yet they do exist in all cases.

Furthermore, most workers in the informal economy have not made a free choice to work in this way: they do so simply because the formal economy has not created formal jobs for all those who wish to work. This is especially true in most developing economies which have undertaken structural adjustment and privatization mostly on the advice of the international financial institutions. While these policies have done away with hundreds of thousands of allegedly inefficient jobs, they have not been as successful in creating as many formal jobs as they have destroyed. Thus, for a great majority of informal workers, working in the informal economy is essentially a survival strategy.

Towards a legal definition of the 'informal economy'

The first studies that attempted to focus on the informal economy were the research papers and field studies that the ILO carried out in the early 1970s within its World Employment Programme. In 1987, the 14th International Conference of Labour Statisticians proposed a statistical definition, the main purpose of which was to help ILO Members gather data for international comparison.[5] Some years later, in 1991, the Report of the ILO Director-General to the International Labour Conference proposed a definition which tried to give an economic dimension to the informal sector, as it was called then. Later on, in 2002, the ILO Conference held a general discussion on Decent Work and the Informal Economy.[6] It adopted conclusions where attempts were made at defining the informal economy from an institutional viewpoint. It would seem worthwhile to compare how this question was addressed in 1991 and how it was tackled in 2002.

Box 2.1 Definitions of the informal economy

ILO Report, 1991 definition

The term informal sector may be understood to refer to very small-scale units producing goods and services, and consisting largely of independent, self-employed producers in urban areas of developing countries, some of whom also employ family labour and/or a few hired workers or apprentices, which operate with very little capital or none at all; which utilize a low level of technology and skills; which therefore operate at a low level of productivity; and which generally provide a very low and irregular income, and highly unstable employment to those who work in it.

---

5 It has been reviewed in 2003 by the 17th International Conference of Labour Statisticians; see its Final Report online at http://www.ilo.org. According to the Conference:

(5) Employees are considered to have informal jobs if their employment relationship is, in law or in practice, not subject to national labour legislation, income taxation, social protection or entitlement to certain employment benefits (advance notice of dismissal, severance pay, paid annual or sick leave, etc.). The reasons may be the following: non-declaration of the jobs or the employees; casual jobs or jobs of a limited short duration; jobs with hours of work or wages below a specified threshold (e.g. for social security contributions); employment by unincorporated enterprises or by persons in households; jobs where the employee's place of work is outside the premises of the employer's enterprise (e.g. outworkers without employment contracts); or jobs for which labour regulations are not applied, not enforced, or not complied with for any other reason. The operational criteria for defining informal jobs of employees are to be determined in accordance with national circumstances and data availability.

6 ILO, *Decent work and the informal economy*, Report VI, International Labour Conference, 90th Session, Geneva, 2002.

ILO Conference, 2002

The term informal economy refers to all economic activities by workers and economic units that are – in law or in practice – not covered or insufficiently covered by formal arrangements. Their activities are not included in the law, which means that they are operating outside the formal reach of the law; or they are not covered in practice, which means that – although they are operating within the formal reach of the law, the law is not applied or not enforced; or the law discourages compliance because it is inappropriate, burdensome, or imposes excessive costs.

These definitions help, but do not completely solve the problem of establishing clearly who is a worker in the informal economy. Data collected from several countries tell us that the informal economy may account for as much as 80–90 per cent of all workers in many African countries, and 50–60 per cent in many Latin American countries. However, undertaking international comparisons of data may result in misleading conclusions as the data are frequently based on different criteria. Some countries consider that all undeclared (though not illicit) work is informal, while others do not. Some data automatically categorize all workers in micro-enterprises employing less than five workers as informal workers, while others put the threshold at 10 workers; others still do not use the workforce threshold as a criterion at all. Domestic work and home work are included within the definition of the informal economy in many countries but not in all.[7]

The only point that does not seem to be at issue is that the informal economy is vast and the trend is that it is expanding, in both developing and developed economies. In general, it possesses the following features:

- Most informal workers are unregistered and unrecorded in official statistics. However, informal work is sometimes recorded in household and labour force surveys.
- Informal workers have little or no access to credit, to markets integrated in the formal economy, to formal education or training institutions. Frequently they are also excluded from public services and amenities.
- Informal workers are neither recognized, supported nor regulated. This is a basic feature that distinguishes the informal sector from small enterprises that work within the boundaries of the law.

---

7 See this discussion in ILO, *Decent work and the informal economy*, 2002, op. cit., pp. 25–6.

- In most cases the workers are beyond the scope of action of trade unions and employers' organizations, although they can organize and in fact in a number of countries they have established associations, including unions.

It should be added that much if not most informal work is carried out so openly that it would be very difficult to argue that it is in breach of the law.[8]

In short, the informal sector is neither recognized nor repressed. Moreover there are different degrees of informality: whereas some informal activities clearly correspond to the above features, others may abide by a number of regulations, thus being formal in a certain sense and informal in another one.

Policy issues

Reducing poverty is the overall concern for any government policy aimed at addressing the informal economy. The application of labour law in this domain is often only one element of a broader and holistic policy approach, which embraces an entire set of different policy elements, ranking from socioeconomic to fiscal. The core objective is to reduce the deficit of decent work by gradually widening the application of national labour laws reflecting international labour standards in theory and practice, even if this may hamper the capacity of the informal economy to absorb unemployed workers, as has been acknowledged in the ILO Employment Policy (Supplementary Provisions) Recommendation, 1984 (No. 169):

> 29.(1) While taking measures to increase employment opportunities and improve conditions of work in the informal sector, Members should seek to facilitate its progressive integration into the national economy. [However] (2) Members should take into account that integration of the informal sector into the formal sector may reduce its ability to absorb labour and generate income. Nevertheless, they should seek progressively to extend measures of regulation to the informal sector.

It should also be taken into account that the informal economy accommodates considerable diversity in terms of workers, enterprises and entrepre-

---

8 Some years ago, while leaving the premises of the Ministry of Labour in a Central American country, the author observed intensive informal economy activity (street vending, repairing, shoe-shining, hairdressing, windscreen washing, musical performances, acrobatics, a parrot-show, letter-writing, motorbike taxis, delivery services, craftwork and so forth) just across the street. He then asked a labour inspector whether the labour inspection services monitored this type of activity. The inspector replied: 'They are outside our domain. They are informal workers.'

neurs with identifiable characteristics. A not necessarily complete list would include the following: (a) casual and self-employed workers; (b) micro-entrepreneurs; (c) home workers; (d) domestic helpers; (e) wage earners in informal sector micro-enterprises; (f) unpaid family workers; and (g) apprentices in informal enterprises. Nonetheless, depending upon the situation, some of these groups can be classified either in the formal or in the informal economy. For example, many micro-enterprises are well integrated in the formal economy while others are not. The same would apply to self-employed workers, home workers and domestic helpers. Whether or not their work is legally recorded would determine their classification as either formal or informal economy workers.

Yet it would be naive to pretend that the problem of the informal economy could be solved simply by recording and officially registering all its workers. Apart from being unrealistic, this would not alleviate poverty in the informal economy or remedy the deficit of decent work. Besides, in many cases conventional national labour law, of which the scope of application would require the existence of an employment relationship, would apply to many informal workers, most notably to those who have an employer, but it would not fully apply to self-employed workers. Also, it is essential to take into consideration all the practical difficulties that undermine the enforcement of labour law, or of certain labour law rules.

It has been suggested that the scope of national labour law be widened so as to cover different types of workers, such as the many apparently self-employed informal workers at the end of a chain of formal trade. This approach motivated the discussion[9] and the adoption of Recommendation No. 198 on the Employment Relationship, which gives guidance for policy-makers on how to define an employment relationship, and which thus allows for the broadening of the scope of application of national labour laws in practice. This would enable a large number of informal workers to benefit from labour protection.

Many informal economy workers, such as street vendors, messengers, pizza deliverers and the like, actually depend on businesses in the formal economy. Indeed, in many countries they have employee status, while in many others they are presumed to be self-employed. In principle there should be no objection to these informal workers – who are apparently dependent workers, though not formally employed in a business – being perceived as employed and, in this sense, 'formalized' so that they can benefit from labour law and social protection. This approach may, however, be

---

9 See ILC, 95th Session, 2006, discussion on the report of the Committee on the Employment Relationship.

challenged by neo-liberal thinkers who would rather advocate overall deregulation of the labour market, on the grounds that this would be the only way
to do away with 'special treatment' and thus put an end to discrimination
against informal economy workers.

It may be observed that this issue is closely connected with the ongoing
debate about the cost of labour law protection, so it can be assumed that
those who advocate labour law protection will oppose those who campaign
for deregulation. Such a debate would be particularly relevant for labour-
intensive activities, for labour law-related costs account for the largest share
of the overall operating costs of micro-enterprises in the informal economy.
Bearing this in mind, it has been argued that it would not be good policy to
enforce labour law in the informal economy because this could lead to that
sector losing its capacity to absorb manpower that otherwise would remain
unemployed. Labour-protection advocates, on the other hand, would observe
that overall deregulation would result in the worsening of the situation for
workers in the formal economy without any positive effect on informal workers.

With reference to this question, the ILO Conference Report on the
Dilemma of the informal sector in 1991 emphasized that 'there can be no question of the ILO helping to "promote" or "develop" an informal sector as a
convenient, low-cost way of creating employment unless there is at the same
time an equal determination to eliminate progressively the worst aspects of
exploitation and inhuman working conditions in the sector'. The Conference
discussion stressed that the dilemma should be addressed by 'attacking the
underlying causes and not just the symptoms through a comprehensive and
multifaceted strategy' (Report VI, p. 1).

To sum up, it would seem very difficult to reach consensus on the specific
strategies which could be followed with respect to the informal economy.
However, it has been agreed that the decent work deficit be reduced, and a
gradual transition of the informal economy to the formal economy be undertaken. This message is also supported by a significant number of ILO standards which cover all kind of workers, regardless of the existence of an
employment relationship. In particular, the rights covered by the ILO
Declaration on Fundamental Rights and Principles at Work have been defined
as a minimum social floor which should apply to all workers regardless of
their working status in the formal or informal economy.[10] This approach has
been followed in India, for example, in the form of recommendations by the

---

10 ILO, *The informal economy: Enabling transition to formalization*; Background document to
the Tripartite Interregional Symposium on the Informal Economy: Enabling Transition to
Formalisation, Geneva, 27–29 November 2007.

Group on Women Workers and Child Labour to the Second National Commission, established in 1999 (box 2.2).

The gradual widening of the application of national labour law in theory and practice has been defined as one necessary cornerstone of policies to address the needs of informal workers, but strategies can not be limited to this alone. Decent work for all workers, regardless of status, requires integrated policies touching upon rights at work, social protection, social dialogue and employment promotion. In short, the question how to efficiently protect the unprotected remains an ongoing challenge.

Box 2.2 Recommendations to extend national labour legislation to informal women workers in India[11]

The Second National Labour Commission in India set up in late 1999 was mandated to recommend 'umbrella legislation' for the informal workforce. It involved organizations of informal workers in drafting the legislation. Below are some of the major recommendations of the Group on Women Workers and Child Labour.

A. *Minimum Wages Act*
- Broaden definition of worker to accommodate more categories of informal workers
- Include piece rates, not just time rates, under minimum wage

B. *Equal Remuneration Act, 1975*
- The Equal Remuneration Act (ERA) should be amended to promote equal remuneration between all workers – men and women, formal and informal, as follows:
- Extend application of the Act to cover unequal remuneration not just within units/establishments but across units/establishments by occupational group, industry or sector, or region
- Replace clause 'same work or work of a similar nature' by clause 'work of equal value'
- Provide guidelines and mandate training for labour inspectors – for example, to help them to identify discriminatory practices pertaining to the ERA

---

11 Report of the Study Group on Women Workers and Child Labour to the National Commission on Labour (2001), cited in M. A. Chen, R. Jhabvala and F. Lund, *Supporting workers in the informal economy: A policy framework*, ILO Working Paper on the Informal Economy 2002/2 (Geneva, ILO, 2002).

C. *Sector-specific Acts*

Bidi and Cigar Workers (Conditions of Employment) Act, 1996
- Include those who work under the 'sale-purchase' system in the definition of 'employee'
- Fix a national minimum wage for bidi rolling to be adopted by all States

D. *Women-specific measures*

Maternity Benefit Act
- Coverage needs to be expanded

Industrial Disputes Act
- Include prohibitions against all forms of sexual harassment
- Give proportionate representation to female employees in the Worker Committee

Workmen's Compensation Act, 1923
- Provide coverage for all female workers under medical insurance schemes

Factories Act, 1948 (and other Acts with childcare provisions)
- Mandate provision of crèches in all factories employing more than ten workers (either men or women)

Employees State Insurance Act, 1948 – cash benefit to insure women for pregnancy
- Extend coverage to units of ten workers and to workers who earn less than Rs3,000 per month

E. *Advisory, worker and tripartite committees or boards* (mandated under these Acts)
- Empower and expand the activities of these institutions to review and regularize irregular tactics by employers, such as shifting from subcontract to sale-purchase arrangements to avoid employer status
- Include at least one woman from all sides (employer, formal employees, informal workers and government)
- Include representatives of trade unions of informal women workers and formal women workers

Atypical work: from rejection to integration in labour law

We have already examined the emergence of *atypical work* from the mid-1970s onwards. The prosperity of the post-war years – and doubtless also the very low unemployment rates at that time – led to the development of a model employment relationship according to which workers performed work or provided services to an employer under a contract of employment of indefinite duration. Their work was performed for the benefit of a single employer and within the premises of a company or an establishment. In addition, workers were protected against unfair dismissal and generally expected to spend most of their working life – or at least a great part of it – in the same enterprise. For these reasons, career development and seniority were given great emphasis. At that time, part-time work, home-based work, as well as contracts of employment for a specified period of time or for the performance of a specified task, also existed, as did special statutes. These forms of employment which deviated from the prevailing models had more than a token presence in some industries and economic activities, but in general they only accounted for a small share of overall employment.

By the end of the 1970s, what had been a well-established pattern of employment started to erode as a result of the emergence of many different working arrangements which lacked some or several of the attributes mentioned above. Perhaps what attracted the greatest attention was the supply of workers through temporary work agencies (TWAs), which led to the establishment of a triangular relationship between a worker, his or her legal employer (the TWA) and a third party, the user enterprise for whom the worker actually worked. This kind of arrangement did away with the traditional employer–employee relationship on which the concept of the individual employment relationship had been built. Though it would not be accurate to say that temporary work was a completely new phenomenon – the TWA Manpower had existed since 1948 – the percentage of temporary work in the overall employment figures was quasi-confidential until the 1960s. Nevertheless it acquired a quite remarkable visibility in the following decade, to the point that several countries, for instance Belgium, France, Germany and the Netherlands, considered it necessary to recognize and regulate it.[12]

During most of the 1970s and 1980s, an overwhelmingly majority of labour law academics were deeply hostile to this and to other forms of non-

---

12 During the 1960s, other countries such as Spain and Sweden prohibited temporary work. This prohibition was largely based on a (non-binding) opinion of the International Labour Office, which considered that the activity of temporary work enterprises fell within the framework of the Fee Charging Employment Agencies Convention (revised), 1949 (No. 96), which provided for the suppression or if not the strict regulation of private intermediation in the labour market. The ILO later reviewed its position with respect to private placement in general and temporary work in particular, and in 1997 it adopted the Private Employment Agencies Convention (No. 181), which legitimates the activity of temporary work enterprises.

conventional employment relationships. For example, most of the academics attending the World Congress of Labour and Social Security Law in Caracas in 1985 expressed great concern because of the emergence of *atypical employ-ment*, to which the notion of *precariousness* was always attached. Opposition to precarious work and atypical forms of employment was also on the agenda of labour organizations as well as on those of many left-wing governments.

It cannot be denied that, in terms of the *standard employment relationship*, the status of atypical workers is generally more unfavourable. However, it should also be recognized that rejection across the board of atypical employment frequently contains an element of ideology. First, atypical work is considered to be precarious work, but this is not always the case. On the contrary, it is presumed that the standard employment relationship is never precarious – which is unrealistic because no law can guarantee life employment, at least in the private sector. Secondly, it is presumed that the proliferation of atypical employment forms part of right-wing government programmes, which would be ideologically interested in undermining labour law. Yet the facts show that atypical employment has risen under both left-wing and right-wing govern-ments; indeed, many labour law reforms which have institutionalized some forms of atypical employment have been adopted under left-wing govern-ments. Thirdly, it should be acknowledged that some forms of atypical employ-ment are actually sought out by the workers themselves; this is the case, for example, with voluntary part-time work and, in some cases, with temporary work, which incidentally can have a positive impact on the labour market. It is recognized that temporary work serves in many cases as a springboard for work-ers to get a permanent job after one or several temporary placements.

Thus the view that rejects all forms of atypical employment is no less ideo-logical than that which assigns pejorative connotations to labour law protec-tion and therefore advocates more *labour flexibility* as an efficient means of improving productivity, thus fuelling the economy and creating jobs. The fact is that labour flexibility very rarely creates new and authentic jobs, while it has doubtless made many of the existing ones precarious, just as labour law protection very rarely, if at all, has been able to protect jobs that the market is no longer able to sustain.

Indications now suggest that the antagonism between *standard* and *atypi-cal* employment relationships is fading away. On the one hand, nowadays, the patterns of employment established in the post-war years match the real-ity of and respond to the labour market's needs in many cases but not in others; this gives a raison d'être to atypical employment. On the other hand, it is undisputed that the standard employment relationship is still the prevail-ing pattern of employment in the most dynamic and competitive economies of the world (while it is not, and in fact it never has been, in a majority of developing countries). Moreover, despite the increasing share of non-standard forms of employment, nothing suggests that they will eventually replace what is still regarded as the standard pattern. What has occurred is that, although in a minority position, atypical employment nowadays takes a greater share of overall employment and has thus become a standard and structural component of the labour market.

It is on that premise that labour law now attempts to bring together both typical and atypical employment. Government policies and legislative strategies seem to be attempting to provide atypical employment with a legal framework, the purpose of which is twofold. First, it recognizes that in a globalized world there is a greater need for labour mobility. Both the Dutch law on flexibility and security of 1999 (also known as the *flexicurity law*) and the reform of the labour market in Italy in 2003 (known as the *Biagi reform*) would seem to provide sound examples of this trend.

In the same way, the Framework Agreement on Fixed-term Work (1999) concluded by the European Trade Union Confederation (ETUC), the Union of Industrial and Employers' Confederations of Europe (UNICE, now BUSINESSEUROPE) and the European Centre of Enterprises with Public Participation and of Enterprises of General Economic Interest (CEEP), which was further transposed into a European Community Directive on fixed-term work, recognizes that 'contracts of an indefinite duration are, and will continue to be, the general form of employment relationship between employers and workers', but also that 'fixed-term employment contracts respond, in certain circumstances, to the needs of both employers and workers'. Thus the agreement forbids employers to treat fixed-term workers in a less favourable manner than permanent workers solely because they have a fixed-term contract, unless the difference in treatment can be justified on objective grounds. It further prevents the abuse of fixed-term work by introducing a number of safeguard measures (for example, renewal of fixed-term contracts should be justified by objective reasons, the number of renewals should be limited and there should be a maximum total duration for successive fixed-term employment contracts and relationships). A similar approach is followed in the Framework Agreement on Part-time Work concluded by UNICE, CEEP and ETUC, which has also been transposed into a European Community Directive addressed to the EU Member States.[13] The ILO anticipated this in

---

13 Council Directive 1999/70/EC of 28 June 1999 concerning the Framework Agreement on Fixed-term Work concluded by ETUC, UNICE and CEEP, *Official Journal of the European Communities (OJ)*, L 175, 10 July 1999, pp. 43–8. See also Council Directive 97/81/EC of 15 December 1995 concerning the Framework Agreement on Part-time Work concluded by UNICE, CEEP and the ETUC, *OJ*, L 14, 20 January 1998, pp. 9–11.

1997 when it adopted the Private Employment Agencies Convention (No. 181). The Convention acknowledged the role of private placement and provided an institutional framework for both the regulation of temporary work agencies and the protection of the workers hired by these enterprises and further supplied to the user enterprises.

Box 2.3 From rejection to recognition of private placement and temporary work: the Private Employment Agencies Convention, 1997 (No. 181), and Recommendation (No. 188)

With the adoption of the Private Employment Agencies Convention, 1997 (No. 181), the ILO reversed its tradition of mistrust of private placement that had begun in 1919 with Recommendation No. 1. Under that Recommendation, ILO Members were urged to 'take measures to prohibit the establishment of employment agencies which charge fees or which carry on their business for profit ... and where such agencies already exist ... they be permitted to operate only under Government licences, and that all practicable measures be taken to abolish such agencies as soon as possible'. Later, in 1933, the ILO adopted the Fee-Charging Employment Agencies Convention (No. 34), whereby such agencies were to be abolished within three years from the coming into force of the Convention for the Member concerned.

In view of the poor ratification rate of Convention No. 34, a revision was undertaken after the Second World War, in 1949, in the form of Convention No. 96, which provided that ratifying States had the choice, either to prohibit fee-charging employment agencies under Part II of the Convention or to (tightly) regulate them in keeping with Part III of the Convention (licensing, renewable on a yearly basis at the discretion of the public authorities, fees approved or fixed by the competent authority). In 1966, in reply to a request made by the government of Sweden, the Office gave a non-binding opinion which concluded that temporary work agencies should be included in the definition of fee-charging employment agencies as provided for in Convention No. 96, and should therefore be either prohibited or tightly regulated.

For many countries, however, both the position of Convention No. 96 and the Office opinion had become dated by the early 1980s. Critics pointed out that in many countries the relations between public and private placement had evolved from antagonism to cooperation. Also, Convention No. 96 ignored the increasingly positive role of temporary work agencies, which were able to cope efficiently with both the temporary needs of enterprises and the personal choices of many workers, not to mention that temporary work also operated, in many cases, as a springboard to stable employment. Acknowledging these problems, the ILO Conference held a General Discussion in 1994 on the role of private employment agencies in the functioning of the labour market. The Conference came to the unanimous conclusion that Convention No. 96 needed to be revised, something which was done in 1997 by Convention No. 181.

Under the new Convention the term 'private employment agency' (PEA) applies to both firms which 'offer services for matching offers of and applications for employment, without the private employment agency becoming a party to the employment relationships which may arise therefrom' and temporary work agencies which employ workers 'with a view to making them available to a third party, who may be a natural or legal person [i.e. the user enterprise] which assigns their tasks and supervises the execution of these tasks'.

The Convention implicitly recognizes that both forms of private placement are legal and legitimate. While Members are not required to demand that a PEA be in the possession of a licence, they must, however, take measures to ensure that workers recruited by or through a PEA are not victims of abuses. In particular, trade union and collective bargaining rights are to be respected; child work cannot be used or supplied; and a PEA shall 'treat workers without discrimination on the basis of race, colour, sex, religion, political opinion, national extraction, social origin, or any other form of discrimination covered by national law and practice, such as age or disability'.

The Convention includes measures on the processing and protection of workers' personal data (this is indeed the sole international binding standard that specifically addresses the protection of workers' personal data). It also provides that private employment agencies shall not charge fees or costs to workers (some exceptions are, however, permitted in the interest of the workers concerned). Protection of migrant workers recruited or placed by PEAs and collaboration between PEAs and the public employment service are also addressed by the Convention. No less noteworthy is a provision (Article 12) which requires that Members shall:

> determine and allocate the respective responsibilities of private employment agencies providing the services referred to in paragraph 1(b) of Article 1 and of user enterprises in relation to (a) collective bargaining; (b) minimum wages; (c) working time and other working conditions; (d) statutory social security benefits; (e) access to training; (f) protection in the field of occupational safety and health; (g) compensation in case of occupational accidents or diseases; (h) compensation in case of insolvency and protection of workers claims; (i) maternity protection and benefits, and parental protection and benefits.

Dependent-independent workers and the 'defocusing' of the employment relationship

---

**Box 2.4 The conversion of dependent employment
relationships in the self-employed provision of services**[14]

There was a kind of 'end of the world' feeling in eyes and in the voice of a senior and distinguished teacher of languages in the largest Hungarian university when she came to ask for my legal advice: she had been confronted with the alternative to become an 'entrepreneur' providing teaching services to her former students through a contract between the university and her 'enterprise' or lose her job. The university, due to serious budget cuts, decided to offer formerly free language tuition as a paid service to the students and to shift the business and employment risk of the activity to the previous teachers by requiring them to form small private companies with which the university would contract for the services. The teacher insisted that she had been a faculty member, a public employee of a state university for about a quarter of century and she found it an absurd idea to be a university teacher as a private enterprise. She could hardly believe there was nothing in the law books that would have prevented the university from making such a move.

The attention that in the 1980s was centred on work then called 'atypical' has today been shifted towards other forms of work arrangements. More particularly it is much discussed whether or not a certain number of new (and sometimes not so new) work arrangements fall within the scope of labour law. There is no doubt that some of these forms fall into a grey area, which makes it very difficult to determine accurately whether or not they correspond to the definition of what has traditionally been understood as an 'employment relationship'. Some other forms of work arrangement clearly fall within the field of civil and commercial law, and in these cases workers are deemed to be self-employed rather than employees. For example, the German Commercial Code provides that a person who is essentially free to organize his own work and thus to determine his working time is presumed to be self-employed. However, many of those who are presumed to be self-employed are in fact economically dependent on the person or the business for which they

---

14 Csilla Kollonay Lehoczky, 'Ways and effects of deconstructing protection in the post-socialist new member States – based on Hungarian experience', in G. Davidov and B. Langille (eds), 2006, op. cit., pp. 220–1.

perform work or provide services. It follows that these workers actually take all the risks but fail to benefit from any of the advantages normally associated with being an entrepreneur. Still, there are other apparently self-employed workers who are in fact subordinated employees whose employment relationship has been deliberately disguised under the form of a civil or a commercial law arrangement (false contractors).

Labour law doctrine and case law have reacted differently vis-à-vis these new (and not so new) arrangements. For a long time it was accepted that work could be either subordinated or independent, and that labour law was concerned only with the first of these. 'Subordinated work' implied the performance of personal work or the provision of personal services under the direction of an employer or his or her representative; other features of subordinated work were the disciplinary prerogatives of the employer: continuity of the relationship, performance of work within an established time-frame and regular remuneration on the basis of the hours of work performed or the worker's output. Anything that did not fit within those parameters was 'independent work', which was dealt with under civil or commercial law but did not fall within the scope of labour law.

Though simple, coherent and fit for the social environment in which it was originally formulated, today this approach has become simplistic and inadequate. The traditional view of individuals simply obeying an employer's or a supervisor's orders in determining the organization of their work or working time would seem to be well adapted to manual work in a factory environment but does not correspond to other forms of work organization where employees enjoy more freedom in deciding how and when they perform their work. Mere subordination is thus no longer a sufficient criterion to determine who is to be deemed an employee and who is not. In addition, such a criterion would be unjust and unfair as an increasing number of workers actually perform work or provide services under objective conditions of dependency, though not under traditional subordination, and consequently can be denied protection which is otherwise granted to those who have recognized employee status (i.e. subordinated workers in the traditional sense of subordination). These workers are obviously in a much more vulnerable situation than those who benefit from labour law protection. The ILO has referred to this phenomenon as a 'loss of focus' or 'defocusing' of the employment relationship.[15] As in photography, the term suggests that the 'labour law

---

15 This expression was used for the first time in a report submitted to a Meeting of Experts on Workers in Situations Needing Protection held in May 2000. ILO, *The employment relationship: Scope*, Basic technical document, Meeting of Experts on Workers in Situation Needing Protection (Geneva, 2000), Ch. 3, pp. 134–5.

viewfinder' points in one direction but the workers who need labour law protection are out of that viewfinder's range – they are 'out of focus'.

While the lack of protection of the worker is the common denominator in these situations, the variety of situations in which that phenomenon occurs makes it impossible for a common solution to be proposed for all of them. This was one of the reasons why the ILO Conference was not able to adopt standards on what at the time was called 'contract labour' when the subject came before it in the 1997 and 1998 Sessions, as the standards then proposed were attempting to encompass too many diverse situations.

However, after further work, the Conference and the Office were able to identify a number of situations where workers could be left unprotected because their employee status was unclear or simply denied, namely the following, which were endorsed by the 91st Session of the International Labour Conference in 2003:

- the law is unclear, too narrow in scope or otherwise inadequate;
- the employment relationship is disguised under the form of a civil or a commercial arrangement;
- the employment relationship is ambiguous;
- the worker is in fact an employee, but it is not clear who the employer is, what rights the worker has, and against whom those rights can be enforced;
- lack of compliance and enforcement.

The ILO Conference further agreed that:

> Clarity and predictability in the law are in the interests of all concerned. Employers and workers should know their status and, consequently, their respective rights and obligations under the law. To this end, laws should be drafted in such a way that they are adapted to the national context and provide adequate security and flexibility to address the realities of the labour market and to provide benefits to the labour market. While laws can never fully anticipate every situation arising in the labour market, it is nonetheless important that legal loopholes are not created or allowed to persist. Laws and their interpretation should be compatible with the objectives of decent work, namely to improve the quantity and quality of employment, should be flexible enough not to impede innovative forms of decent employment, and promote such employment and growth. Social dialogue with tripartite participation is a key means to ensuring that legislative reform leads to clarity and predictability and is sufficiently flexible.[16]

---

16 See ILO, *Report of the Committee on the Employment Relationship*, Provisional Record No. 21, International Labour Conference, 91st Session, Geneva, 2003; Conclusions concerning the Employment Relationship, adopted by the Committee, paras 5 and 6.

Who is protected by labour law?

In short, it has become essential that an effort be made to redraw the boundaries of labour law, something which is now being undertaken in the form of laws and regulations, collective agreements and case law in many countries. Thus some labour laws have been drafted to broaden the definition of who is an employee in order to include situations where the nature of the work performed or the service rendered, or the type of relationship existing between the work or service provider and the person for whom the work is performed or services are provided, has fallen into a grey area (for example, when a worker is not totally subordinated to the company nor is totally independent either). It is worthwhile noting here that the principle of the 'realities of working relationships' becomes the leading criterion in determining whether a given arrangement between a worker and the person for whom the work is performed is an employment relationship or a contract for civil or commercial services. This is, for example, the approach followed in the law of countries such as Canada (Province of Ontario),[17] New Zealand, South Africa and a majority of Latin American countries, whereas in Ireland the social partners have identified a group of indicators to determine whether an employment relationship exists (see box 2.5).

Box 2.5 Ireland: Code of practice for determining employment or self-employment status of individuals[18]

EMPLOYEE	SELF-EMPLOYED
An individual would normally be an employee if he or she:	An individual would normally be self-employed if he or she:
– is under the control of another person who directs as to how, when and where the work is to be carried out;	– owns his or her own business;

---

17 Under the Labour Relations Act of the Province of Ontario 1995, a 'dependent contractor' means a person, whether or not employed under a contract of employment, and whether or not furnishing tools, vehicles, equipment, machinery, material, or any other thing owned by the dependent contractor, who performs work or services for another person for compensation or reward on such terms and conditions that the dependent contractor is in a position of economic dependence upon, and under an obligation to perform duties for, that person more closely resembling the relationship of an employee than that of an independent contractor; ('entrepreneur dépendant'); text available online at http://www.e-laws.gov.on.ca.

18 Department for Enterprise, Trade and Employment, Programme for Prosperity and Fairness, Employment Status Group, *Code of practice for determining employment or self-employment status of individuals* (Dublin, July 2001); available at: http://www.entemp.ie.

– supplies labour only;

– receives a fixed hourly/ weekly/monthly remuneration;
– cannot subcontract the work. If the work can be subcontracted and paid by the person subcontracting the work, the employer/employee relationship may simply be transferred on;
– does not supply materials for the job;

– does not provide equipment other than small tools of the trade. The provision of tools or equipment might not have a significant bearing on coming to a conclusion that employment status may be appropriate having regard to all the circumstances of the case;
– is not exposed to personal financial risk in carrying out the work;
– does not assume responsibility for investment and management in the business;
– does not have the opportunity to profit from sound management in the scheduling of engagements or in the performance of tasks arising from the engagements;

– is exposed to financial risk, by having to bear the cost of making good faulty or substandard work carried out under the contract;
– assumes responsibility for investment and management in the enterprise;
– has the opportunity to profit from sound management in the scheduling and performance of engagements and tasks;

– has control over what is done, when and where it is done and whether he or she does it personally;
– is free to hire other people, on his or her terms, to do the work which has been agreed to be undertaken;

– can provide the same services to more than one person or business at the same time;
– provides the materials for the job;

– has a fixed place of business where materials, equipment, etc. can be stored;

– provides equipment and machinery necessary for the job, other than the small tools of the trade or equipment which in an overall context would not be an indicator of a person in business on their own account;

– works set hours or a given number of hours per week or month; – works for one person or for one business; – receives expenses payments to cover subsistence and/or travel; – is entitled to extra pay or time off for overtime.	– costs and agrees a price for the job; –provides his or her own insurance cover; – controls the hours of work in fulfilling the job obligations.

Different legal strategies have been proposed to deal with the expanding definition of the employment relationship. One of these consists in the broadening of the criteria that are commonly used to define subordination. More recently, the worker's integration in a collective organizational scheme designed by and for others has also been taken as an indicator of subordination, as was pointed out in a well-known study sponsored by the European Commission, *Beyond employment: The transformation of labour and the future of labour law in Europe*, commonly known as the Supiot Report after the name of the report's coordinator.[19]

[The] broadening of the concept of subordination has made dealing with the concept more uncertain and above all more complex. Hence, when workers are afforded a certain degree of independence in the performance of their duties, other indications of their possible subordination must be sought to establish the legal status of their contracts. This technique, called 'indication clustering', has become a common feature in labour law in European countries. Rather than verifying that all indications conform to the situation under consideration, it consists of inferring, from the existence of several of such indications, that the resulting relationship involves subordination.

The UNIZO test provides us with an interesting example of this approach. UNIZO (Unie van Zelfstandige Ondernemers) is an organization representing small enterprises and self-employed people in Belgium (predominantly in Flanders). It has developed a formula, largely based on criteria established through case law, to determine mathematically whether a person is an employee or self-employed. As shown in table 2.1, there are 12 criteria, each

---

19 EC, *Transformation of labour and future of labour law in Europe*, final report (Brussels, 1998).

of which is allocated a given number of points, the total sum of which is 100. If the result of the formula is below 40, the person is not considered to be self-employed. If it exceeds 60, the person is considered to be a self-employed person. If the result is between 40 and 60, a commission should decide whether or not the worker is self-employed. The formula reads as follows:

Table 2.1 UNIZO criterion points

	Criterion	Points
1	Substantial participation in the profits	13
2	Significant professional investments	13
3	Responsibility and authority to decide whether to keep the company profitable by investing in capital equipment	13
4	Variable income without a minimum guaranteed income	9
5	Possibility of working for several clients	9
6	Presenting to a third party as a company	9
7	Has own infrastructure and equipment	4
8	Not subject to control/sanctions	4
9	Freedom to purchase or fix prices	4
10	Organizes own working time	9
11	Real possibility of recruiting own staff	9
12	Possibility of being engaged as self-employed person	4
	TOTAL	100

Box 2.6 Judicial redress when an employment relationship has been disguised under the form of a civil contract of services

Jorge O. Amora v. Asian Development Bank[20]
The applicant had served for many years with the Asian Development Bank (ADB) under a 'Memorandum of Agreement' (MOA), which was periodically extended until 21 April 1993, when it was replaced by a regular appointment. Among other terms the MOA specified:

– [He] shall be under the direction of such officer or officers as the Bank may in its absolute discretion nominate from time to time . . .
– In consideration of his services, the Bank shall pay [him] a monthly remuneration of Pesos Seven Hundred Fifty (P750.00) only payable semi-monthly. [...]

---

20 *Jorge O. Amora* v. *Asian Development Bank*, Administrative Tribunal of the Asian Development Bank, Decision No. 24 (6 January 1997).

The MOA also contained the following clauses:

– Nothing contained in the terms and conditions herein . . . shall be construed as establishing or creating any relationship other than that of independent contractor between the Bank and [him].
– [He] shall not be entitled to any compensation, allowances, benefits or rights from or against the Bank other than expressly provided therein . . .

Upon his retirement the complainant brought a complaint before the ADB Administrative Tribunal. In order to deal with his several claims the Tribunal considered that it must first determine his employment status from 24 August 1979 to 20 April 1993, through an analysis and evaluation of his contractual relations with the Bank during that period.

The Tribunal considered that usually a contract signed by the parties is binding upon them. There are, however, some circumstances in which a contract may be set aside or varied by a competent tribunal. This happens, for example, *when the contract fundamentally disregards reality*.

The Tribunal concluded that in the case at stake 'the MOAs did not reflect the true relationship between the Bank and the applicant'. It held that:

recourse to successive short-term or temporary contractual appoint-ments to jobs which are essentially of a permanent nature is not a fair employment practice, particularly if such appointments can be shown to have been made only to deny employees security of tenure or other conditions and benefits of service. Such appointments are permissible only if they have a clear functional justification and rationale in the exigencies of management and the nature of the job in question, and are subject to limitations based on norms of good administration.

It further held:

There are several tests which traditionally are applied in order to determine whether a person is an independent contractor, engaged under a contract for services, or an employee, working under a contract of service.

Although every MOA under which the Applicant worked contained references to his services, it is quite clear that he was not engaged under a contract for services to perform a specified piece of work, for a stipulated fee or price, under his own responsibility and according to his own methods, without being subject to the control of the Bank (except as to the results of his work), and investing his own resources, in regard to tools, equipment, materials and the like.

The MOAs did not describe the work which the Applicant was required to do; he was to work, in the Bank's premises, under the direction of the Bank's officers and in accordance with their instructions; he was not to be paid for the job or the result, but was to receive a regular, stated monthly remuneration; indeed, he even received increments midway through several contracts, just like an ordinary employee; he had to work full-time in accordance with the Bank's working hours, and could even be required to work overtime or on shifts; and he was entitled to annual, medical and casual leave. One of his obligations was at all times [to] refrain from actively engaging in any political activity [...]. All along, the Applicant was neither carrying on an independent business nor could he assign the performance of the work to anyone else. On the contrary, his work was part of, or ancillary to, the Bank's business.

The Tribunal finds that all the relevant tests applicable to the situation under consideration indicate that the Applicant was not an independent contractor. On the contrary, all these features, being totally inconsistent with the Applicant's status as an independent contractor, are consistent only with his being an employee of the Bank. [...]

Thus the intention of the parties as manifested in the terms and conditions of each MOA was that the Applicant was to be an employee. However, every MOA had an interpretation clause, that nothing contained in [those] terms and conditions [...] shall be construed as establishing or creating any relationship other than that of independent contractor. That is irreconcilably contrary to reality, and must be disregarded.

From the foregoing, the Tribunal concludes that for nearly 15 years, notwithstanding the interpretation clause in each MOA, the relationship between the Bank and the Applicant under every MOA was that of employer and employee.

In addition, there would seem to be a trend to extend certain forms of labour protection to borderline situations between employment relationships and the performance of work or provision of services under a civil or a commercial contract (box 2.6 gives an example of judicial redress in such a situation). In response to this trend, the EC Directive of 18 December 1986 on the coordination of the laws of the Member States relating to self-employed commercial agents (86/653/EEC)[21] requires that they receive a minimum

---

21 *OJ*, L 382, 31 December 1986, pp. 17–21.

remuneration; it also provides that the termination of an agency contract shall be subject to a period of notice.

Likewise, the United Kingdom's National Minimum Wage Act 1998 applies not only to wage-earners but also to other workers who perform work or render services personally even though they do not have the formal legal status of employees. In South Africa, the Basic Conditions of Employment Act 1997 allows the public authorities to decide on a total or partial extension to workers whose legal situation has been defined as that of 'dependent contractors'. In Germany, economically dependent workers who are in a similar situation to that of employees (*Arbeitnehmerähnliche Personen*) are recognized as being entitled to a number of rights which are typically granted to wage-earners only – for example paid leave, safety and hygiene standards, collective bargaining, access to the labour courts – but not all of them. Under French law, shop managers (*gérants de fonds de commerce*) are legally considered as independent workers in their relations with third parties but as wage-earners with respect to suppliers. Moreover, the French Labour Code specifically grants employee status to workers in a number of occupations, such as home-based workers, nursery nurses, freelance journalists and public performance artists, who, in the light of the conditions in which they carry out their activities, might be considered independent workers.[22]

Last but not least, mention should be made of the Biagi reform in Italy, which has regulated the *collaborazione coordinata e continuativa*, whereby a status close to that of employee has been acknowledged in respect of a certain group of 'parasubordinated' workers. The Supiot Report, mentioned earlier, together with the various reports on the Scope of the Employment Relationship that the ILO submitted to the 91st (2003) and 95th (2006) Sessions of the Conference,[23] are indispensable sources for the study of this problem. More recently, the European Commission has started to use the term 'economically dependent workers' to refer to those workers who are formally self-employed but depend on a single source for their income (box 2.7).[24]

---

22 Similarly, the Labour Code of Luxembourg (Article L. 121-1) gives a list of apparent grey areas where employee status is recognized. These include directors of enterprises or sections thereof, supervisors, wardens, salespersons, sales representatives and so forth.

23 ILO, *The scope of the employment relationship*, Report V, International Labour Conference, 91st Session, Geneva, 2003 and ILO, *The employment relationship*, Report V(1), International Labour Conference, 95th Session, Geneva, 2006.

24 European Industrial Relations Observatory: '*Economically dependent workers*', *employment law and industrial relations*; available online at http://www.eiro.eurofound.ie.

Box 2.7 Economically dependent workers[25]

The concept of 'economically dependent worker' falls between the two established concepts of employment and self-employment. It refers to those workers who do not correspond to the traditional definition of employee because they do not have an employment contract as dependent employees. However, although formally 'self-employed', they are economically dependent on a single employer for their source of income.

The status of these workers falls in between self-employment and dependent employment, and they have some characteristics of both forms. First, they are formally self-employed, in that they usually have a sort of 'service contract' with the employer. Second, they depend on one single employer for all or much of their income. They are often similar to employees in a number of ways. They may lack a clear organizational separation, working on the employer's premises and/or using the employer's equipment. There may be no clear distinction of tasks: they may perform similar tasks to existing employees, or of those formerly undertaken by employees, before the work was outsourced. Finally, their 'services' fall outside the traditional professions, in that they often do not require specific skills or professional knowledge or competence.

Despite these similarities to employees, such economically dependent workers do not generally benefit from the protections granted to employees both by law and collective bargaining, including provisions on health and safety, such as working time provisions. The categories of employee and self-employed workers are reasonably clearly defined, and the distinction in most, but not all EU Member States, tends to exclude the latter from employment protection law, including working time regulations.

The problem arises with new categories of work, which do not clearly fall into either category of employment or self-employment: 'economically dependent worker'. Member States have adopted a variety of strategies to deal with this problem, including treating them as employees and therefore falling within the scope of employment protection legislation, extending protection to specified categories of such workers and listing criteria that enable identification of the workers as either employees or self-employed.

In a number of Member States, trade unions have been active in establishing organizations specifically targeted at 'economically dependent workers'.

---

25 Eurofound, 'Economically Dependent Workers', in *European Industrial Relations Dictionary* (Dublin).

The challenge today consists – no more and no less – in widening the definition of the workers who are to be protected by labour law, and providing the legal means to organize such protection, for it is not certain that all of these workers can be protected in the same way as those who have recognized employee status. If we continue the analogy of the viewfinder, we could say now that this work would consist in providing labour law with something like a wide-angle lens to enlarge the scope of labour law to protect not only workers in that grey area but also those who are objectively employees but not legally subordinated workers.

Thus, in Spain, self-employed workers are represented by associations affiliated with the biggest workers' and employers' associations, the Union of Professionals and Self-Employed Workers (Unión de Profesionales y Trabajadores Autónomos, UPTA), affiliated to the General Workers' Confederation (Unión General de Trabajadores, UGT) and the National Federation of Self-Employed Workers (Asociación de Trabajadores Autónomos, ATA). In September 2006, following negotiations, an agreement was worked out which was subsequently presented to the Council of Ministers as a draft bill for a statute on self-employed workers. This paved the way for a law on Self-employed Work being passed in July 2007.[26] Broadly, this law provides for the following:

- rules on occupational risk prevention for cases in which workers use raw materials or tools belonging to others;
- economic guarantees for self-employed workers who are subcontracted. The main company is responsible for the debts of contractors to self-employed workers;
- specific rights for economically dependent self-employed workers (those who receive 75 per cent of their income from a single client or company), such as 18 days' holidays per year and compensation for unjustified termination of the contract by the worker's 'client';
- dispute settlement procedures; it should be noted that self-employed workers are placed within the sphere of social law;
- social security for self-employed workers brought closer to that of workers with employee status;
- protection against temporary incapacity;
- collective rights;
- non-discrimination.

---

26 Law 20/2007, of 11 July 2007, Charter of Self-Employment Work, *Boletín Oficial del Estado*, núm. 166 of 12 July 2007.

Finally, the law provides for the establishment of a State Council of Self-Employed Workers formed by representatives of associations, trade unions and employer organizations.

Box 2.8 The ILO Employment Relationship Recommendation, 2006 (No. 198)

In June 2006 the ILO Conference adopted the Employment Relationship Recommendation (No. 198). After a difficult debate, the workers' group and an overwhelming majority of governments voted for the Recommendation, while most of the employers' delegates voted against it.

The Recommendation provides policy guidance for the Members, to be reviewed at appropriate intervals, and allows, if necessary, for the clarifying and adapting of the scope of relevant laws and regulations in order to guarantee effective protection for workers who perform work in the context of an employment relationship. This policy should at least include measures to:

(a) provide guidance [...] on effectively establishing the existence of an employment relationship and on the distinction between employed and self-employed workers;

(b) combat disguised employment relationships in the context of, for example, other relationships that may include the use of other forms of contractual arrangements that hide the true legal status, noting that a disguised employment relationship occurs when the employer treats an individual as other than an employee in a manner that hides his or her true legal status as an employee, and that situations can arise where contractual arrangements have the effect of depriving workers of the protection they are due;

(c) ensure standards applicable to all forms of contractual arrangements, including those involving multiple parties, so that employed workers have the protection they are due;

(d) ensure that standards applicable to all forms of contractual arrangements establish who is responsible for the protection contained therein.

In the context of the transnational movement of workers, Members should consider adopting appropriate measures with a view to providing protection for and preventing abuses of migrant workers who may be affected by uncertainty as to the existence of an employment relationship. Also, where workers are recruited in one country for work in another, the Members concerned may consider concluding bilateral agreements to prevent abuses and fraudulent practices which have as their purpose the evasion of the existing arrangements for the protection of workers in the context of an employment relationship.

National policy for protection of workers in an employment relationship should not interfere with true civil and commercial relationships, while at the same time ensuring that individuals in an employment relationship have the protection they are due.

The Recommendation further states that the determination of the existence of an employment relationship should be guided primarily by the facts relating to the performance of work and the remuneration of the worker, notwithstanding how the relationship is characterized in any contrary arrangement, contractual or otherwise, that may have been agreed between the parties. Also, specific indicators of the existence of an employment relationship may be defined. These might include:

(a) the fact that the work is carried out according to the instructions and under the control of another party; involves the integration of the worker in the organization of the enterprise; is performed solely or mainly for the benefit of another person; must be carried out personally by the worker; is carried out within specific working hours or at a workplace specified or agreed by the party requesting the work; is of a particular duration and has a certain continuity; requires the worker's availability; or involves the provision of tools, materials and machinery by the party requesting the work;

(b) periodic payment of remuneration to the worker; the fact that such remuneration constitutes the worker's sole or principal source of income; provision of payment in kind, such as food, lodging or transport; recognition of entitlements such as weekly rest and annual holidays; payment by the party requesting the work for travel undertaken by the worker in order to carry out the work; or absence of financial risk for the worker.

Members should establish specific national mechanisms in order to ensure that employment relationships can be effectively identified within the framework of the transnational provision of services. Consideration should be given to developing systematic contact and exchange of information on the subject with other States.

Disguised employment relationships

Objectively dependent workers can also be denied labour law protection when their employee status is disguised beneath the form of a non-labour relationship. This is clearly fraudulent, and was tackled by the ILO Conference in 2003 in the following terms:

Disguised employment occurs when the employer treats a person who is an employee as other than an employee so as to hide his or her true legal status. This can occur through the inappropriate use of civil or commercial arrangements. It is detrimental to the interests of workers and employers and is an abuse that is inimical to decent work and should not be tolerated. False self-employment, false subcontracting, the establishment of pseudo-cooperatives, false provision of services and false company restructuring are among the most frequent means that are used to disguise the employment relationship. The effect of such practices can be to deny labour protection to the worker and to avoid costs that may include taxes and social security contributions. There is evidence that it is more common in certain areas of economic activity but governments, employers and workers should take active steps to guard against such practice anywhere they occur.[27]

In a number of Latin American countries, for example, the fraud consisting in hiring workers through labour-only cooperatives is quite a widespread practice, particularly in Brazil, Colombia and Peru. In the case of Brazil, the legal basis for labour cooperatives is a provision of the *Consolidaçao das Leis do Trabalho* (the Labour Code of 1943), which states that there is no employment relationship between a labour-only cooperative and its members; nor does such a relationship exist between the member and a user enterprise. It would seem that this provision was enacted in law following an initiative by landless peasant organizations, who were interested in promoting cooperativism. However, in practice many employers used it to hire workers through the intermediation of a labour cooperative. Quite often, cooperativists do not know even the name of their cooperative or where it is located. Many judicial decisions, in Brazil and other Latin American countries, have concluded, however, that these apparent cooperativists are actually subordinated workers of a user enterprise, and have therefore decided that a direct employment relationship does exist between them, as illustrated in box 2.9.

Box 2.9 Workers hired through a labour cooperative[28]

The claimant was a physician who had worked for the respondent, Comfenalco (an institution that pays family allowances and also provides

---

27 ILO, *Provisional Record 21*, Fifth item of the agenda: The scope of the employment relationship, International Labour Conference, 91st Session, Geneva, 2003, Conclusions, para. 7.

28 *Florez* v. *Caja de Compensación Familiar Comfenalco*, judgment of the Supreme Court of Colombia, Labour Cassation Chamber of 6 December 2006.

medical care for teachers in the public education sector), under a contract of employment between 1991 and 2001. In 1992 he was compelled to become a member of a labour cooperative named Coopesalud which had made a contract with the respondent for the purpose of providing medical care to the members of Coopesalud. However, this change in his legal status did not imply any change in the nature of the services he was to provide to the members of Comfenalco. Some years later he initiated litigation against Comfenalco on the grounds that he was actually in an employment relationship, and thus entitled to the rights granted to employees under the Labour Code, including being registered for social security benefits.

The respondent argued that the claimant was a cooperativist who worked pursuant to a civil contract it had concluded with the cooperative Coopesalud. It denied that the claimant had employee status.

At first instance, the judge held that the claimant had been in an employment relationship with the respondent, and his claim was legitimate and legal. The judgment was appealed. The Court of Appeal dismissed the appeal and decided that the respondent was obliged to register the claimant with the relevant social security department and to pay the contributions to the latter for the duration of the employment relationship. It held that the so-called cooperative operated in fact as a temporary work agency in breach of the law. It recalled that temporary work is permitted only under very specific conditions (replacement of workers on leave, increase of work, marketing, etc.). It considered it 'unbelievable' that employers use intermediaries such as labour cooperatives to avoid their responsibilities, and concluded that this was a fraud which should not be tolerated. Consequently it held that the respondent was the claimant's real employer. However, the Court of Appeal did not order the respondent to pay certain indemnities under the Labour Code for it had not been proved that it had acted in bad faith. The claimant then brought the case to the Supreme Court.

The Supreme Court assessed the evidence which had been made available in the litigation. It acknowledged that the claimant worked under the defendant's supervision and that his obligations were similar to those which are normally expected from a worker in an employment relationship. It was clear from the evidence that an actual employment relationship had existed, which had been illegally disguised under a civil law form. It considered that the fact that the respondent had illegally used the intermediary of a labour cooperative proved its bad faith. It recalled that the law permitted an organization to conclude certain contracts with labour cooperatives provided they were not used with the purpose or the effect of denying rights which were granted under the Labour Code. Such was not the case in this complaint. It concluded that the claimant was entitled to all the rights and indemnities under the Labour Code, including his affiliation to the social security system.

Decentralization of production and its impact on labour and employment relations: who is an employer?[29]

Social sciences have for the past three centuries successively depicted society as a 'machine' (in the eighteenth century), a 'body' (in the nineteenth century), and a system (in the twentieth century).[30] Today, the images of society that seem to prevail are those of the 'labyrinth' and the 'network', which reflect a profound change from the twentieth-century model represented by Max Weber's pyramid-like organization, described at the end of the nineteenth century and encapsulated in the metaphor of the 'iron cage'.[31] From an organizational viewpoint, enterprises were structured and operated similarly to the State;[32] they had well-established boundaries and were managed under a central authority. They were techno-structures that handled the entire production process: raw materials came in through one door and went out through another door as manufactured products.

At the end of the twentieth century, new socioeconomic developments challenged Weber's *iron cage*, both at the State level (federalism and quasi-federalism, the strengthening of local powers, the increasing loss of power of the state in relation to supranational political entities like the EU) and at that of business organizations which now tended to operate like networks of independent and semi-independent units under flexible forms of coordination. On the other hand, at the bottom of the pyramid, increasing organizational and societal fragmentation was taking place as outsourcing and externalization models were used more widely. Repetitive tasks became a thing of the past, and savings were made by reducing levels of functional work at the bottom of the pyramid.[33] Today, the terms *labyrinth* and *network* describe

---

29 This section is largely based on Raffaele de Luca Tamajo and Adalberto Perulli, *Labour law (in its individual and collective dimensions) and productive decentralization (outsourcing of work and contracting of labour)*, General Report to the XVIII World Congress of the International Society for Labour and Social Security Law, Paris, 2006.

30 See Bernard Mandeville, *The fable of the bees* (Oxford, 1714) (the machine concept is also central for David Hume and other founders of conventional political economy); Émile Durkheim (1893), *De la division du travail social* (Paris, Les Presses universitaires de France, 8e édition, 1967); translated as *The division of labour in society* (New York, Macmillan, 1933); and Talcott Parsons, *The structure of social action* (New York, McGraw-Hill, 1937).

31 Max Weber, *Die protestantishe Etik und der 'Geist' des Kapitalismus* (Gutersloh, 1905); translated into English by Talcott Parsons as *The protestant ethic and the spirit of capitalism* (London, Allen & Unwin, 1930).

32 For example, G. Poggi, *La vicenda dello stato moderno, profilo sociologico* (Bologna, Il Mulino, 1978).

33 Richard Sennett, *The culture of the new capitalism* (New Haven, Conn., Yale University Press, 2006).

better than any others the structure of many companies, especially transnational enterprises, and that of the organization of work within them. We can use the term *network society*[34] to describe the spread of organizational models based on socioeconomic alliances in which one can find values such as globalization, business links and associations. Corporate organizations have been moving from centralized and bureaucratic models, set up as isolated 'citadels', to relational structures, set up as networks. Work which is organized as a consequence of this new pattern takes the shape of a worldwide archipelago that mirrors the worldwide economy. Transnational corporations have several interconnected centres (regional and national) rather than one single centre.

Production patterns within this new organizational model are characterized by *outsourcing*,[35] which is frequently made up of two phases: *outsourcing* and *insourcing*. In the first phase, a company transfers to a third party some production or other processes which were formerly under its direct control. Such a transfer may be of assets, machinery, know-how and staff. In the second phase, the same company reacquires the transferee's output in order to reassemble it in its own complex production process. For example, an enterprise sells a truck to one of its former salaried truck-drivers, and signs a contract whereby the truck-driver will provide the enterprise with the same services as when he or she was an employee of that same enterprise. Whereas the work to be performed has not changed, the legal framework of the relationship between the enterprise and the truck-driver has indeed changed significantly, for the truck-driver has become an independent contractor. Thus the enterprise no longer has liability as an employer would: it does not pay for idle time, time off or overtime; it does not pay social security contributions; it does not grant paid leave or maternity leave; and it is not liable vis-à-vis third parties in the case of road accidents for which its former truck-driver could be held to be responsible while driving for his or her 'client'.

We hardly need to add that the outsourcing/insourcing strategy can take far more sophisticated forms than the one provided in the example above. However, the effect of this strategy is in all cases the same: by externally acquir-

---

34 Manuel Castells, *The information age: Economy, society and culture*, Vol. I, *The rise of the network society* (Oxford, Blackwell Publishers, 1966).

35 While the term 'outsourcing' is more frequently used in English, 'externalization' appears in French, and in Spanish this phenomenon is described variously as 'outsourcing', 'externación' and 'terciarización'. Whichever term is used, all refer to a varied collection of practices which share some common features but not all. As none of them have a legally sanctioned definition, we will use 'outsourcing' in this book to refer to all of these practices.

ing goods or services provided by third parties who manage their own risks – even though they might be using the same production factors as the transferor before them – a progressive substitution of internal production is established.

Companies are increasingly relying on outsourcing for the supply of production and provision of services closer and closer to the core of their activities. This process can be extended so that larger companies are no longer involved in direct production at all. Instead their role becomes one of market management, research and innovation – of coordinating the production of other companies they have subcontracted to. An example of this would be a large multinational sportswear firm that has no production plants of its own in any country of the world.[36]

Outsourcing is thus increasingly used in the supply of labour. We can distinguish several distinct patterns, all of which share a common feature: outsourced workers are not in an employment relationship with a user enterprise for which they perform work or provide a service.

The first pattern is that of workers who are employees of a firm providing a well-defined service to a user enterprise, often within the premises of that business. Cleaning, maintenance and surveillance have for many years been the most well-known forms of this arrangement, in which an in-house service is outsourced. However, in more recent years, the number and the variety of services provided by third parties have increased considerably and diversified as enterprises outsource more and more sophisticated services. A key feature of this pattern consists in the fact that the employees are under the direct supervision of the service-provider, not that of the user enterprise.

In the second, workers are leased staff of a third party, which is legally speaking their employer, but they work under instructions and the direct supervision of the user enterprise. Leasing of workers by a temporary work enterprise is the best-known example of this arrangement. Other forms of staff leasing include labour-only subcontracting (in France it is known as *marchandage*), something which is forbidden in many countries but not in others (for example, *tâcheronnage* – where the contractor takes over the whole task – is permitted in Francophone African countries as it has been a long-established practice there). A variant of this practice is the provision of workers through a labour-only cooperative, and this is widely used in a number of Latin American countries. Workers supplied by labour-only cooperatives are regarded as members of the cooperative and are not deemed to be in an

---

36 When, on 13 April 2005, the spokesperson of a sports clothing and footwear multinational announced the firm's new transparency policy of listing all the companies producing its goods worldwide, a BBC journalist inquired why the company did not simply hire the people directly. The reply was that this was 'no longer a viable business model'.

employment relationship with the user enterprise. As we have seen, the legality of this practice is questionable in many of these countries. A number of judicial decisions have held that this is merely a fraud, and the courts have deemed the worker in fact to be in an employment relationship with the user enterprise.[37] A well-known case of staff leasing is that of the Cuban employer entity (*entidad empleadora*). There is a rule in Cuba that no private employer can hire workers under a private-law contract of employment. However, as joint ventures with the Cuban State as well as foreign investors do have a need to hire workers, Cuban legislators have designed a scheme whereby workers are supplied by an employer entity to which they are legally subordinated. Amongst other provisions, Cuban law provides that the user enterprise will pay the *entidad empleadora* in hard currency while the latter will pay its workers in local currency. Cases involving the leasing of workers by China to factories in Saipan, and by the military government of Myanmar to a US multinational have also attracted huge publicity, and have even been brought before the US courts.[38]

The third pattern of outsourcing is when individual workers perform work or provide a service to a user enterprise under a civil or commercial arrangement, not an employment relationship. This can be done by former employees of the enterprise, which, legally speaking, has become the workers' client after having been their employer (see the example of the truck driver above).

The decentralization of production is in sharp contrast with the Fordist paradigm which was the prevailing type of work organization during the second part of the twentieth century. The new paradigm is as yet not perfectly defined, and so tends to be generically referred as post-Fordist. It has some fundamental characteristics that highlight a reversal in the production logic that prevailed during the past century. The first element consists in the progressive overtaking of goods-oriented production by knowledge-based production. The computer revolution has brought in a new era in which the central elements (tools, manual labour and raw materials) are replaced by intelligence, computerized information and more generally by services. This can be seen in the fact that, at the end of the twentieth century, more than half of the labour force in industrialized countries was producing and managing data and information rather than goods. A second element is linked to the substitution of a strategy of complex government by one of hierarchical

---

37 See note 28 above for the decision of the Colombian Supreme Court, Labour Cassation Chamber, in the case *Florez* v. *Comfenalco*.

38 See Lance Compa, 'Pursuing international labour rights in U.S. courts. New uses for old tools', in *Relations Industrielles/Industrial Relations* (Québec, 2002), Vol. 57, No. 1, pp. 48–76.

control. The rapid ageing of technical and scientific knowledge provides the third element.

This development has a strong bearing on production processes, which are repeatedly reorganized and increasingly decentralized. On the one hand, the enterprise retains a core, which is made up of a number of key competences. On the other hand, it outsources the other processes to third parties (contractors, suppliers, franchisees, self-employed service providers). Similarly, units that are distinguished by their specializations (workshops, engineering and design, distribution) increasingly use external workers and skills obtained by outsourcing.[39] Fordist patterns of work organization are replaced by post-Fordist engineering, which is characterized by deverticalized models of production networks, which do not need to be organized in factories.

Though we lack sufficient data, it is a fact that the decentralization phenomenon has expanded to many countries at an intense rate over the last few years. It has affected both developed and developing economies. Its growth has varied in shape and intensity, and it has modified the territorial, economic and normative particularities of all production sectors. Some methods of outsourcing are seen in both the public and the private sector. They are used in relation to both ancillary and incidental activities, as well as for the core activities of the company. Today it is possible to say that the hypothesis of a production-free and employee-free company that would simply own name brands and enter into contracts at one end with producers, and at the other end with customers is no longer just a theory.

This phenomenon has had profound effects on the organization and use of labour. The decentralization of production can take many forms, of which outsourcing/insourcing of production and services and staff leasing are just a few examples. Indeed, it is rather difficult to identify invariable models of decentralization, although the model that consists of contracting out to associated or legally independent external companies would seem to exist everywhere. This model is particularly prevalent in some branches of the metal trades (for example, automobile and shipyards), as well as in service-oriented sectors such as banks and insurance, telecommunications and transportation. In such sectors the principal company can have a strong grip on its suppliers. In effect, even when they have different shareholders, the suppliers remain highly influenced by the prevailing or exclusive business relation linking them to the client company.

---

39 See Ministerio de trabajo (ed.), 'Descentralisacion productiva y nuevas formas organizativas del trabajo', in *Proceedings of the Tenth National Congress of the Spanish Society of Labour Law* (Madrid, 2000).

But this is not the only pattern for the decentralization of production. A second and emerging pattern is made up of networking companies where cooperation and federation prevail over hierarchy, inducing each sector to enhance its own skills and extend its own market, while benefiting from the links that the companies have with each other or with external businesses. The best-known and most prominent examples of networking are in the industrial districts where many legally distinct and truly independent enterprises share services, infrastructures and sometimes know-how (patents, licences, research, and so forth).

'Service businesses' or 'multi-service businesses' also represent a form of networking. This is characterized by a company or a group of companies which can provide principal enterprises and their subsidiaries with a series of structured services. Large multi-service businesses are a particularly interesting phenomenon, since they often have more employees than the principal enterprise and they sell their services to more clients. In those cases, the level of control exerted by the principal enterprise compared with that of its ancillary companies is considerably reduced. It is difficult to determine which entity is more secure and strong in the contractual relationship, and which company is able to offer the best guarantees in terms of work.

The challenges of outsourcing for labour law

Traditionally, labour law has not had great difficulty in defining an employer, because it was simply the physical or legal person for the benefit of whom a worker performed work or provided services in conditions of dependency or subordination. This definition was well adapted to the Taylorist–Fordist company. Where third parties intervened in the employer–employee relationship, the law also had an appropriate response, generally provided for in the concepts of *contractor* and *intermediary*. The contractors were entrepreneurs who assumed their own risks, possessed capital, equipment, technology, their own customers, and so forth. They took up the supply of services to one or several user enterprises under a contract for services, and took on and supervised the work of their own workers who did not have a direct employment relationship with the user enterprise. Sometimes, but not always, legislative provisions like Article 42 of the Estatuto de los Trabajadores (the Spanish workers' charter) required that the user enterprise fulfil certain duties, such as verifying that the contractors had registered their workers regularly and meeting other labour-related obligations. The user enterprise was also responsible for the enforcement of safety and health standards when contractors' employees worked on the user's premises. In contrast, an intermediary was just a middleman who simply took on and sometimes also supervised the work of the employees for the benefit of the user enterprise. In such cases, most laws considered that workers of an intermediary were in a direct employment relationship with the user enterprise so that both the user enterprise and the intermediary had joint and several responsibilities in respect to the labour and social security rights to which the intermediary's workers were entitled. According to some laws, labour-only subcontracting, unless exceptionally authorized (for example in the case of temporary agency work), was an offence liable to prosecution under criminal law; this was the case with *marchandage* in French law.

These concepts are difficult to sustain in the move to decentralize production that we are faced with today. Legally speaking, the employer of a worker is not always the same person that takes the decisions on which the worker's work and conditions of employment depend. In comparative law and practice some solutions have been worked out, which permit the protection of third parties' employees. This is the case, for example, with workers supplied by temporary work agencies, a situation that in many countries has been addressed by both statute law and case law.

The ILO has elaborated international standards on the subject: many provisions of the previously mentioned Private Employment Agencies Convention, 1997 (No. 181), and its accompanying Recommendation (No. 188), focus on the lease of workers by temporary work enterprises. These standards provide that ILO Members should adopt measures to apportion the respective obligations of a TWA and the respective user enterprise in relation to the workers that the TWA makes available to the user enterprise. But it is much more difficult to address the relationship between workers and employers within a group of enterprises where the controller company transfers to its subsidiaries the risks that an employer must normally assume for its employees as a result of their subordination or dependency. Further, the decisions that affect the workers, for example a merger, the closing down or the delocalization of a plant, are taken in remote decision-making centres, often in other countries or continents.

Though labour law has had great difficulty in apprehending these realities, it has already begun to offer some solutions. An example of this would be EC Directive 94/45/EC of 22 September 1994 on the establishment of a European Works Council or a procedure in Community-scale undertakings and Community-scale groups of undertakings for the purposes of informing and consulting employees, which specifies that the term 'group of undertakings' means a controlling undertaking and its controlled undertakings'. Group negotiation is now expressly acknowledged under French law, where, in accordance with the law of 4 May 2004, it is possible to conclude a collective agreement or accord between the employer of the dominant company or one or several representatives of the employers included in the agreement's scope on the one side, and the trade unions representing the wage earners in the group or in the whole of the enterprises included in that scope on the other side. There is still a long way to go before these solutions can become universally applied, although it is interesting to note that in some countries rules were set in place a long while ago to make it possible for parent companies to be liable for the labour-related obligations of their subsidiaries.[40]

Another important question relates to the determination of the employer's liability with respect to health and safety issues at the workplace. This issue would not seem to raise any difficulties when all the workers at a given work site are employees of the same employer. But this is not always the case. Thus health and safety legislation, for example the US Occupational and Safety and Health Act (OSHA) 1970, put health and safety liability primarily on the shoulders of the person or the firm who had control over the work environment and hence the ability to prevent or abate occupational hazards, even when the workers performing work there were not their employees. Such an approach is more controversial, however, when members of a 'peripheral' workforce, such as temporary agency workers, are represented within the scope of a given bargaining unit (see box 2.10).

Box 2.10 The representation of temporary workers under the US National Labor Relations Act[41]

The National Labor Relations Act 1935 gives employees a right to organize unions of their own choosing and bargain collectively with their employer. When a group of workers wants to form a union, the agency that administers the Act, the National Labor Relations Board (NLRB), determines the appropriate unit for collective bargaining and conducts an election to determine whether a majority of the employees in the unit wants to be represented by the union. In 1990, the NLRB ruled that long-term temporary employees could not be included in a bargaining unit with a user

---

40 For example, under Article 2.2 of the Brazilian Consolidation of Labour Laws, 1943, 'whenever two or more enterprises, even when each of them have their own legal personality, are under the direction, control, or administration of another one so that they make an industrial, commercial or any other kind of group, the principal enterprise and its subordinated enterprises shall be joint and severally responsible for the purposes of employment relations'.

41 Katherine V.W. Stone, *Legal protections for workers in atypical employment relationships in the United States*, Report prepared for the XVIIIth World Congress of the International Society for Labor and Social Security Law, Paris, 2006 (unpublished). Professor Stone is affiliated to the School of Law, University of California at Los Angeles (UCLA).

employer's regular employees unless both the provider-agency employer and the user employer consented. Thereafter, the Board refused to consider any unit that combined temporary and regular employees without the consent of both employers. Because it is highly unusual for an employer to consent to its employees forming a union, the dual consent requirement made it virtually impossible for temporary workers to unionize.

In 2000, in Sturgis & Textile Processors, the NLRB reversed its former position and held that regular employees and temporary employees could be in the same bargaining unit so long as they shared a community of interest. The Board also stated that temporary employees could unionize in a bargaining unit of all the employees of a single temporary work agency. As a result, the NLRB began to permit temporary employees to be included in bargaining units that are comprised of temporary and regular employees of a single employer, or that are comprised of all the employees of a single temporary agency. This ruling greatly expanded the possibilities for temporary workers to claim labour law protection.

However, in 2004 the NLRB again reversed its position in the case of Oakwood Care Center and N & W Agency,[42] and reinstated the dual consent requirement for temporary workers' organizing efforts. As a result, temporary workers are now not able to organize in units with the permanent workers they work alongside. Rather, if they want to unionize, they must do so together with the other workers employed by their temporary work agency. Yet agency workers are often dispersed and have little contact with each other. Thus, as a practical matter, temporary workers lack representation or a collective voice.

---

42 *H.S. Care L.L.C., d/b/a/Oakwood Care Center and N&W Agency, Inc.* v. *New York's Health and Human Service Union, 1199, Service Employees International Union, AFL-CIO,* Case 29-RC-10101 (19 November 2004).

Chapter 3

Security of employment

Unfair dismissal: a controversial issue

Termination of employment and, more particularly, the protection of workers against unfair dismissal has been for many years one of the most sensitive issues in labour law and is still very controversial today. On the one hand, protection against dismissal is seen by most workers as a crucial guarantee, as dismissal can lead to dire financial consequences, particularly if dismissed workers cannot claim unemployment insurance, as is the case in a great many countries. In addition, protection against dismissal can play a systemic role in labour law to the extent that it effectively protects workers against abuse by the employer in the employment relationship. Thus in a *termination-at-will system*, such as is used in the United States, workers who refuse to accept changes imposed by the employer to the terms or conditions of their contracts of employment can be easily dismissed. By contrast, in a legal system where workers are protected against unfair dismissal, in principle this is not possible, or at least it is made more difficult. It is true that, even in the absence of statutory protection (or in certain cases of protection developed through case law), workers can still be protected against dismissal by their trade union, and in fact in a number of countries security of employment is an important negotiating issue. However, not all workplaces are unionized; on the contrary, in a great number of countries the majority of workers are not unionized, so that trade unions are not in any position to protect workers against abuses, including that of unfair dismissal.

On the other hand, neo-liberal thinkers and those in business circles tend to consider that, along with increasing labour costs, protection against dismissal imposes constraints on the ability of enterprises to react rapidly to market fluctuations and technological change, thus limiting their productivity and competitiveness. It is also argued that protection against dismissal actually prevents employers from creating jobs, for they fear they will not be able to make workers redundant should they face a fall in demand. This is an argument which should not be disregarded, and has indeed given strength to those who assert that labour law protects those workers who have a job to the detriment of those who do not.[1] One could argue, of course, that statutory protection against dismissal has never prevented an employer from making workers redundant when it was necessary on economic, technological or other structural grounds. Yet it cannot be denied that dismissal procedures are sometimes cumbersome – and very frequently they are also time-consuming. The OECD's *Employment Outlook 2004* emphasizes that the possible negative and positive aspects of employment protection regulation must be very carefully assessed. For the time being, evidence that an overall easing of the hiring and firing rules can have a significant effect on employment creation continues to be disputed (see box 3.1).

Box 3.1 The role and effects of employment protection regulation (EPL)[2]

- Employment protection regulation fulfils its stated purpose, namely protecting existing jobs. Indeed, evidence [...] suggests that EPL tends to limit firms' ability to fire workers. At the same time, EPL would reduce the re-employment chances of unemployed workers – thereby exerting upward pressure on long-term unemployment. Indeed, in deciding whether to hire a worker, employers will take into account the likelihood that firing costs will be incurred in the future. In sum, EPL leads to two opposite effects on labour market dynamics: it reduces inflows into unemployment, while also making it more difficult for jobseekers to enter employment (i.e. lower outflows from unemployment).
- The net impact of EPL on aggregate unemployment is therefore ambigu-ous a priori, and can only be resolved by empirical investigation. However, the numerous empirical studies of this issue lead to conflicting results, and moreover their robustness has been questioned. On the other hand, it is possible to detect a link between EPL and employment rates for specific groups. Some studies [...] suggest the possibility of a negative link between strict EPL and the employment rates of youth and prime-age women, while there may be positive links to the employment rates of other groups. This is consistent with the ... findings of the effects of EPL on labour market dynamics. Indeed, youth and prime-age women are more likely to be subject to entry problems in the labour market than is the case with other groups, and they are therefore likely to be dispropor-tionately affected by the effects of EPL on firms' hiring decisions.

---

1 See this discussion in ILO, *Termination of employment digest* (Geneva, International Labour Office, 2000).

2 OECD, *OECD Employment Outlook, 2004* (Paris, 2004), p. 63.

- Differences in the strictness of EPL for regular and temporary jobs may be an important element in explaining the rise in the incidence of temporary work for youth and the low skilled (this is less the case for other groups, notably prime-age men). This means that facilitating the use of temporary work arrangements, while not changing EPL on regular employment, may aggravate labour market duality. It may also affect career progression and productivity of workers trapped in temporary forms of employment, which are typically characterized by weak job attachments and limited opportunities for upgrading human capital.
- Any overall assessment of EPL has to weigh costs against benefits. EPL may foster long-term employment relationships, thus promoting workers' effort, co-operation and willingness to be trained, which is positive for aggregate employment and economic efficiency. In addition, by promoting firms' social responsibility in the face of adjustment to unfavourable economic circumstances, a reasonable degree of employment protection could be welfare-improving, i.e. it can help balance concern for workers' job security with the need for labour market adjustment and dynamism. Thus, some recent studies suggest that an optimal policy would combine some EPL with effective re-employment services and active labour market policies aiming at counteracting the negative effects of EPL on firms' hiring decisions.

Far from being just a scholarly debate, this question has been at the heart of many government policies, which recently have more or less traded employment security for job creation or, to be more accurate, for the hope of job creation – as it is undisputed that in a market economy it is the market not the law, that creates, modifies and destroys employment. As already noted, there is no evidence to support the assumption that deregulatory labour reforms alone can be sufficient to improve a country's employment levels, though there are reasons to believe that flexibilization of the law governing dismissal, coupled with active labour market policies, including unemployment insurance schemes, can meet both the employers' requirement of flexibility and the workers' need of protection. This is, for example, the strategy that has been followed in Denmark, whose 'flexicurity' approach has drawn wide interest in the European Union and beyond. Nevertheless the EU is made up of 27 countries, many of which do not have labour market structures, institutional frameworks and overall labour relations practices comparable to those of Denmark, which would suggest that flexicurity policies would not be as feasible there as they are in Denmark.

At the EU level, flexicurity has been identified as an important element to reinforce the implementation of the Lisbon Strategy.[3] In the Common Principles of Flexicurity, which were endorsed by the European Council in December 2007, it was underlined that flexicurity involved a deliberate combination of flexible and reliable contractual arrangements, effective labour market policies and modern social protection systems. It should promote overcoming labour market segmentation and be tailored to the specific conditions of each Member State, which should develop its own flexicurity arrangements.[4] It is not certain if this flexicurity approach will be a successful instrument in attaining the objectives of the Lisbon Strategy: in its 2007/08 report on employment, the Council of the European Union stated that, while flexicurity approaches are being developed, the performance within the various underlying components has been still unsatisfactory within the Member States.[5] Moreover, even the European Parliament has expressed serious concerns, highlighting the one-sidedness of the flexicurity approach initiated by the European Commission and, in particular, the absence of a detailed cost–benefit analysis of the approach.[6]

In any event, in a lot of countries (of which the most notorious but not the sole exception is the United States), it is still a well-established principle today that employment beyond the probationary period of a worker cannot be unilaterally terminated by an employer unless there are good grounds for termination, either relating to the worker's capacity or conduct or to the economic needs of the enterprise.

It is worth reflecting at this point that protection against unfair dismissal is by no means a new issue in labour law. In Germany, the Weimar Republic was amongst the first countries to provide for statutory protection in cases of dismissal under the Works Councils Act 1920. That law provided that dismissed employees could have recourse before the works council if the dismissal: (a) was discriminatory; (b) was not justified; (c) was the result of the employee's refusal to perform work other than that agreed upon in the contract of employment; or (d) had to be considered as inequitable and not justified by the employee's behaviour or by the economic situation of the establishment.

---

3 See Commission of the European Communities, *Towards common principles of flexicurity: More and better jobs through flexibility and security*, Communication from the Commission to the European Parliament, the Council, the European Economic and Social Committee and the Committee of the Regions, COM (2007) 359 final.

4 Ibid.

5 Council of the European Union, Joint Employment Report 2007/2008, available at http://ec.europa.eu.

6 European Parliament Resolution of 29 November 2007 on Common Principles of Flexicurity (2007/2209 (INI)).

A number of countries, including Norway, Spain and many Latin American countries, also adopted legislation before the Second World War with a view to protecting workers against the unjustified termination of their employment. However, it was only after the Second World War that this became a common feature in labour law throughout the world. Protection against unfair dismissal is mentioned in a number of Latin American political constitutions, such as those of Argentina, Brazil, Costa Rica, Guatemala, Mexico, Panama and Paraguay, as it is frequently considered as part of the right to work. By contrast, most US states do not have statutory protection laws specifically focusing on termination of employment and unfair dismissal, as US common law has since the nineteenth century followed the employment-at-will doctrine, after a famous court ruling which can be summarized as follows: the employer can terminate the employment of workers – be they many or few – for a good cause, a bad cause or even for a cause that is morally wrong, without being guilty of a legal wrong.[7] Though a number of exceptions to this rule exist under US law and practice,[8] termination at will is still a basic principle in the United States, and applies to a large majority of the workers in that country. Similarly, until very recently, protection against dismissal in Japan was based on the abuse of rights doctrine developed through the case law of the Supreme Court, but not on any statutory authority. However, under the 2004 revision of the Labour Standards Act it has been established that 'a dismissal shall, where the dismissal lacks objectively reasonable grounds and is not considered to be appropriate in general societal terms, be treated as a misuse of that right and invalid'. Also noteworthy is the situation in Belgium, where only blue-collar workers benefit from statutory protection against dismissal, while white-collar workers do not; on the other hand, white-collar workers are entitled to notice periods that are far longer than those granted to blue-collar workers.

---

7 *Payne* v. *Western & Atlantic Railroad Co.*, 81 Tenn. 507, 519-520, 1884 WL 469 at *6 (Sep. term 1884).

8 For example, workers covered by collective agreements are generally protected against unfair dismissal; however, only 14 per cent to 15 per cent of the labour force in the United States is actually covered by a collective agreement. Similarly, workers enjoy statutory protection against dismissal under anti-discrimination laws. Case law has also developed a number of principles relating to wrongful dismissal. One such principle is the *public policy exception*. Workers have been held to have been wrongfully dismisssed when the grounds for dismissal related to activities which are supported by public policy, such as performing jury service or providing evidence of employer wrongdoing. Other judicial decisions have held that workers have been wrongfully dismissed when dismissal occurred in breach of their explicit or implied terms of employment.

In international law, the principle that the employment of a worker cannot be terminated unless there is a valid reason was recognized in 1963 by the ILO Termination of Employment Recommendation (No. 119); this was strengthened in 1982 by both the Termination of Employment Convention (No. 158)[9] and its accompanying Recommendation (No. 166). In European Community law, termination of employment was addressed in 1975, in Council Directive 75/129/EC of 17 February 1975 on the approximation of the laws of the Member States relating to collective redundancies. The current norm on this subject is Council Directive 98/59/EC of 20 July 1998. ILO Convention No. 158 applies to both individual and collective terminations, and its provisions on collective terminations have clearly drawn inspiration from the EC Directive of 1975. By contrast, unlike Convention No. 158, the 1975 Directive does not contain rules on individual dismissals. The subject of individual dismissal is touched upon in different EC directives in other contexts, for instance equal treatment in employment and occupation (Council Directive 2000/78/EC of 27 November 2000).

A number of other important international instruments, including human rights covenants, also provide for protection against unjustified termination of employment. Thus, under Part II.24 of the European Social Charter (revised in 1966), all workers have the right 'not to have their employment terminated without valid reasons for such termination connected with their capacity or conduct or based on the operational requirements of the undertaking, establishment or service'. Likewise, the Additional Protocol to the American Convention on Human Rights in the area of Economic, Social and Cultural Rights, 'Protocol of San Salvador' (San Salvador, 1988), foresees that all workers have the right to 'Stability of employment, subject to the nature of each industry and occupation and the causes for just separation. In cases of unjustified dismissal, the worker shall have the right to indemnity or to reinstatement on the job or any other benefits provided by domestic legislation'. The EU Charter of Fundamental Rights, 2000, declares in Article 30 that 'Every worker has the right to protection against unjustified dismissal, in accordance with Community law and national laws and practices'. This view has also been supported by the UN Committee on Economic, Social and Cultural Rights, which, in its general comment on the right to work as defined by Article 6 of the International Covenant on Economic, Social and Cultural Rights,

---

9 Convention No. 158 has so far been ratified by 34 countries only. Despite this relatively low rate of ratification, many of its rules and principles have clearly been embedded in the law of many ILO Members.

mentions the lawfulness of dismissal as an integral part of this right, making reference to ILO Convention No. 158.[10]

An increasing number of exceptions to unfair dismissal protection

While most countries of the world still maintain the basic rule that a worker cannot be dismissed in the absence of a valid reason, many of them have introduced labour law reforms which have had the effect of providing an increasing number of exceptions, such as the following.

(1) **Dismissal protection legislation either does not apply or its rules have been relaxed for small enterprises.** This exception has been used in Germany for example, where the Protection Against Dismissal Act 1951 (*Kündigungsschutzgesetz*) initially did not apply to enterprises with a workforce of up to five workers, excluding apprentices. However, under a reform introduced in December 2003, this threshold was increased to 10 employees (those who, until December 2003, worked in establishments with more than five and up to 10 employees did not lose dismissal protection under the new law).[11] Still more far-reaching was the reform adopted in Australia under the Workplace Relations Amendment (Work Choices) Act 2005, in which the threshold was put at 100 employees, which in practice meant that a great majority of Australian workers could be denied statutory protection against dismissal.[12] Similarly, in France, a law on the *Contrat Nouvelle Embauche* (New Job Contract) was adopted in 2005, which relaxed the rules on dismissals in small enterprises (those with a workforce of less than 20 employees) during the first two years of employment. However, in two leading decisions of the Courts of Appeal of Bordeaux and Paris, this contract was held to be incompatible

---

10 *The right to work*, General Comment No. 18 of the UN Committee on Economic, Social and Cultural rights, adopted on 24 November 2005, on Article 6 of the International Covenant on Economic, Social and Cultural Rights, available at http://www2.ohchr.org.

11 For more details, see Achim Seifert and Elke Funken-Hötzel, 'Wrongful dismissals in the Federal Republic of Germany', in *Comparative Labor Law and Policy Journal* (Urbana-Champaign, University of Illinois College of Law, 2004), Vol. 25, No. 4, pp. 487–517.

12 As Australia has ratified the ILO Termination of Employment Convention,1982 (No. 158), it is very likely that this reform will be challenged on the grounds that the Convention permits only the exclusion of 'limited categories of employed persons in respect of which special problems of a substantial nature arise in the light of the particular conditions of employment of the workers concerned or the size or nature of the undertaking that employs them'.

with the Termination of Employment Convention, 1982 (No. 158), which had been ratified by France. The decisions were appealed against in June and July of 2007, but upheld by the Court of Cassation.[13]

(2) **The length of the period of probation has been extended.** Some 10 years ago, the duration of the probationary period (the initial period of service during which either party can dissolve the contract of employment at very short notice or no notice at all, without the need to state any cause of termination) was generally between one month and three months. Nowadays it frequently lasts up to six months, though in a number of countries the duration of the probationary period depends on the nature of the work that a worker is expected to provide under the contract of employment. For example, in Romania, the probationary period cannot exceed five working days for unskilled workers; for other employees it cannot be longer than 30 days, but it can be up to 90 calendar days for management positions and up to six months in respect to those with a higher education qualification. In Belgium, probation may not be longer than 14 days for blue-collar workers but it can extend to one year in the case of highly paid white-collar workers.

(3) **The qualifying period of service for employees to be able to challenge their dismissal before a court or a tribunal has been extended.** Nowadays it is generally no shorter than six months, though it can be up to one year in a number of countries, for example in the United Kingdom.

(4) **The use of fixed-term contracts of employment has increased.** Unlike contracts for unspecified duration, a fixed-term contract comes to an end naturally on the expiry of the agreed term, so that the end of a fixed-term contract will not be legally treated as a dismissal. On the other hand, a worker who has been taken on under a fixed-term contract cannot normally be dismissed, except for gross misconduct or some other very serious reason during the term of the contract – which can be an important guarantee in countries with very light statutory protection against dismissal.

Limitations on the abuse of fixed-term employment contracts

The law has always provided for the possibility of an employer taking on workers under fixed-term contracts of employment; yet this was and still is limited on a number of grounds. Thus the law has frequently required an objective reason for an employer being authorized to hire a worker under a fixed-term contract, usually because of the temporary nature of the work.

---

13 Case No. 1210 of 1 July 2008, Social Chamber of the Court de Cassation.

French law, for example, prescribes that a fixed-term contract of employment may not be used with the purpose or effect of permanently filling a position which is not of temporary nature. Such an approach is shared by many countries, either as a result of clear statutory provisions or following precedents established in case law. The Termination of Employment Convention, 1982 (No. 158) also requires that ratifying states take adequate safeguards 'against recourse to contracts of employment for a specified period of time the aim of which is to avoid the protection resulting from this Convention'. Thus fixed-term contracts would be authorized for the performance of time-limited tasks or to replace workers who are temporarily absent from work. In the absence of such reasons, the law has generally provided that, despite any terms of employment that have been agreed upon, a fixed-term contract was to be treated as a contract of employment for unspecified duration, so that the worker would be protected against unfair dismissal. However, under successive reforms, many countries have widened the scope of use for fixed-term contracts of employment, either by expanding the number of reasons that allowed employers to hire workers under fixed-term contracts, or simply by authorizing these contracts even when they could not be justified objectively. The duration of these contracts has also been extended in a number of countries; for example they can now extend up to three years in Belgium and the Netherlands.

The use of fixed-term contracts was allowed, and even encouraged, when it was thought that they would lead to the creation of new jobs, especially for the benefit of certain categories of workers who were likely to have greater difficulty in entering into the labour market. Thus in Spain, under several reforms introduced from 1981, enterprises were authorized to use fixed-term contracts in an extended range of circumstances, such as the launching of new ventures and the hiring of job-seekers, as well as in a number of training for employment schemes. These contracts also benefited from State subsidies, which largely contributed to their success. However, after a number of years of operation, it became apparent that a dual labour market had been created as some 30 per cent of the labour force was permanently employed on fixed-term contracts. Since 1997, labour law reforms have sought to reverse this trend by encouraging employers to take on workers on permanent contracts of employment. Significant changes were introduced into Spanish labour law in 2006, reflecting the outcome of a socioeconomic national tripartite agreement. The protection of vulnerable groups of workers has been strengthened and chains of fixed-term contracts have been prohibited.

Germany has also authorized the use of fixed-term contracts without objective reasons with the aim of hiring workers over 52 years of age. This was, however, judged by the European Court of Justice (ECJ) to be contrary to

EC law in that it discriminated against workers on the grounds of age.[14] Argentina, to a large extent, copied Spain's 1981 scheme in its law on employment of 1991, which was further extended in 1995. The 1995 law permitted the use of fixed-term contracts with respect to young job-seekers, workers with disabilities, workers aged over 45 years and women. It was repealed some years later as it became apparent that it did not create new employment opportunities while it made the existing ones more precarious. In Colombia, a reform introduced in 1990 permitted employers to hire workers either under a contract of employment without limit of time or under a fixed-term contract, without restrictions. Last but not least, under the Labour Code of the Russian Federation, 2001, enterprises employing less than 40 employees were allowed to hire out their entire workforce under fixed-term contracts (though it should be noted that the reverse of this is that dismissal is highly restricted under the Russian Labour Code).

When relaxing the rules on fixed-term contracts, there is certainly a risk that they might be used with the main purpose of preventing workers from enjoying protection against unfair dismissal. In practice, abuse can occur when workers are hired under a succession of fixed-term contracts, which may or may not be separated by short breaks between them. To prevent such abuse, a number of countries have provided that when a worker has been working for an employer during a given period of time, under an array of fixed-term contracts, then the contract of employment is deemed to be concluded for an unspecified period of time. This rule is now mandatory in the European Union under Council Directive 1999/70/EC of 28 June 1999 concerning the framework agreement on fixed-term work concluded by ETUC, UNICE and CEEP.[15] It also applies when a sequence of successive fixed-

---

14 See the ECJ ruling in Case C–144/04 *Werner Mangold* v. *Rüdiger Helm*, judgment of the Court (Grand Chamber) of 22 November 2005. (The case concerned age discrimination and is discussed further in Chapter 5 of this book.)

15 The relevant provisions of this agreement reads as follows:

> To prevent abuse arising from the use of successive fixed-term employment contracts or relationships, Member States, after consultation with social partners in accordance with national law, collective agreements or practice, and/or the social partners, shall, where there are no equivalent legal measures to prevent abuse, introduce in a manner which takes account of the needs of specific sectors and/or categories of workers, one or more of the following measures:
>
> (a) objective reasons justifying the renewal of such contracts or relationships;
> (b) the maximum total duration of successive fixed-term employment contracts or relationships;
> (c) the number of renewals of such contracts or relationships.

term contracts is broken by a period of non-employment when the purpose of breaking up the chain of contracts is precisely to avoid the application of that rule. In a judgment of July 2006, the ECJ ruled that this agreement:

> is to be interpreted as precluding the use of successive fixed-term employment contracts where the justification advanced for their use is solely that it is provided for by a general provision of statute or secondary legislation of a Member State. On the contrary, the concept of 'objective reasons' within the meaning of that clause requires recourse to this particular type of employment relationship, as provided for by national legislation, to be justified by the presence of specific factors relating in particular to the activity in question and the conditions under which it is carried out.[16]

Many countries have introduced legislation which prevents employers from continually renewing fixed-term contracts and introducing breaks in such chains of contracts simply to circumvent legal restrictions. In the Netherlands, for example, it is possible to have three consecutive contracts that may be ended without having to give notice, as long as they fall within a period of three years. The fourth contract, or the contract that brings the total working period to over 36 months, will automatically become a contract for an indefinite term, which gives the worker protection against dismissal. Furthermore, contracts that follow each other within a period of three months are considered to be consecutive, and it is not relevant whether the work done under the different contracts is identical. Still more straightforward is the rule introduced in Chile by the labour law reform of 1990 whereby the maximum duration of a fixed-term contract of employment was limited to 12 months, and it was also provided that a worker who had worked for the same employer during 12 months over a time span of 15 continuous months, under several fixed-term contracts of employment, would be deemed to have been working under a contract of employment of unlimited duration.

How effective are remedies for unfair dismissal?

Despite more or less flexibilization, and no less intense scholarly debate, the labour laws of a large majority of countries remain firmly committed to the principle that a worker may not be dismissed from employment unless there are valid grounds. Yet, there is wide diversity of approaches and solutions

---

16 Case C–212/04 *Adeneler et al.* v. *Ellinikos Organismos Galaktos (ELOG)*, judgment of the Court (Grand Chamber) of 4 July 2006.

when it actually comes to implementing this principle. Thus in a number of countries, the law provides for various procedural safeguards that should be observed before an employer can dismiss an employee – in other countries such safeguards do not exist at all.

Notice provision and procedural safeguards

Giving notice is a quasi-universal procedural requirement, as most countries of the world provide that employers shall give advance notice of their intention to terminate the contract of employment (quite often a parallel obligation is imposed on the worker). This certainly does not constitute a justification for termination per se, and does not release the employer from any applicable obligation to base a dismissal on a justifiable cause. However, it is a very important practice as it minimizes the element of surprise of an otherwise sudden dismissal and enables the worker to start searching for new employment. This is why the law in many countries provides that during the notice period a worker is entitled to a certain amount of paid time off to seek new employment. The Termination of Employment Convention, 1982 (No. 158), requires that a worker whose employment is to be terminated 'shall be entitled to a reasonable period of notice or compensation in lieu thereof', but does not prescribe a minimum entitlement or a minimum period of notice which should be respected to allow the person to look for a new job.

In comparative law and practice, the actual length of notice widely varies, depending on certain factors such as the worker's length of service, age, occupational category and the basis on which the worker is paid. This can range from one or two weeks to several months. For example, in Sweden notice must be of no less than six months when an employee has 10 or more years of service with the same employer. In Belgium there is a big difference between the period of notice that is to be given to blue-collar workers (28 calendar days for workers with up to 20 years of service and 56 calendar days for workers with more than 20 years of service) and the notice to be given to white-collar workers (three months for workers with less than five years of service, six months from five to 10 years of service, nine months from 10 to 15 years of service, 12 months from 15 to 20 years of services and 15 months from 20 years of service on). It should, however, be recalled that, unlike manual workers, white-collar workers in Belgium cannot claim compensation for unfair dismissal.

Procedural safeguards can also include a preliminary meeting between the employer and the employee who is to have his or her employment terminated, or consultations between the employer and the relevant staff representatives. Most notably, in Austria and Germany, employers must seek the advice of the works council (*Betriebsrat*) before they can terminate a worker's employment; in France, workers must be summoned to a hearing with the employer or the employer's representative before their employment can be terminated; in Sweden, the Employment Protection Act 1982 provides for consultations between the employer and the relevant local trade union when the employee to be dismissed is a union member; while in the Russian Federation the same consultation is to be undertaken with the trade union authorities. In some countries, as in the Netherlands for example, it is mandatory for the termination of employment to be authorized by the employment service, though nowadays such a requirement is less frequent.[17]

Appeal and recourse

Though preliminary consultations or hearings are not required in many other countries, it should be recalled that in all cases dismissed employees have the right to challenge their dismissal before a court or other independent body (for example an arbitrator in countries such as Canada or the United States) after it has taken place. It should be added that when employees challenge their dismissal before a court or an arbitrator, it is a quasi-universal rule that the burden of the proof of the validity of the termination of employment falls on the employer. The most important exception in this respect would be that in US common law, where employment-at-will is the basic rule. Dismissed employees who want to bring a case before a court are required to submit proof that they were protected by an exception and had been *wrongfully* dismissed.

No less diversity exists with respect to unfair or unjustified dismissal. In light of the wording of the Termination of Employment Convention, 1982 (No. 158), one might presume that the annulment of a dismissal and the subsequent reinstatement of workers would be the appropriate remedy when a court or other body is satisfied that a dismissal is not justified. Reinstatement with back pay is, for example, the current remedy that is ordered by arbitrators in Canada and the United States when a union brings a complaint on behalf of a worker protected by a collective agreement, who has been dismissed from employment without a valid cause. However, reinstatement is not feasible in many cases and not convenient in many others, or simply it is not the wish of the employee or acceptable to the employer. The Termination of Employment Convention, 1982 (No. 158), acknowledges this problem and provides that when the bodies before which an employee has appealed find that termination is unjustified and 'are not empowered or do

---

17 In some cases these rules do not apply when employees are summarily dismissed on the grounds of their gross misconduct.

not find it practicable, in accordance with national law and practice, to declare the termination invalid and/or order or propose reinstatement of the worker, they shall be empowered to order payment of adequate compensation or such other relief as may be deemed appropriate'. In its 1995 General Survey on the Termination of Employment Convention, 1982 (No. 158),[18] the Committee of Experts stated in this regard that in the event of termination of employment having impaired a basic right, the reinstatement of the worker in his or her job with payment of unpaid wages and maintenance of acquired rights would be the best solution. However, it would seem that monetary compensation is in practice the most frequent remedy, even in countries such as Croatia, Germany, Italy, Mexico, the Russian Federation and many others where reinstatement with back pay is the statutory remedy to be applied by default.

It would seem that reinstatement is increasingly used when workers have been dismissed on grounds that are prohibited by law, for example when they have been discriminated against on the grounds of sex (including pregnancy), colour, race, disability, political opinion or trade union activity. In such cases, the court would consider annulment of the dismissal and actual reinstatement to be the appropriate remedy, rather than statutory compensation, as it is seen as a matter of public policy rather than a mere conflict between the individual interests of employers and employees. This was the approach followed by the Court of Cassation in France, for example in the *Clavaud* case (see Chapter 5)[19] in respect of the protection of the right to freedom of expression; and in Argentina by the National Labour Chamber of Appeal in a case brought by an employee who had been dismissed allegedly because of her trade union activism, described in box 3.2.

Box 3.2 Annulment of a dismissal and reinstatement with back pay is the appropriate remedy for a discriminatory dismissal[20]

In a decision taken in June 2006, the National Labour Chamber of Appeal of Argentina (Chamber V) examined a complaint brought by an employee

---

18 ILO, *Protection against Unjustified Dismissal*, General Survey on the Termination of Employment Convention (No. 158) and Recommendation (No. 166), 1982, Report III, International Labour Conference, 82th Session, Geneva, 1995.

19 *SA Dunlop France c. Clavaud*, Cass. Soc., 28 February 1988, *Droit Social*, 1988, p. 428, with note by Couturier.

20 National Labour Chamber of Appeal (Chamber V). Judgment 68536, file No. 144/05. Case *Parra Vera, Máxima C/ San Timoteo S.A. S/ Acción de Amparo (Judgment No. 40)*, 14 June 2006.

with more than 20 years of service, who had been dismissed from employment, allegedly on the grounds of company reorganization. The claimant provided evidence that she was deeply involved in trade union activism, though she was not a designated trade union official or staff representative (who benefits from strengthened protection under Argentinian law). Furthermore, it was demonstrated that the alleged reorganization only affected one job in the enterprise, precisely that of the claimant.

The Tribunal held that the defendant had failed to prove that the employee had been dismissed on grounds other than her trade union activity. It concluded that the dismissal was unjustified as the reasons for dismissal cited by the defendant (i.e. company reorganization) were not supported by the evidence.

With regard to the remedy, under Argentinian law, employees who have been dismissed without just cause are only entitled to statutory compensation at the rate of one month's pay for each year of service. In principle the claimant was not entitled to request reinstatement. However, in the light of international law that is binding on Argentina (most notably the ILO Freedom of Association and Protection of the Right to Organise Convention, 1948 (No. 87), and the Social Protocol of San Salvador to the American Human Rights Convention), the Court took the view that annulment of the dismissal, not statutory compensation, was the appropriate remedy to be provided when the dismissal is held to be discriminatory on grounds that are prohibited by law. It therefore declared that the dismissal was void and ordered reinstatement with back pay.

When reinstatement is not ordered, or is not actually carried out, the normal remedy is monetary compensation, which can be of two types: either civil or common law *damages* or *statutory compensation* at a fixed rate. Common law damages are normally awarded by civil courts in the United States when they are satisfied that an employee has been wrongfully dismissed. It should be recalled, however, that under the US employment-at-will doctrine, protection against unjustified dismissal works as an exception – it is not a *positive* right – so that very few workers actually bring a wrongful dismissal complaint before a court and still fewer complaints actually succeed. Yet when a complaint does succeed, the amount of damages is usually huge as the damages are generally awarded to put claimants in the position they would have been in had the tort not taken place. On such an understanding, they are assessed in the light of presumed prejudices suffered by the employee, for example loss of future earnings or loss of company pension or other benefits, and the moral prejudice arising from psychological stress, humiliation or harm to the worker's reputation.

Additional punitive damages would be awarded if the dismissal was malicious or it had been pronounced in open and flagrant violation of the worker's rights. An essential feature of damages is that they are awarded at the court's discretion.

By contrast, statutory compensation consists of a fixed amount of money that is predetermined by the law. Typically it is calculated on the basis of the worker's length of service, and sometimes also on the worker's age. A very common rate is one month's pay per year of service, sometimes with an upper ceiling of 12 or 18 months of pay,[21] though in some countries it is much higher. Under the Swedish Employment Protection Act 1982, when an employer refuses to comply with a court order that notice of termination or a summary dismissal is invalid, or that a fixed-term employment contract should be valid for an indefinite term, they must pay compensation to the employee: six months' pay for less than five years of employment, 24 months' pay for at least five years but less than 10 years of employment, and 32 months' pay for 10 or more years of employment. If the employee is aged 60 or over, these amounts are increased to 24, 36 or 48 months' pay respectively.

Lastly, it is worth noting that a recent trend tends to consider statutory compensation as a floor, not a ceiling, especially when an employee has been dismissed or otherwise prejudiced on grounds that are prohibited by law. This is clearly the approach followed by the European Court of Justice in cases of discrimination on the grounds of sex:

> EEC Directive 76/207, the purpose of which is to put into effect in the Member States the principle of equal treatment for men and women as regards the various aspects of employment, in particular working conditions, including the conditions governing dismissal, leaves Member States, when providing a remedy for breach of the prohibition against discrimination, free to choose between the different solutions suitable for achieving the objective of the Directive. Nevertheless it does entail that if financial compensation is to be awarded where there has been a discriminatory dismissal in breach of Article 5(1), such compensation must be adequate, in that it must enable the loss and damage actually sustained as a result of the discriminatory dismissal to be made good in full in accordance with the applicable national rules.

---

21 For a detailed overview of termination procedures, avenues for redress and statutory compensation in 72 jurisdictions, see the ILO *Termination of employment digest*; available online at http://www.ilo.org.

Accordingly, the interpretation of Article 6 of Directive 76/207 must be that reparation of the loss and damage sustained by a person injured as a result of discriminatory dismissal may not be limited to an upper limit fixed a priori or by excluding an award of interest to compensate for the loss sustained by the recipient of the compensation as a result of the effluxion of time until the capital sum awarded is actually paid.[22]

22 Case C–271/91 *Helen Marshall* v. *Southampton and South-West Hampshire Area Health Authority (No. 2)*, Judgment of the Court of 2 August 1993, [1993] ECR I–4367.

Chapter 4

Global trade and labour law

Is substandard labour a legitimate comparative advantage?

The relationship between international trade and labour norms is not by any means a new subject. Indeed, the links between trade and labour were already implied in David Ricardo's theory on comparative costs, formulated in the eighteenth century, and it was in 1788 that Jacques Necker, a Swiss banker and Minister of Finance for the French King Louis XVI, argued that the abolition of Sunday as a day of rest could give a competitive edge to a country's economy provided other countries did not do the same.[1] Later on, during the nineteenth century, several industrialists such as the British Robert Owen and the French Daniel Legrand launched calls for an international regulation of labour on the understanding that countries that wished to improve the situation of their working classes would suffer from competition by other countries which did not. This reasoning was common wisdom for a long time, and in fact still stands. It is very likely that fear of international competition was one major reason that prevented many countries from undertaking measures to correct what even in the nineteenth century were considered the excesses of liberalism. It is worth noting that during the nineteenth century, apart from measures aimed at limiting child labour and night work by women in factories, the State only legislated to reduce working time in the civil service, where there was no risk of international competition.

What came later, in the form of successive congresses of the international trade union movement and of private associations like the International Association for the Legal Protection of Workers, until the ILO was created in 1919, is widely known, and has been extensively addressed in many textbooks.[2] Apart from humanitarian preoccupations, it is clear that when the ILO was established the problem of the links between international trade and

---

1 Quoted in N. Valticos, 'Droit international du travail' in *Traité de droit du travail*, publié sous la direction de G.H. Camerlynck (Paris, Dalloz, 1983), Vol. 8, p. 3.

2 See, for example, Bob Hepple, *Labour laws and global trade* (Oxford, Hart Publishing, 2005), pp. 24–30; Jean-Michel Servais, *International labour law* (The Hague, Kluwer Law International, 2005); Antony Alcock, *History of the International Labour Organization* (London, Macmillan, 1971).

the improvement of working conditions at the national level was an important concern in the mind of the drafters of the Treaty of Versailles. This is why the Preamble of the ILO Constitution declares that 'The failure of any nation to adopt humane conditions of labour is an obstacle in the way of other nations which desire to improve the conditions in their own countries'.

Nearly 30 years later, in 1948, the idea of providing for protection of workers' basic rights in trade agreements was taken up in the Havana Charter, which was intended to launch the International Trade Organization. The ITO Treaty, however, did not enter into force as the US Congress denied ratification. Until the World Trade Organization (WTO) was created in 1994, international trade relations were regulated under a Protocol of Provisional Application of the General Agreement on Tariffs and Trade (GATT), signed in Geneva in 1947, which was further developed under successive negotiation rounds.

Neither the GATT agreement nor the WTO Treaty was concerned about the protection of labour rights.[3] Yet the debate on the links between international trade and national regulations, including labour law, remained an outstanding issue in post-Second World War international trade relations. Thus while the Treaty of Rome of 1957 was meant to address international economic relations, it did not prevent the European Economic Community from dealing with labour issues to the extent that they directly affected the establishment or functioning of the Common Market.[4] It is worth recalling that the sole social provision in the original Treaty of Rome was Article 141 EC (ex Article 119 EC), which enshrined the principle of equal pay between men and women for equal work or work of equal value. Yet such a principle came into the Treaty's text on the ground of economic considerations only; this was because France, which had already ratified the Equal Remuneration Convention, 1951 (No. 100), in 1958, feared competition from its Common Market interlocutors who had not ratified the Convention, and could therefore allow female workers to be paid less than their male counterparts, thus giving a competitive edge to industries that employed female workers, most notably the textile industry. It took a further 20 years before the European

---

3 See Cleopatra Doumbia-Henry and Eric Gravel, 'Free trade agreements and labour rights: Recent developments', in *International Labour Review*, Vol. 145 (2006), No. 3, p. 186.

4 See old Article 100 EC (new Article 94 EC), which provides the following: 'The Council shall, acting unanimously on a proposal from the Commission and after consulting the European Parliament and the Economic and Social Committee, issue directives for the approximation of such laws, regulations or administrative provisions of the Member States as directly affect the establishment or functioning of the common market.' At least until the Social Protocol was annexed to the Treaty of Maastricht, 1992, and was later integrated into the Treaty of Amsterdam in 1997, this text was practically the sole legal basis for the development of EC law on labour issues.

Court of Justice, in a preliminary ruling in the case *Defrenne II*, took the view that Article 141 EC (ex Article 119) had both economic and social founda- tions (see box 4.1).[5] In short, what today is regarded as a human rights issue – equal pay for men and women – was in 1957 just a labour–trade problem.

Box 4.1 *Gabrielle Defrenne v. Société Anonyme Belge de Navigation Aérienne (Sabena)*[6]

Article 119 (EC) pursues a double aim.

First, in the light of the different stages of the development of social legislation in the various Member States, the aim of Article 119 is to avoid a situation in which undertakings established in States which have actually implemented the principle of equal pay suffer a competitive disadvantage in intra-community competition as compared with undertakings established in States which have not yet eliminated discrimination against women workers as regards pay.

Secondly, this provision forms part of the social objectives of the Community, which is not merely an economic union, but is at the same time intended, by common action, to ensure social progress and seek the constant improvement of the living and working condi- tions of their peoples, as is emphasized by the Preamble to the Treaty.

This aim is accentuated by the insertion of Article 119 into the body of a chapter devoted to social policy whose preliminary provi- sion, Article 117, marks 'the need to promote improved working conditions and an improved standard of living for workers, so as to make possible their harmonization while the improvement is being maintained'.

This double aim, which is at once economic and social, shows that the principle of equal pay forms part of the foundations of the Community

---

The relationship between labour standards and international trade came to the forefront again in recent years, in the context of the opening up of the

---

5 To a certain extent the recognition of links existing between trade and labour was also expressed in the 1937 decisions by the US Supreme Court, which considered that the US Federal Congress had competence to regulate on labour and social issues to the extent that these address questions of interstate trade. In the Supreme Court's view, such a competence existed under Article 8 of the US Constitution, which provided that the Congress can legis- late on issues relating with trade between states and with the Indian nations (*NLRB* v. *James and Laughlin Steel Corporation*; *Helvering* v. *Davis*; *Steward Mach Co.* v. *Davis*; *US* v. *Darby*).

6 Case 43/75 *Defrenne* v. *Société Anonyme Belge de Navigation Aérienne* [1976] ECR 455.

economy internationally and the general spread of labour-saving production technologies, which led to an unprecedented growth of trade between countries with different labour standards and labour costs. While these trading links had always existed, they had never attained the volume that they achieved in the last few decades. Still more important than quantitative increase of trade was the diversification of what was traded between countries. In effect, in earlier decades the world had known, on the one hand, flows of trade of comparable production between countries with comparable labour regulation and labour costs and, on the other hand, flows of trade of non-comparable production between countries with non-comparable labour regulation and labour costs. Traditionally, countries of the global North with strong labour regulation and high labour costs offered high value-added production while cheap labour countries (in the global South) offered raw materials and low value-added production, so that the North–South gap in labour costs did not affect international trade competition in practice. Furthermore, in the relatively rare cases where there was risk of competition between high-wage and low-wage countries, the former protected themselves by means such as custom duties or import quotas, as was the case in the steel and the textile industries.

That situation started to undergo drastic changes at the beginning of the 1980s, when a number of countries from the global South (at that time especially from South-East Asia) began to compete with countries from the global North in the high value-added bracket of the market. Though perhaps less important than other elements, relatively low wages and weak labour regulations, including in some cases severe restraints on freedom of association,[7] were among the assets which allegedly gave these countries a competitive advantage. As a consequence, the jobs and conditions of work of workers in countries with higher labour costs and labour standards were put under threat. First, goods from low-wage countries had a competitive advantage over both local production and exports to third countries. Secondly, industries in countries with high labour costs and high labour standards had an interest in delocalizing production processes to countries with low wages and low labour standards.

Moreover, increasing international competition came together with strong international advocacy, especially from the Bretton Woods institutions, for

---

7 See, for example, the complaints brought before the Committee on Freedom of Association (CFA) by the International Metalworkers Federation against the government of Malaysia on the grounds of serious restriction on freedom of association in the electrical/electronic industries, Cases 911 and 1552. CFA reports are available on the ILO database ILOLEX at http://www.ilo.org and in the *Official Bulletin* of the ILO.

structural adjustment and overall market deregulation, including that of the labour market. It was suggested that strong, comprehensive and well-implemented labour standards negatively affected international competitiveness, and discouraged investors from coming into a country to invest capital and create jobs. This implied a call for deregulation, which apparently did not take into account the fact that no country would become more competitive if all countries came to adopt the same or comparable deregulation measures (something which is commonly referred to as a 'race to the bottom').

It was against this background that first the international trade union movement, followed by several governments, considered that it was essential that international trade accept some rules relating to the treatment of labour in the different countries. Though they did not challenge the fact that countries have different labour rules and different labour costs, they questioned that these rules and costs were being kept artificially low in order to give certain countries a competitive advantage at the time they were gaining international markets. In particular, they questioned those rules which denied the fundamental rights of the workers, which in some countries such as the United States, for example, are commonly referred to as the 'internationally recognized workers' rights'.

Box 4.2 The economic and moral dimension of labour laws[8]

Labour laws are at the centre of debates about how to respond to economic globalization. When, in April 2006, the French government caved in to massive street protests against the *contrat première embauche* (CPE), students and trade unions were triumphant that they had preserved the philosophy of universal job security. But *The Economist* (and many economists) criticized the French State – unlike France's buoyant private sector – for failing to face up to, and accept, the consequences of global capitalism, which demands the end of what were described as 'rigid", 'over-protected' labour markets. In May 2006, when General Motors cut 900 jobs at its Vauxhall plant, and warned of possible closure in Britain, trade unions blamed Britain's weak job security laws which make it cheaper to dismiss workers as redundant in Britain than elsewhere in the EU, a charge denied by Gordon Brown, the then Chancellor of the Exchequer.

Who is right? For extreme free trade advocates who favour the removal of all barriers on free trade and investment, accompanied by the deregulation of labour markets, the issue is simple. Labour laws are seen as much a

---

8 Bob Hepple, 'Labour laws in the context of globalization', unpublished paper prepared for this comparative overview (2007), based on his book, *Labour law and global trade* (Oxford, Hart Publishing, 2005).

determinant of comparative advantage as natural endowments, resources and preferences. At the other extreme, protectionists argue for safeguarding national markets and domestic labour laws against external pressures for 'flexibilization'. Most politicians in developed and developing countries are seeking a path between these extreme versions of free trade and protectionism. For me, as a scholar and practitioner of labour law, the question is how global processes can be better regulated in order to deliver both economic growth and social justice embedded in the rule of law. There is a rapidly expanding body of literature on the subject, mainly written by economists, political theorists and trade specialists. I ventured into this controversial area in my recent book on *Labour laws and global trade*[9] for two reasons. First, because of a belief that the rules and practices governing productive work are as essential as property rights for the functioning of the market economy. Secondly, labour laws also have an important moral dimension – the idea embodied in the ILO Constitution, that 'labour is not a commodity'. They thus provide an excellent case study of the possibilities for creating a legal framework within which economic integration in a globalized market economy can be reconciled with the ideals of social justice.

Strategies to address the relationship between international trade and labour rights

International and supranational rules

Different strategies can be imagined with such a purpose in mind. All of them are intended to provide an international dimension to labour law or at least to some of its key institutions. The first and most well known is the traditional approach, which led to the creation of the ILO in 1919. It consists in the elaboration of international labour standards that impose on Member States the obligation to guarantee minimum rights and conditions of work to their workers. Its logic rests on the fact that if all the States respect these standards, none of them will improve their commercial competitiveness by such means as the denial of the workers' rights in their own country. Its weakness stems first from the fact that ILO Conventions are binding upon Member States only on ratification, which is not mandatory. Thus, despite worldwide acceptance, the ILO fundamental Conventions have not yet been ratified by all of the ILO Members (see box 4.1). Most notably, the Freedom of Association and Protection of the Right to Organize Convention, 1948

---

9 Bob Hepple, *Labour laws and global trade*, op. cit., on which this chapter draws extensively.

(No. 87), has so far been ratified by 149 of the 182 ILO Members,[10] but not as yet by Brazil, China, India, Iran, Saudi Arabia, Thailand, the United States and Vietnam, for example, which means that in practice some 50 per cent of the workers in the world – and still more worrying, the workers of some of the countries that account for a very large share in international trade – are not protected under this Convention. Secondly, even after ratification, the effectiveness of ILO standards at the national level may vary depending on the means which can be made available in each country to give effect to them, not to mention the real willingness of a Member to actually apply them. Thirdly, apart from a provision included in the ILO Constitution, which was used only once in the whole history of ILO,[11] the breach by a Member of obligations arising out of the ratification of an ILO Convention can result in moral sanctions only, and it is widely known that international moral pressure is effective in many but not in all cases. In short, there are reasons to hold that, despite an overall remarkable rate of success, the ILO standard-based approach suffers from some shortcomings. Yet the point is that, apart from the supranational approach taken by the European Union, which is limited to just one region in the world, no other strategy has so far been supported by an international consensus as wide as the one which supports the ILO approach.

A second approach is that of supranational law, that is, the establishment by an international authority of labour standards that would be directly binding on each State, with no need for ratification. Supranational standards are applied by the national judge in the same way as national laws or regulations; in the case of conflict between national and supranational law, the judge is required to set national law aside and decide the case on the basis of supranational law.

Apart from constitutional limitations (it is clear that a State that would be ready to accept supranational authority would need to review its Constitution), the greatest hurdle to this approach stems from the fact that it calls for very strong political will, as it implies that States agree to give up some of their sovereign policy-making and law-making powers. Technical difficulties are also apparent as a supranational law would need to apply in very different national environments, and the variety of national approaches

---

10 Data as at 21 November 2008.

11 In accordance with Article 33 of the ILO Constitution, 'the Conference can request to the international community that it adopts such action as it may deem wise and expedient to secure compliance with a ratified international convention a country fails to implement'. Until now this provision has been used only once, in a case prompted by Myanmar's violation of the Forced Labour Convention, 1930 (No. 29).

Table 4.1 Ratification of the ILO fundamental Conventions by G8 countries, plus Brazil, China and India[12]

Country	Convention No. 87	Convention No. 98	Convention No. 100	Convention No. 111	Convention No. 29	Convention No. 105	Convention No. 138	Convention No. 182
Brazil	–	X	X	X	X	X	X	X
Canada	X	–	X	X	–	X	–	X
China	–	–	X	X	–	–	X	X
France	X	X	X	X	X	X	X	X
Germany	X	X	X	X	X	X	X	X
India	–	–	X	X	X	X	–	–
Italy	X	X	X	X	X	X	X	X
Japan	X	X	X	–	X	–	X	X
Russian Federation	X	X	X	X	X	X	X	X
United Kingdom	X	X	X	X	X	X	X	X
United States	–	–	–	–	–	X	–	X

is something which must be taken into account while developing international or supranational law. Moreover, supranational law cannot be effective without a supranational interpretative body; otherwise there is a risk that it will be interpreted in diverse ways by different courts in the different countries in which it is applied. This means that countries that accept supranational regulation must also accept supranational judiciary.

So far, supranational law is a key feature only in the European Community system (the impact of which on the labour law of EU Member States is discussed in Chapter 6). Other regions in the world do not yet seem ready to follow a comparable approach.

Harmonization

A third strategy consists in the harmonization of labour legislation. Through harmonization, countries that share the same market are encouraged to adopt comparable labour laws so that none of them obtain comparative advantages by having less favourable labour legislation than their competitors. Attempts at harmonizing labour law have been made within the framework of some

12 Updated at 21 November 2008. While not G8 Members, Brazil, China and India are permanent members of the ILO Governing Body as most important industrial nations.

regional trade agreements, like the Andean Community and MERCOSUR,[13] so far without success.

A different form of harmonization is offered by the project for a uniform Labour Code by the Organization for the Harmonization of Business Law in Africa (OHADA), a grouping of 16 francophone African countries and Equatorial Guinea. The OHADA Secretariat has already elaborated a draft OHADA Labour Code. Rather than addressing specific labour law issues that are relevant for business law (for example redundancy proceedings, the effects of mergers and transfers of businesses on the contract of employment or the position of workers' claims in insolvency proceedings), the OHADA text is a comprehensive Labour Code and attempts to regulate most if not all of the topics which are generally dealt with by the labour codes of French-speaking Africa. If eventually approved by all of the OHADA members, it would replace the labour laws of each of them.

Harmonization under the OHADA approach raises a number of problems, however. First, while the overall existing labour laws of OHADA members bear many similarities, an ILO study has also drawn attention to many differences on a great number of issues.[14] It follows that OHADA would have difficulty in presenting its members with a proposal that would be agreeable to all of them. Secondly, it is doubtful that all of the OHADA members would be ready to relinquish all their labour law – though they would perhaps not be against having a single law on some specific issues. Thirdly, attention should be paid to the fact that many ILO Conventions have been ratified by some of the OHADA members but not by others. However, for the OHADA text to be in compliance with international law, it would seem indispensable that it be compatible with all the Conventions ratified by each and every one of the OHADA members. By failing to do that, there is a risk that some members would be in breach of some ILO Conventions that they had ratified. On the other hand, if the OHADA text is fully compliant with all ILO Conventions ratified by each and every one of the OHADA members, many of the latter would become indirectly bound by ILO standards that they have not accepted. Furthermore, if a member were to ratify a new ILO Convention after the OHADA text had been passed as a law, it would be necessary to undertake a review of that text to make it compatible with the Convention. When taken together, these problems seem sufficient to cast some doubt on the prospects for the OHADA approach bearing fruit.

---

13 MERCOSUR is a common market founded in 1991 by Argentina, Brazil, Paraguay and Uruguay.

14 See Jean-Marc Béraud, 'Etude préalable à l'adoption d'un Acte uniforme en Droit du Travail dans le cadre de l'Organisation pour l'Harmonisation en Afrique du Droit des Affaires (OHADA)', IFP/Dialogue Document No. 2 (Geneva, ILO, 2003).

The social clause: from WTO to ILO

A fourth strategy is the social clause, which can have a multilateral or a unilateral source. In the first case, the social clause may be part of a treaty or an international trade agreement: it would endow the treaty or the agreement with the mechanisms to investigate and, if appropriate, to impose fines or trade restrictions on countries which have denied or violated internationally recognized workers' rights with the aim or the effect of improving international competitiveness.

The debate on the social clause is not new. For example, as mentioned earlier in this chapter, a social clause was envisaged in the draft Charter of the International Trade Organization (Havana Charter, 1948) but this never came into force. Only certain elements of the Havana Charter were later incorporated into the GATT agreement, which did not contain any specific provision concerning labour apart from a rule which allowed for the prohibition of imported goods produced by prison labour.

However, even in the 1970s, the United States brought the issue of labour standards before the Tokyo Round, though with no success. Nonetheless, from the 1980s, social clauses became a common feature in unilateral trade schemes like the US and EU Generalized System of Preferences (discussed later in this chapter).

The social clause again came to the forefront during the Uruguay Round negotiations (1986–94) that gave birth to the World Trade Organization (WTO). It was supported by the United States and some countries of the European Union. International trade unions also lobbied intensively for its adoption. However, the social clause did not appear in the Final Act signed in Marrakesh in 1994, mainly because it was strongly challenged by many countries, especially developing countries, which alleged that it would actually be used by North countries with protectionist purposes. It was again rejected in the WTO Singapore Conference in 1996, which adopted a Declaration which emphatically stated that while the WTO was competent on trade issues it was also committed to respect for internationally recognized core labour standards (see box 4.3). However, it added that labour issues fall within the competence of the ILO, not of the WTO, and that labour standards should not be used for protectionist purposes. Thus the debate on the links between global trade and labour rights came back full circle to the ILO.

Box 4.3 Ministerial Declaration of the WTO

Adopted 13 December 1996, Singapore

We, the Ministers, have met in Singapore from 9 to 13 December 1996 for the first regular biennial meeting of the WTO at Ministerial level, as called for in Article IV of the Agreement Establishing the World Trade Organization, to further strengthen the WTO as a forum for negotiation, the continuing liberalization of trade within a rule-based system, and the multilateral review and assessment of trade policies, and in particular to:

- assess the implementation of our commitments under the WTO Agreements and decisions;
- review the ongoing negotiations and Work Programme;
- examine developments in world trade; and
- address the challenges of an evolving world economy.

Core labour standards

We renew our commitment to the observance of internationally recognized core labour standards. The International Labour Organization (ILO) is the competent body to set and deal with these standards, and we affirm our support for its work in promoting them. We believe that economic growth and development fostered by increased trade and further trade liberalization contribute to the promotion of these standards. We reject the use of labour standards for protectionist purposes, and agree that the comparative advantage of countries, particularly low-wage developing countries, must in no way be put into question. In this regard, we note that the WTO and ILO Secretariats will continue their existing collaboration.

The ILO Declaration on Fundamental Principles and Rights at Work, 1998

With the debate back in its own court, the ILO formulated a strategy on the foundation of three pillars: it actively promoted the ratification of the eight fundamental Conventions; it adopted a Declaration on Fundamental Principles and Rights at Work; and it developed the Decent Work Agenda. Here we will discuss the purpose and effects of the Declaration.

In 1994 the ILO Director-General submitted to the Conference a report entitled *Defending values, promoting change*, on the ILO's 75th anniversary.[15] The Director-General undertook an in-depth review of the goals and principles of the ILO, and discussed some of the challenges it had met arising out of globalization, technological change and the end of the Cold War. The role and effectiveness of ILO standards, the shortcomings arising out of the lack of universal ratification of the fundamental Conventions and the possible need to complete ILO standards with some other forms of instruments and means of action were amongst the problems tackled in this report.

The subsequent discussion of the report by the Conference showed that while there was worldwide support of the rights and principles embodied in the ILO fundamental Conventions, a number of countries were not considering ratification of some of them; secondly, with regard to the application and enforcement of ILO standards, a great number of countries of the global South rejected any social clause that could lead to the imposition of trade sanctions on a country which failed to respect workers' fundamental rights; and thirdly, many speakers also rejected strongly the possibility of introducing some form of 'social labelling' under the aegis of the ILO, something which had been raised (as something to explore, not as a concrete proposal) in the ILO report.

It was clear, however, that there was consensus on one point: globalization and worldwide political and technological changes had had a deep impact on workers' rights and working and living conditions throughout the world. This was obviously of great concern for the ILO and called for something more than a mere debate at a session of the Conference. As a result, the Conference debate was followed up by a Working Party on the Social Dimensions of the Liberalization of International Trade. Amongst other questions, the Working Party was asked to explore possible ways to enable the ILO to have a say in the worldwide debate on the interplay between international trade and labour rights.

One of the hottest topics in this debate – namely the possible establishment of a link between international trade and social standards through the use of a social clause accompanied by mechanisms for imposing sanctions – was very rapidly abandoned. In effect, no consensus could be reached on this question as the introduction of a legally binding and operational social clause within the framework of ILO (something which would have called for a far-reaching reform of ILO procedures, including perhaps a constitutional amendment) met with strong opposition from many governments and

---

15 ILO, *Defending values, promoting change: Social justice in a global economy*, Report of the Director-General, International Labour Conference, 81st Session, Geneva, 1994.

employers' members, though it did receive support from some other governments and workers' members. This decision largely espoused the position of
a majority of developing countries, which feared the possible use of a social
clause with protectionist goals.

The same concern was also echoed at the Social Summit of Copenhagen in
1995, which concluded with a final Declaration in which a firm commitment
was made to: '(i) Pursue the goal of ensuring quality jobs and safeguard the
basic rights and interests of workers, and to this end freely promote respect
for relevant International Labour Organization Conventions, including those
on the prohibition of forced and child labour, the freedom of association, the
right to organize and bargain collectively, and the principle of non-discrimination'. Thus both the rejection of the social clause by the WTO in Singapore
and the Summit Declaration provided the ILO with clear indications on the
direction it should follow when tackling this issue.

At some point in the debate, the possibility was mooted for establishing –
with the ILO Governing Body – a committee similar to the Committee on
Freedom of Association, to receive complaints concerning breaches of the
principles embodied in fundamental Conventions other than those on freedom of association and collective bargaining, especially regarding forced
labour, including child labour and discrimination, even when these
Conventions had not been ratified by a Member.[16] However this idea was
objected to by a great majority of governments.[17]

In view of the above, it became clear that all that the Members were ready
to accept at this stage was a legally non-binding instrument, which could
nevertheless strengthen the ILO's position in the worldwide debate on the
social and labour effects of globalization. This approach was further elaborated in the Director-General's Report submitted to the 85th Session of the
Conference, 1997: *The ILO, standard setting and globalization*.[18] It evoked the
possibility of setting up a promotional mechanism to strengthen the universal application of core rights or, in a more general way, of a possible procla-
mation of the ILO's doctrine concerning social measures to go hand in hand
with globalization. As this proposal received strong support from the
Conference, the Governing Body decided to include in the 86th Session of the
Conference, 1998, an item headed 'Consideration of a possible Declaration of

---

16 See, for example, ILO, *The strengthening of the ILO's supervisory system*, Governing Body,
267th Session, Geneva, Nov. 1996, GB.267/LILS/5.

17 See ILO, *Reports of the Committee on Legal Issues and International Labour Standards*, 267th
Session, Geneva, Nov. 1996, GB.267/9/2.

18 ILO, *ILO standard setting and globalization*, Report of the Director-General, International
Labour Conference, 85th Session, 1997.

principles of the International Labour Organization concerning fundamental rights and its appropriate follow-up mechanism'. After a difficult debate and a tight vote[19] the Conference adopted the Declaration (see box 4.4).

Box 4.4 ILO Declaration on Fundamental Principles and Rights at Work

Whereas the ILO was founded in the conviction that social justice is essential to universal and lasting peace;

Whereas economic growth is essential but not sufficient to ensure equity, social progress and the eradication of poverty, confirming the need for the ILO to promote strong social policies, justice and democratic institutions;

Whereas the ILO should, now more than ever, draw upon all its standard-setting, technical cooperation and research resources in all its areas of competence, in particular employment, vocational training and working conditions, to ensure that, in the context of a global strategy for economic and social development, economic and social policies are mutually reinforcing components in order to create broad-based sustainable development;

Whereas the ILO should give special attention to the problems of persons with special social needs, particularly the unemployed and migrant workers, and mobilize and encourage international, regional and national efforts aimed at resolving their problems, and promote effective policies aimed at job creation;

Whereas, in seeking to maintain the link between social progress and economic growth, the guarantee of fundamental principles and rights at work is of particular significance in that it enables the persons concerned to claim freely and on the basis of equality of opportunity their fair share of the wealth which they have helped to generate, and to achieve fully their human potential;

Whereas the ILO is the constitutionally mandated international organization and the competent body to set and deal with international labour standards, and enjoys universal support and acknowledgement in promoting fundamental rights at work as the expression of its constitutional principles;

Whereas it is urgent, in a situation of growing economic interdependence, to reaffirm the immutable nature of the fundamental principles and rights embodied in the Constitution of the Organization and to promote their universal application;

---

19 The Declaration was approved with 273 votes in favour, none against, and 43 abstentions: the required quorum was 264, and had there been fewer than 264 votes it would have been rejected. For a report of the debates, see ILO, *Report of the Committee on the Declaration of Principles*, International Labour Conference, 86th Session, Geneva, 1998.

The International Labour Conference,

1. Recalls:

(a) that in freely joining the ILO, all Members have endorsed the principles and rights set out in its Constitution and in the Declaration of Philadelphia, and have undertaken to work towards attaining the overall objectives of the Organization to the best of their resources and fully in line with their specific circumstances;

(b) that these principles and rights have been expressed and developed in the form of specific rights and obligations in Conventions recognized as fundamental both inside and outside the Organization.

2. Declares that all Members, even if they have not ratified the Conventions in question, have an obligation arising from the very fact of membership in the Organization, to respect, to promote and to realize, in good faith and in accordance with the Constitution, the principles concerning the fundamental rights which are the subject of those Conventions, namely:

(a) freedom of association and the effective recognition of the right to collective bargaining;

(b) the elimination of all forms of forced or compulsory labour;

(c) the effective abolition of child labour; and

(d) the elimination of discrimination in respect of employment and occupation.

3. Recognizes the obligation on the Organization to assist its Members, in response to their established and expressed needs, in order to attain these objectives by making full use of its constitutional, operational and budgetary resources, including by the mobilization of external resources and support, as well as by encouraging other international organizations with which the ILO has established relations, pursuant to Article 12 of its Constitution, to support these efforts:

(a) by offering technical cooperation and advisory services to promote the ratification and implementation of the fundamental Conventions;

(b) by assisting those Members not yet in a position to ratify some or all of these Conventions in their efforts to respect, to promote and to realize the principles concerning fundamental rights which are the subject of those Conventions; and

(c) by helping the Members in their efforts to create a climate for economic and social development.

4. Decides that, to give full effect to this Declaration, a promotional follow-up, which is meaningful and effective, shall be implemented in accordance with the measures specified in the annex hereto, which shall be considered as an integral part of this Declaration.

5. Stresses that labour standards should not be used for protectionist trade purposes, and that nothing in this Declaration and its follow-up shall be invoked or otherwise used for such purposes; in addition, the comparative advantage of any country should in no way be called into question by this Declaration and its follow-up.

To understand the role and the place of the Declaration within the ILO, it is worth first recalling what this instrument is *not* meant to be. From a legal viewpoint, it is *not* an ILO standard, first because its adoption has followed a procedure comparable to that of a resolution (that is, by discussion and adoption by simple majority at the Conference, not by a qualified two-thirds majority as for a Convention or a Recommendation); and secondly because it is not legally binding. It simply states that all ILO Members, from the very fact of membership in the Organization, have an obligation to respect, 'to promote and to realize [in good faith and in accordance with the Constitution] the principles concerning the fundamental rights' which are addressed in the ILO fundamental Conventions. Obviously those Members that have ratified the said Conventions are also obliged to *apply* them; however those which have not are only obliged to *respect, to promote and to realize* the principles embedded in these Conventions. It should be added that unlike the Declaration of Philadelphia, 1944, the 1998 Declaration is not a part of the ILO Constitution.

In short, the Declaration is a promotional instrument, and strictly speaking does not create new obligations on the Members. This is why it simply *declares* (or acknowledges) that the obligation to respect the core principles on which the ILO is based arises from the very fact of membership of the ILO. Also, unlike ILO Conventions, no complaints or representations can be made against a Member on the grounds that it has not respected the principles of the Declaration, the impact of which is assessed through a *follow-up*, not a *supervisory* procedure. On the other hand, the Declaration does not affect the ILO's traditional standard-setting and supervisory mechanisms, to which it simply offers added value, but is by no means meant to be an alternative. Actually the Declaration goes hand in hand with the ILO standards system. Most noteworthy is that it has helped in undertaking promotional activities for the ILO fundamental Conventions, which in many cases have paved the way for the ratification by some countries which had been reluctant to do so. Also it has been highlighted in many international instruments, including human rights covenants, as well as in an increasing number of corporate social responsibility initiatives, so that its moral impact cannot be called into question.

The Declaration's follow-up is made up of two components. The first of these is an annual review of the reports submitted by the Members on the fundamental Conventions they have not ratified (Members who have ratified the fundamental Conventions do not need to submit a separate report). These reports are compiled by the International Labour Office and reviewed by a group of experts (not by the ILO Committee of Experts on the Application of Conventions and Recommendations). The second component is a Global Report, prepared by the Office each year on a different group of ILO fundamental Conventions.[20] This report is submitted to and discussed by the Conference. These are indeed state-of-the-art reports, the reading of which provides invaluable information on the situation regarding these rights, and the main problems they face in being fully respected and promoted throughout the world.

A no less important element of the Declaration is the obligation that it puts on the Office's shoulders, to use all its resources to assist the Members in order to attain the objectives of the Declaration. In keeping with this mandate, the Office has established a special programme on the promotion of the Declaration which has received strong support from the ILO constituents and has drawn on financing from many sources.

Finally, it should be observed that the ILO Declaration, like that of the WTO in Singapore, clearly rejects the use of labour standards for protectionist trade purposes.

Labour-related provisions in multilateral and bilateral trade agreements

The first workers' rights protection schemes appeared in the early 1980s in US tariff preference laws (addressed in the next section). However, since 1993 the United States has also linked workers' rights protection to free trade agreements (FTAs) using three basic models. The first model, the North American Free Trade Agreement (NAFTA), includes workers' rights provisions in a side agreement, the North American Agreement on Labour Cooperation (NAALC), with sanctions limited to a failure to enforce standards of occupational safety and health, child labour or minimum wages. The second model, the free trade agreement between the United States and Jordan, put labour provisions within the body of the agreement and made

---

20 The first report – on Freedom of association and collective bargaining – was submitted in 2000; the second year's report was on Forced labour; the third year's was on Elimination of child labour; and the fourth year's was on Equality.

them subject to sanctions via the FTA's dispute resolution procedures. The third model is embodied in the Dominican Republic and Central America Free Trade Agreement (DR-CAFTA),[21] which includes labour rights provisions in the body of the agreement, but permits sanctions only if a country fails to enforce its own labour laws.

Canada has also signed free trade agreements, with Costa Rica and Chile respectively, which include a subsidiary agreement on labour cooperation.[22] Both contain clauses that reaffirm a commitment to respect workers' fundamental rights and provide that each of the parties shall ensure that its domestic labour law is enforced.

North American Agreement on Labor Cooperation

The North American Agreement on Labor Cooperation (NAALC) is perhaps the most well-known of these instruments. NAALC is a labour protocol annexed to the North American Free Trade Agreement (NAFTA), signed in 1993 by Canada, Mexico and the United States. It was devised by the US Government in response to union-sponsored advocacy against NAFTA ratification. US trade unions feared that NAFTA would lead to massive offshoring of plants from Canada and the United States to Mexico, allegedly a country with cheap labour and a low level of law enforcement. To cope with this, the US Government proposed adding NAALC to NAFTA on the understanding that it would help improve the enforcement of labour law by Mexico.

While it is meant to promote a number of labour law principles,[23]

---

21 This agreement was originally negotiated between the United States and Costa Rica, El Salvador, Guatemala, Honduras and Nicaragua and was then known as CAFTA. The Dominican Republic later joined CAFTA negotiations, which became DR-CAFTA. The Agreement (a law for the United States but a Treaty for the other members) was signed in 2004 and came into force in 2006 for some countries (by January 2008 only Costa Rica had not yet ratified DR-CAFTA; however, after it was approved by referendum in October 2007 the way is now clear for its ratification by that country). For an analysis of NAFTA and other FTA negotiated by the US government, see Mariluz Vega Ruiz, *Legal considerations on labor regulations in free trade agreements in the Americas* (Lima, Cuadernos de Integración Andina, 2004).

22 Available online, respectively at http://www.sice.oas.org (for Canada–Costa Rica) and at http://www.hrsdc.gc.ca (for Canada–Chile).

23 Namely the following: (1) freedom of association and protection of the right to organize; (2) the right to bargain collectively; (3) the right to strike; (4) prohibition of forced labour; (5) labour protection for children and young persons; (6) minimum employment standards; (7) elimination of employment discrimination; (8) equal pay for women and men; (9) prevention of occupational injuries and illnesses; (10) compensation in cases of occupational injuries and illnesses; (11) protection of migrant workers.

NAALC does not provide for the establishment of specific international labour standards, nor does it make a clear reference to ILO Conventions. This is perhaps due to the fact that Canada and the United States have together ratified far fewer ILO Conventions than Mexico.[24] Had NAALC laid down that the three NAFTA countries were to apply the ILO Conventions they had ratified, Mexico would have been put in a more stringent position than its NAFTA partners, while the latter would have been under pressure to ratify a greater number of ILO Conventions. Instead, NAALC provides that the three members of NAFTA shall be committed to enforce their domestic law. Thus NAALC proposes that no deregulation be made in the form of non-enforcement of labour law. To this end, NAFTA members are to take a number of measures, for example through labour inspection, labour-management consultation, mediation, conciliation and arbitration. They shall also be required to initiate, 'in a timely manner, proceedings to seek appropriate sanctions or remedies for violations' of labour law.

NAALC is administered by a Commission for Labour Cooperation, which comprises a Ministerial Council and a Secretariat, and is assisted by national administrative offices (NAO) in each of the three countries. Labour and management organizations participate in NAALC in a consultative capacity only, though they can initiate complaints, which in NAALC terminology are called 'public communications'. These must be submitted before a NAO of a country other than the one where the problem has arisen (that is, a complaint against Mexico can be submitted before the US or Canadian NAO but not that of Mexico). If it is declared receivable, the 'communication' may be addressed through ministerial consultations, 'which shall make every attempt to resolve the matter through cooperation, including the exchange of publicly available information to enable a full examination of the issue' (NAALC, Article 22). If, after ministerial consultation, a matter has not been resolved, any of the parties may request the establishment of an Evaluation Committee of Experts (ECE), which can only analyse, 'in the light of the objectives of the Agreement and in a non-adversarial manner, patterns of practice by each Party in the enforcement of its occupational safety and health or other technical labour standards' (Article 23). However, the petitioners are excluded from this phase of the proceedings and no ECE may be convened if the matter is not trade-related or is not covered by mutually recognized labour laws.

It should be observed that freedom of association is not included within the definition of 'other technical labour standards'. Further procedures may

---

24 As of 21 November, Mexico had ratified 78 ILO Conventions, far more than Canada (30 ratifications) and the United States (14 ratifications) together.

include additional consultations, and if the matter remains unresolved, 'the establishment of an arbitral panel to consider the matter where the alleged persistent pattern of failure by the Party complained against to effectively enforce its occupational safety and health, child labour or minimum wage technical labour standards is trade related and covered by mutually recognized labour laws'. This means that an arbitral panel may not be convened when the matter relates to freedom of association, forced labour or discrimination. If, in its final report, a panel can determine that there has been a 'persistent pattern of failure by the Party complained against to effectively enforce its occupational safety and health, child labour or minimum wage technical labor standards, the disputing Parties may agree on a mutually satisfactory action plan, which normally shall conform with the determinations and recommendations of the panel' (Article 38). If no agreement is reached on such a plan, any disputing party may request that the panel be reconvened, to determine whether the party complained against is fully implementing the action plan. If it is not, 'the panel shall impose a monetary enforcement assessment'. If the party fails to pay this monetary enforcement assessment, any complaining party or parties may suspend the application of NAFTA benefits to the party complained against 'in an amount no greater than that sufficient to collect the monetary enforcement assessment'.

So far, fewer than 30 communications (complaints) have been submitted under NAALC, most of these in the years that immediately followed the adoption of the agreement (two such complaints are summarized in box 4.5). Most of the complaints related to trade union and collective bargaining rights, and they did not go beyond the phase of ministerial consultations. None of the other complaints led to the appointment of an ECE, let alone that of an arbitral panel, and non-financial penalties have never been imposed under NAALC. At present, the Canadian trade unions have decided not to submit new complaints under NAALC as they do not want to give credibility to what they consider a meaningless procedure. It would seem that only in one case have the Canadian unions reaped some success after having submitted complaints under NAALC. Activists in the United States seem to share this view, as they consider that NAALC has not led to real changes in national laws, nor has it improved compliance.

Box 4.5 Two complaints submitted against Canada under NAALC[25]

Two complaints have been brought against Canada under NAALC. The first arose after the closure of a McDonald's restaurant in Québec, allegedly to avoid the unionization of staff. The complainants submitted that McDonald's had exploited some loopholes in the law of Québec that permit employers to delay certification proceedings and then close facilities to avoid unionization. The US NAO accepted the case for review but shortly thereafter an agreement was reached between the submitters and the Québec government to include this issue in an ongoing review of the Québec Labour Code. As a result, the complaint was withdrawn and the file was closed. In 2001 administrative changes were made to the Code that accelerated the certification process but nothing was done to address plant closure to avoid unionization.

The second complaint was about a provision in federal legislation that rural route mail couriers were not deemed to be employees for the purposes of the application of collective bargaining laws, thus depriving them of access to a statutory collective bargaining scheme. The US NAO refused to accept the complaint because it did not raise a question related to the enforcement of law. The rural route mail couriers subsequently achieved voluntary recognition after a lengthy and expensive organizing drive by the postal workers' union.

The treatment given to labour-related complaints under NAALC contrasts sharply with complaints that can be lodged under NAFTA by private investors in relation to trade issues. NAFTA foresees the removal of tariff and non-tariff barriers (such as import licences) between the three participating countries. It also protects investors by guaranteeing treatment no less favourable than treatment that is granted to national investors, and gives most-favoured-nation status to each of the participating countries. Private investors are also protected against expropriation, nationalization or comparable measures. Investors who complain against measures which are incompatible with these principles can lodge a complaint before an international tribunal, whose decision is binding. There is almost no need to add that this is a far stricter procedure than the one that is provided under NAALC with regard to 'communications' relating to workers' rights.

---

25 Eric Tucker, 'Great expectations defeated? The trajectory of collective bargaining regimes in Canada and the United States post-NAFTA', in *Comparative Labor Law & Policy Journal* (2004), Vol. 26, No. 1, p. 130.

Nonetheless, NAALC should receive some credit, in that, apart from its ineffectiveness as a law-enforcement mechanism, it has enabled a number of worthwhile initiatives to develop in the field of research and exchange of information on good labour relations practices. It has also encouraged the development of transnational union activism.

DR-CAFTA

Under the DR-CAFTA agreement, each country pledges: (1) to 'not fail to effectively enforce' its own labour laws in a manner affecting trade; (2) to strive to ensure that both ILO core labour principles and internationally recognized workers' rights are recognized and protected by domestic law; (3) to strive to 'not waive' or 'derogate from' its own labour laws to encourage trade or investment; (4) to respect the sovereignty of the other countries; and (5) to establish mechanisms for cooperative activities and labour-related trade capacity building with the other countries. Of these shared commitments, only sustained failure to enforce one's own labour laws is subject to binding dispute settlement and ultimately to fines or sanctions. The maximum fine in a particular dispute is set at $15 million per year per violation, which is to be directed towards remedying the labour violation.

It is still too early to assess the effectiveness of this agreement to actually promote and protect the respect of the workers' fundamental rights. However, it should be pointed out that neither DR-CAFTA nor NAALC provides an impartial and objective mechanism for assessing the effective application of the labour rights they are meant to protect, especially with respect to freedom of association, which can only be dealt with by government-level consultations.[26] Unlike the DR-CAFTA, the ILO does have an effective supervisory system that can determine compliance with a ratified Convention, namely the Committee of Experts on the Application of Conventions and Recommendations and the complaints procedures under Articles 24 and 26 of the ILO Constitution. However, when the relevant Convention has not been ratified and there are no other monitoring bodies, assessing conformity is obviously more difficult. As has already been indicated, Canada and the United States have ratified far fewer ILO Conventions than their free trade partners. More specifically, the United States has ratified only two of the eight ILO fundamental Conventions, and Canada has as yet not ratified Conventions No. 29, No. 98 and No. 138. By contrast, all of the Central American countries, Chile and the Dominican Republic have ratified the eight ILO fundamental Conventions and Mexico has ratified six of them

---

26 See Vega Ruiz (2004), op. cit., p. 25.

(though it has not ratified Conventions No. 98 and No. 138). This limits considerably the possibility of having even-handed mechanisms to assess and compare how workers' rights are effectively protected in all of these countries.

However, it is to the DR-CAFTA's credit that it has been accompanied by important US funding to help improve the enforcement of labour laws, with five particular priorities:

1. To modernize the labour justice system – with a focus on building public awareness and knowledge of labour and international labour standards, particularly among judges, academics, and others involved in labour law administration and justice.
2. To strengthen the ministries' capacity to enforce labour laws, conduct inspections and resolve labour disputes.
3. To reduce discrimination against women and harassment in the export processing industries (*maquiladoras*).
4. To establish benchmarking, verification and monitoring processes.
5. To support the Environmental Cooperation Agreement.

Other agreements in the Americas

The Social and Labour Declaration (*Declaración Sociolaboral*) of MERCOSUR signed in 1998 by the Presidents of Argentina, Brazil, Paraguay and Uruguay, and the CARICOM Declaration of Labour and Industrial Relations Principles, adopted in 1995 by the Standing Committee of Ministers responsible for Labour,[27] also came about in response to a political will to make mainstream fundamental principles and rights at work in the operation of regional free trade agreements. However, so far there is no evidence that this strategy has been effective.

Unilateral social clauses: the Generalized System of Preferences

Unilateral social clauses (those rules that a State can include in its national law on foreign trade) have generally had greater effectiveness. This practice was initiated in the early 1980s by the US government. So far there are four US trade relations schemes which include a labour clause: the Caribbean Basin Trade Partnership Act 1983; the Generalized System of Preferences (GSP), established in 1976 and which since 1984 has included a labour clause; the Andean Trade Promotion and Drug Eradication Act 1991; and the African Growth and Opportunities Act, which was passed in 2000.

---

27 Text available online at http://www.caricom.org.

The Generalized System of Preferences (GSP) is certainly the most well known of these schemes. It provides, inter alia, that the US Government can withdraw custom duties exemptions to imports coming from countries that do not take steps to respect internationally recognized workers' rights, including the following: the right of association; the right to organize and collective bargaining; a prohibition on the use of forced or compulsory labour; a minimum age for the employment of children; and acceptable conditions of work with respect to minimum wages, hours of work and occupational safety and health. However, the GSP does not contemplate sanctions for labour law violations in the field of discrimination.

The risk of having custom preferences withdrawn from a country like the United States is not something to be taken lightly. Thus, the possibility of having GSP privileges withdrawn was very likely a determining factor behind the revision of labour law in Costa Rica (1993), the Dominican Republic (1992), El Salvador (1994) and, some years later, Guatemala. These countries had in effect been called on to revise their labour laws with a view to better protecting freedom of association, and a failure to do so meant their trade privileges under the GSP would be withdrawn.

The European Union runs a programme similar to the United States' GSP (see box 4.6), but in contrast to the GSP it makes explicit reference to the ILO fundamental Conventions. The EU has already used GSP labour-related provisions, with respect to Myanmar, which was excluded from trade preferences on the ground of widespread use of forced labour by the government.

Box 4.6 User's Guide to the European Union's Scheme of Generalized Tariff Preferences[28]

Special incentive arrangements for the protection of labour rights
While it is safe to say that GSP preferences have a positive impact on development, hopes that trade liberalization and export-led economic growth would result in sustainable patterns of development have not always materialized. Growing international competition tends to favour a race to the bottom, in particular in respect of labour and environmental standards. The most appropriate way for promoting the respect of these standards are incentives in the form of additional tariff preferences. This policy has been implemented in the framework of the EU's GSP. [...]

---

28 Excerpts from EC, *User's guide to the European Union's scheme of Generalized Tariff Preferences* (Brussels, 2003).

The special arrangements for the protection of labour rights are available upon request. Requests have to include the laws of the requesting country incorporating the substance of the eight ILO Conventions as well as the measures taken in order to implement those laws. It is not required that the country has signed and ratified those Conventions. It is sufficient that the substance of the standards concerned is incorporated in the domestic legislation. [...]

The examination of requests is carried out by the Commission. Upon receipt of a request, the Commission publishes a notice in the Official Journal of the European Communities inviting interested parties to submit their comments and to share any relevant information. The examination takes into account, in particular, reports of the relevant organizations and agencies (ILO, international trade unions etc). The authorities of the requesting country are involved in the examination at all stages and provided with any possibility to participate.

However effective, GSP labour clauses raise an ethical problem relating to the fact that they are developed and applied unilaterally. Thus a country that has established a GSP labour clause is the sole judge in determining when and which country would be subject to a GSP investigation and may eventually be deprived of trade benefits. This means that risks of having double standard practices are not to be ruled out.

United States–Cambodia bilateral textile agreement

In 1999 the United States and Cambodia signed an agreement relating to trade in cotton and other textiles, which, among other provisions, required that Cambodia substantially comply with its own labour law and support labour standards. The agreement did not anticipate a substantial revision of the Labour Code of Cambodia which had been developed with substantial ILO assistance and was generally considered to be exemplary.[29] It provided that 'the Government of the United States will determine whether working conditions in the Cambodian textile and apparel sector substantially comply with such (i.e. the Cambodia) labour law and standards'.

ILO-sponsored monitoring was a unique feature of this agreement. To this end an international cooperation project under ILO management (Better Factories Cambodia) received financial support from the US Government and

---

29 See Alisa di Caprio, 'Are labor provisions protectionist? Evidence from nine labour-augmented US trade arrangements', in *Comparative Labor Law & Policy Journal* (2004), Vol, 26, No. 1, p. 10.

other international donors, and was put under ILO management. The project developed a checklist of more than 500 items based on Cambodian labour law and ILO standards, which was endorsed by the Government as well as by employers and unions in the garment industry. The ILO trained a number of local staff to work as factory monitors to undertake unannounced visits on-site. The Government required that textile factories register with the project and accept monitoring in order to obtain export permits.

Monitors are authorized to make unannounced visits. To ensure accuracy, workers and management are interviewed separately and in confidence. Interviews with workers usually take place away from the factory. Monitors also talk with factory shop stewards and union leaders.

Factory managers receive reports of the findings which include suggestions for improvement. Suggestions are specific, touching on issues as diverse as child labour, freedom of association, employee contracts, wages, working hours, workplace facilities, noise control and machine safety. After time for discussion and follow-up action, the monitors visit the factory again to check progress. Findings from the monitoring are made public through the reports. Factories are named and their progress with implementation is identified in all reports made after the second visit. Synthesis reports on the work of this project are periodically produced and published. In October 2006 the number of factories registered with the project was 305, with 317,142 workers. In the six months prior to the release of its 17th report in October 2006, the project monitors had made 212 visits. Since the project was established it has been able to assess a good rate of improvement in the textile factories in Cambodia.[30] According to a US scholar, 'the US–Cambodia Bilateral Textile Agreement is commonly cited as one of the great successes of labour provisions in trade agreements. Working conditions have generally improved in the country, and factories have been more vigilant in implementing labour laws.'[31]

Corporate social responsibility (CSR)

***

Box 4.7 Making labour standards work: the need for increasing cooperation between private stakeholders and the State

Who should be responsible for the eight-year-old boy sewing soccer balls for over 12 hours a day in a Third World country? Is it his national

***

30 ILO, *Seventeenth synthesis report on working conditions in Cambodia's garment sector*, Better Factories Cambodia Synthesis Report (Phnom Penh, 2006).

31 Alisa di Caprio, op. cit., p. 11.

government, who regulates labour standards and has failed to adopt international conventions with respect to child labour? Is it the International Labour Organization (ILO), the United Nations specialized agency in labour, who has created international labour standards and Recommendations regarding the implementation of those standards? Is it the governments of Canada and the United States, who have developed trade relations with a Third World country to facilitate and encourage the flow of goods, capital and investment seamlessly across continents? Or is it the Multinational Enterprise (MNE) that has either established production facilities in a Third World country or hired a domestic subcontractor to produce its goods for export internationally? In a progressively globalizing world, the boundaries between public and private are becoming increasingly blurred, making it less clear as to who has responsibility in the adoption and implementation of fundamental labour standards. Fifty years ago, it seemed quite natural to organize and assign responsibilities in the international context to distinct national governments, international organizations, and private enterprises. Today, however, it is not so easy (nor advantageous) to carve out these roles in such a regimented and mutually exclusive manner.

As international trade law and policy continue to expand to new regions of the world with various international, regional and bilateral agreements, it is simultaneously creating a variety of new social problems in developing countries. These countries are oftentimes willing to trade off labour standards for enhanced trade opportunities, with the high cost being absorbed primarily by un-empowered workers. Recognizing that the primary interests of the host-country governments are not always correlated with those of its workforce, greater responsibility for the interests and rights of workers must be assumed by the other actors, such as home-country governments, non-governmental organizations, international organizations, and, finally, MNEs themselves.

It is in this context that the movement towards corporate social responsibility has evolved. In an effort to combat the negative externalities that trade relations have had on workers, MNEs and other actors have begun to develop alternative strategies to promote labour standards. Traditional models of corporate social responsibility (CSR) have included the development of Corporate Codes of Conduct, Multi-Stakeholder Codes, such as the Fair Labor Association, and Model Codes, such as the UN Global Compact. While these traditional CSR models have obtained marginal success in the promotion of labour standards, newer ideas and strategies are evolving that

> solicit greater commitment from MNEs and their home governments, and, as a result, offer promising opportunities to more effectively promote core labour standards on an international level.[32]

Corporate social responsibility (CSR) has been defined as 'a concept whereby companies integrate social and environmental concerns in their business operations and in their interaction with their stakeholders on a voluntary basis'.[33] It is not in fact a new concept, for its roots can be tracked down to a number of socially oriented practices of Christian nineteenth-century industrialists. It has, however, begun to draw wide interest much more recently, and this idea really took off at the end of the 1980s and attracted widespread attention in the last decade of the twentieth century. The basic assumption of corporate social responsibility is that corporations have an obligation to consider the interests of customers, employees, shareholders, communities, as well as to take account of environment-related factors in all aspects of their operations. This obligation is seen to extend beyond their statutory obligation to comply with legislation. It is closely linked with the principles of sustainable development, whose proponents argue that enterprises should make decisions based not only on financial factors such as profits or dividends, but also on the immediate and long-term social and environmental consequences of their activities. In general, the topics that tend to be incorporated into a CSR statement are provisions on bribery and corruption; treatment of employees; the impact of human rights; community involvement and environmental practices. In respect to labour standards, the most common issues addressed are concerns for child labour; forced labour; non-discrimination; freedom of association and the right of collective bargaining; harassment and abuse; occupational safety and health; wages and benefits; and working hours.

Corporate social responsibility instruments can take different forms, namely: (1) unilateral codes of conduct elaborated by an MNE; (2) framework agreements between an MNE and an international trade union; (3) social accountability standards developed by a NGO; and (4) international instru-

---

32 Ashley Weber, *Rethinking corporate social responsibility: Bridging the divide between labour and trade law*, unpublished paper (Toronto, Osgoode Hall Law School, 2006).

33 EC, *Implementing the partnership for growth and jobs: Making Europe a pole of excellence on corporate social responsibility*, Communciation from the Commission, COM (2006) 0136 final (Luxembourg, 2006).

ments like the OECD Guidelines for Multinational Enterprises[34] and the ILO Tripartite Declaration of Principles concerning Multinational Enterprises and Social Policy.[35] The United Nations Global Compact can also be included in this group.[36]

Corporate codes of conduct

Codes of conduct are generally unilateral instruments issued by an MNE. Some codes of conduct have also been elaborated by associations or by groups of employers, and have mainly sectoral scope. An MNE's code of conduct typically takes the form of a charter in which the MNE sets out its responsibilities vis-à-vis the countries where they operate. Many of them also impose commitments on the MNE's business partners such as contractors and suppliers on the implicit or (more rarely) explicit understanding that those contractors who are held to be in breach of the code will no longer be admitted to enter into business with the MNE. This kind of instrument has been used predominantly amongst US-based multinationals and generally does not provide for external monitoring.

Corporate codes of conduct date back to the beginning of the fair labour standards movement by NGOs. They were drawn up in response to accusations of abuse by MNE's subsidiaries and suppliers in developing countries, and there is little wonder that they were very largely motivated by the fear of international campaigning against their brand names. Thus MNEs began to

---

34 Adopted in 1976, and revised in 2000. The OECD Guidelines are part of the OECD Declaration on International Investment and Multinational Enterprises. The Declaration constitutes a political commitment, adopted by the governments of OECD member states, to facilitate direct investment among OECD members. The Guidelines for Multinational Enterprises are divided into separate chapters covering the range of MNE activities. These chapters deal with general policies, information disclosure, competition, financing, taxation, employment and industrial relations, the environment, and science and technology. More information is available on the OECD website at http://www.oecd.org.

35 Adopted in 1977 and amended in 2000. The principles cover MNE activities related to labour matters, such as employment, conditions of work and life, industrial relations, consultation, examination of grievances and settlement of industrial disputes. More information is available at http://www.ilo.org/multi.

36 The Global Compact was launched by the United Nations Secretary-General, Kofi Annan. It calls upon corporations to bring their corporate practices into line with ten principles based on the Universal Declaration of Human Rights (1948), the ILO's Declaration of Fundamental Principles (1998), the Rio de Janeiro Declaration on Environment and Development (1992) and the UN Convention against Corruption (1993). Its main purpose is to advocate core values and good practices to guide business dealings around the world. It does not provide for monitoring.

establish internal codes that addressed fundamental labour standards in the hope that such efforts would ease pressures beating down on them from transnational activism. Perhaps they were also seen by MNEs as the lesser of two evils, as they feared that media attention to such abuses could potentially prompt an increase in government regulation. Thus the MNEs' codes conveyed the message that host-country governments did not need to intervene as MNEs were able to impose fair rules of the game on their subsidiaries and suppliers. However, some MNE codes of conduct have undoubtedly evolved, to the extent that some recent research suggests that they have had a positive impact on the improvement of workers' living and working conditions.[37]

Framework agreements

Unlike the United States' approach to CSR, which has tended to focus on corporate codes of conduct and voluntary compliance, in Europe greater pressure has been placed on making contractual commitments to labour standards. This has been expressed through international (global) framework agreements – instruments negotiated between a multinational enterprise and a Global Union Federation (GUF) in order to establish an ongoing relationship between the parties and ensure that the company respects the same standards in all the countries in which it operates. Sectoral trade unions from the MNE home country also participate in the negotiation of the agreement. The advantage of framework agreements is that they promote social dialogue between the various interest groups, thus giving the workers a voice in setting corporate objectives for labour standards.

Framework agreements are thus one of the possible developments of industrial relations in the era of globalization. Their content varies according to the different requirements and characteristics of the companies and trade unions involved, as well as depending on the industrial relations' traditions between the parties. They all include the four fundamental principles and rights at work and make reference to the ILO core labour standards and the Declaration. Other provisions, which differ from one agreement to the other, refer to various issues covered by ILO standards such as protection of workers' representatives, wages, occupational safety and health, and skills training. Many of these agreements make reference to the entire supply chain, even if supplier companies are not parties to them.

---

37 See this discussion in Richard Locke et al., 'Beyond corporate codes of conduct: Work organization and labour standards at Nike's suppliers', in *International Labour Review* (2007), Vol. 146, No. 1–2, pp. 21–40.

Companies usually commit to inform all their subsidiaries, suppliers, contractors and subcontractors about the agreement. If a subsidiary or associated enterprise is found not to be respecting the global agreement, then the case can be taken up with the MNE's headquarters, which will look for solutions through dialogue. Most framework agreements include follow-up mechanisms involving trade union participation. These mechanisms include specific actions on the part of management and workers' representatives, such as company-wide dissemination (and translation, where necessary) of the agreement or the development of joint training programmes. Some agreements provide for joint missions by the relevant national trade union and global union federation in order to carry out on-site monitoring of the implementation of the agreement. Many of them include mechanisms for the global union federation to bring a complaint if the company violates the terms of the agreement.

By the beginning of 2007 some 50 MNEs operating in different industries had signed international framework agreements with five global union federations. The first one was signed by the French food multinational Danone in 1988; then the hotel chain ACCOR signed the second in 1995. It was only in 2000 that the number of agreements signed per year accelerated to reach 50 at the end of 2006. Amongst these were agreements signed by the Swedish furniture company IKEA; the American banana company Chiquita; the German pencils producers Faber-Castell and Staedler; oil companies in Norway (Statoil), Italy (ENI) and Russia (Lukoil); car producers in Germany and France like Volkswagen, Daimler-Chrysler, Renault and Peugeot-Citroën; the Spanish and French electricity producers Endesa and EDF; telecom companies in Spain (Telefonica) and Greece (OTE); and retailers in France (Carrefour) and Sweden (H&M). On 21 December 2006 France Telecom signed an international framework agreement with the Union Network International (UNI), and telecom unions around the globe. Covering more than 200,000 employees worldwide, the global agreement addresses respect for ILO core standards across the group – including the right to join a union and to bargain collectively and freedom from discrimination and forced or child labour.[38]

---

38 More information on these voluntary codes and framework agreements can be found in the ILO database BASI at http://www.ilo.org.

Box 4.8 IKEA's IWAY Standard[39]

Minimum Requirements for Environment, Social & Working Conditions and Wooden Merchandise when Purchasing Home Furnishing Products

The IWAY Approval Process

Start-up Requirements
Potential IKEA suppliers – prior to starting a business relationship with IKEA – must fulfil the IWAY start-up requirements: no forced or bonded labour, no child labour and no wood from intact natural forests or high conservation value forests.

Performing the IWAY audit
IKEA will conduct an IWAY audit at the supplier ... The first IWAY audit will always be performed by an IWAY auditor from the IKEA Trading Service Office. Future audits may also be performed by IKEA Compliance & Monitoring Group, as well as third party Audit Organizations appointed by IKEA [...] The IKEA supplier shall support on-site audits conducted by any of the above-mentioned parties. This means e.g. allowing for confidential employee interviews and maintaining and allowing access to all documentation and records as required. [...]

7.7 Use of personnel protective equipment
The IKEA supplier shall provide the appropriate Personal Protective Equipment (PPE) to all workers in any harmful or potentially risky work area(s). The IKEA supplier must ensure the PPE is maintained. [...]
  PPE must also be provided for visitors. [...]

9. Wages, Benefits and Working hours

9.1 Contracts
The employees at the IKEA supplier shall be employed according to applicable laws and regulations and there shall be a contract (or appointment letter) written accordingly. [...]
  A written contract must contain everything specified in local legislation, and as a minimum the following: employer, name of worker, birth date,

---

39 Excerpts from IKEA, *IWAY Standard: Minimum requirements for environment, social and working conditions and wooden merchandise when purchasing home furnished products* (Leiden, 2005).

position, salary, working hours, overtime compensation, benefits and notice time. [...]

9.2 Payrolls and attendance records
[...] The IKEA supplier shall – prior to employment – provide written information to the employee (this also counts for temporary workers) regarding wages and the terms of employment. In connection with the payment of wages at regular intervals, the employee shall receive details of the wages, including overtime hours, and other legal or agreed upon deductions. [...]

9.3 Working hours and overtime
Suppliers shall not require their employees to work more than sixty hours per week on a regularly scheduled basis, including overtime. Working time must not exceed the legal limit. [...]

9.4 Minimum wage
The IKEA supplier shall pay its employees with no less than the legal applicable minimum wage. The minimum wage shall be paid as per local legal demands (based on legally stipulated standard working hours).

9.5 Overtime pay
Employees shall be compensated for all overtime hours worked according to the legal requirements. [...]

9.6 Regular payments
Wages shall be paid at regular intervals and on time with respect to work performed, according to local legislation. Wages shall be paid at least monthly. The supplier must not withhold workers' salary.

9.7 One day off in seven
Employees shall have at least one day off in seven.

9.8 Leaves
Employees shall have time off from their job according to applicable legislation, local traditions and standards (e.g. sick/medical leave, annual/earned leave, maternity leave, national holidays etc.).

9.9 Breaks
The IKEA supplier shall provide its employees with appropriate time off for meals and breaks. At least one break per day and shift shall be 30 minutes or more, if not otherwise agreed in writing between the supplier and the employees (e.g. through an agreement with the local union or workers representatives). [...]

10. Child Labour

10.1 Prevention of child labour (Start-up requirement)

Child labour is defined as work performed by children, which interferes with a child's right to healthy growth and development and denies him or her [the] right to quality education. The IKEA supplier shall not make use of child labour.[15] All measures to avoid child labour shall be implemented taking into account the best interests of the child.

The IKEA supplier must abide by the United Nations Convention on the Rights of the Child (1989), and comply with all relevant national and international laws, regulations and provisions applicable in their country of production.[16]

The IKEA supplier shall take the appropriate measures to ensure that no child labour occurs at their own place of production or at sub-suppliers' place(s) of production. [...]

The IKEA supplier shall maintain a Labour force register including date of birth for all the workers.

10.2 Young workers

The IKEA supplier shall protect young persons of legal working age, up until the age of 18, from any type of employment or work which, by its nature or circumstances in which it is carried out, is likely to jeopardize their health, safety or morals.

11.1 Forced and bonded labour (Start-up requirement)

The IKEA supplier shall not make use of forced,[17] prison,[18] bonded,[19] indentured or involuntary labour.[20] [...]

If employment contracts are terminated according to agreed notice time, the IKEA supplier shall not make any salary deductions for workers who leave.

12.1 Discrimination

The IKEA supplier shall, as a general principle, base decisions pertaining to hiring, salary, fringe benefits, promotion, termination and retirement on workers' individual skills and ability to do the job.

The IKEA supplier shall not discriminate with regards to employees based on race, creed, sex, marital or maternal status, age, political affiliation, national origin, sexual orientation or any other basis prohibited by law.

Freedom of Association

13.1 Labour union

The IKEA supplier shall ensure that employees are not prevented from associating freely.

13.2 Collective bargaining
The IKEA supplier shall not prevent employees from exercising collective bargaining. [...]

Harassment, Abuse and Disciplinary Actions

14.1 Punishments and appeal
The IKEA supplier shall not engage in or support the use of corporal punishments, threats of violence, and other forms of mental or physical coercion or engage in sexual harassment.

The IKEA supplier shall not make use of public warning and punishment systems. Reprimands for breach of duty or misconduct shall be a private matter between the employer and the employee and/or his/her representative. The employee at the supplier shall have the right to appeal reprimands/disciplinary actions/dismissal. These appeals shall be recorded. [...]

16.2 Information to sub-suppliers
All sub-suppliers of wood, bamboo and rattan shall be informed about IKEA's minimum requirements for wooden merchandise [...].

[15] *According to ILO Minimum Age Convention, No. 138 (1973), a child is defined as any person less than fifteen years of age, unless local minimum age law stipulates a higher age for work or mandatory schooling, in which case the higher age would apply. [...]*

[16] *If child labour is found in any place of production, IKEA will require the supplier to establish a corrective action plan. The action plan shall take the child's best interests into consideration, i.e. family and social situation and level of education. Care shall be taken not merely to move child labour from one supplier's workplace to another, but to enable more viable and sustainable alternatives for the children.*

[17] *Forced labour is understood as all work or service that a person is compelled to carry out under any threat of punishment or confiscation of any personal belongings, such as ID card, passport etc., and for which work the said person has not offered him/herself voluntarily.*

[18] *Use of state or military prisoners at the supplier or at sub-supplier is prohibited.*

[19] *Bonded labour is understood as labour not only physically bonded, but also bonded by financial debts, loans or deposits.*

[20] *If guest workers or temporary labour are employed on a contractual basis, such workers shall never be required to remain employed against their own will, for any period beyond the agreed time of the contract. The supplier shall pay all commissions and other fees to the recruitment agency in connection with their employment.*

NGOs' social responsibility standards

Unlike unilateral corporate codes of conducts and bilateral framework agreements, social accountability standards (SAs) are instruments produced by non-governmental organizations (NGOs). All of these standards have drawn inspiration from the ILO fundamental Conventions, and sometimes also other ILO standards relating to conditions of work and hygiene and security. For example, SA8000, developed by Social Accountability International and Fair Labor, are already well-known standards, to which many multinational enterprises have adhered (box 4.9).[40]

Box 4.9 A Summary of SA8000 elements[41]

Child Labor

No workers under the age of 15; minimum lowered to 14 for countries operating under the ILO Convention [No.] 138 developing-country exception; remediation of any child found to be working.

Forced Labor
No forced labor, including prison or debt bondage labor; no lodging of deposits or identity papers by employers or outside recruiters.

Health and Safety
Provide a safe and healthy work environment; take steps to prevent injuries; regular health and safety worker training; system to detect threats to health and safety; access to bathrooms and potable water.

Freedom of Association and Right to Collective Bargaining
Respect the right to form and join trade unions and bargain collectively; where law prohibits these freedoms, facilitate parallel means of association and bargaining.

Discrimination
No discrimination based on race, caste, origin, religion, disability, gender, sexual orientation, union or political affiliation, or age; no sexual harassment.

---

40 See the websites of Social Accountability International: http://www.sa-intl.org/index.cfm and the Fair Labor Association: http://www.fairlabor.org. The Fair Labor Association is very active in Central America.

41 Reproduced from the Social Accountability International webpage: http://www.sa-intl.org.

Discipline
No corporal punishment, mental or physical coercion or verbal abuse.

Working Hours
Comply with the applicable law but, in any event, no more than 48 hours per week with at least one day off for every seven-day period; voluntary overtime paid at a premium rate and not to exceed 12 hours per week on a regular basis; overtime may be mandatory if part of a collective bargaining agreement.

Compensation
Wages paid for a standard work[ing] week must meet the legal and industry standards and be sufficient to meet the basic need of workers and their families; no disciplinary deductions.

Management Systems
Facilities seeking to gain and maintain certification must go beyond simple compliance to integrate the standard into their management systems and practices.

NGOs that operate social accountability standards also offer third party monitoring and certification; this provides some degree of social labelling to multinational enterprises and, more importantly, their contractors and suppliers. The interesting feature of norms like the SA 8000 standard is that certification is directed towards factories and suppliers of the product, and not to the brand itself or the retailers. The logic behind this type of certification is that MNEs will seek to enter into business with certified factories, thus creating an incentive for factories to obtain certification. To a large extent social certification would work like ISO standards: it is well known nowadays that obtaining ISO certification is essential for any enterprise that wishes to compete internationally.

ISO standards

The International Organization for Standardization (ISO) has also started work on the development of the ISO 2600 standard, which will address corporate social responsibility. It will include rules on environment protection, human rights, labour practices and organizational governance. However, unlike other ISO standards, ISO 2600 will come in the form of guidance and thus will not include requirements and so will *not* be a certification standard.

In the field of labour, ISO 2600 will provide that organizations should ensure that work performed on their behalf, either directly or indirectly, is performed within the appropriate legal and institutional framework, and that their activities respect, promote and advance internationally recognized standards and fundamental human rights at work. For example, organizations should respect the principle of freedom of association and the right to collective bargaining; provide decent conditions of work for their workers, invest in skills development and encourage good industrial relations; ensure that individuals performing work for them do so within a recognized employment relationship or, alternatively, are legitimately self-employed; and ensure that work done on their behalf is performed in a healthy and safe working environment. Furthermore, organizations should not employ children nor use any form of forced labour, nor allow unfair discrimination in their employment practices, whether based on race, colour, sex, language, religion, political or other opinion, national or social origin, property, birth or other status.

Pros and cons of CSR initiatives

Unlike the law, corporate social responsibility has developed norms of conduct that are focused primarily on the private sector and the voluntary adoption of those norms. The State does not take part in the formulation of CSR initiatives, or in the enforcement of CSR instruments. Thus workers cannot bring a claim before a court on the grounds that their employer has breached a CSR instrument. Furthermore, enforcement of unilateral CSR instruments like codes of conduct is entirely dependent on the will of the MNE that has adopted the code. These features distinguish CSR instruments from traditional legal tools, such as national law and international treaties, placing them in the category of what are known as *soft law* instruments for the promotion of labour standards. It is obvious in these circumstances that CSR instruments cannot be regarded as an alternative to the law. It follows that no State and no government should be relieved from the responsibility of enacting and enforcing laws and regulations to protect workers on the ground that MNEs and other private actors are willing to do that job.

On the other hand, CSR initiatives have the ability to bring together multiple stakeholders, such as MNEs, organized labour, consumers, NGOs, in pursuing a common goal, thus creating and promoting awareness of the social responsibility of the MNEs. From this viewpoint, CSR initiatives should not be regarded as undermining the authority and responsibilities of the State, but rather as flexible responses to the reality of global production networks and the reduced capacity of developing countries to enforce labour laws and regulations in full. In short, CSR initiatives should be considered as an addition rather than an alternative to State action.

Chapter 5

Legal subordination and the fundamental rights of the person: an uneasy cohabitation at the workplace

Human rights and non-specific workers' rights

All States that have written constitutions (the great majority) recognize that certain rights need to be endowed with especially strong protection. Countries that do not have written constitutions, such as Israel,[1] New Zealand and the United Kingdom, acknowledge, however, the existence of certain rights which are given precedence above all other rights.[2] This is largely based on the acceptance of international human rights covenants, many of which have been adopted within the framework of the United Nations,[3] while others have been adopted by specialized UN agencies such as the ILO (the fundamental Conventions), and still some others by regional organizations such as the Council of Europe[4] and the Organization of

---

1 Israel has instead a set of Basic Laws, which set out quasi-constitutional rights. Basic Laws provide a foundation for the courts to set aside statutory provisions which do not conform to the rights so protected. Two Basic Laws adopted in 1992 deal with human rights: the Basic Law on Human Dignity and Liberty and the Basic Law on Freedom of Occupation (later repealed and replaced in 1994). Basic Laws can, however, be repealed or replaced by a majority of the members of the Knesset (the unicameral Parliament).
2 It should be noted that the idea that there are rights that all citizens ought to have was formulated for the first time ever in the English Bill of Rights, 1689.
3 The Universal Declaration of Human Rights, 1948; the International Covenant on Economic, Social and Cultural Rights, 1966; the International Covenant on Civil and Political Rights, 1966; the International Convention on the Elimination of all Forms of Racial Discrimination, 1965; the Convention on the Elimination of all Forms of Discrimination against Women, 1979; the Convention on the Political Rights of Women, 1952; the Convention on the Rights of the Child, 1989; the Slavery Convention, 1926; and the Convention Against Torture and other Cruel, Inhuman or Degrading Treatment or Punishment, 1984.
4 The Convention for the Protection of Human Rights and Fundamental Freedoms, 1950, commonly known as the European Convention on Human Rights.

American States.[5] The United Kingdom, for example, has passed the Human Rights Act 1998 (HRA) in which a list of rights and fundamental freedoms is set out in accordance with the European Convention on Human Rights.[6] While a number of constitutions, such as those of Australia and the United States of America, do not formally declare a list of fundamental rights, they have been implicitly or explicitly recognized as such in a number of landmark judicial decisions. Whether the fundamental rights are also implied beyond the bounds of legislation, because they fall within the domain of *natural law*, is a matter for academic discussion.

Originally, fundamental rights such as those spelled out in the English Bill of Rights of 1689 or the French *Declaration des Droits de l'Homme et du Citoyen* of 1789, were meant to protect the individual against the sovereign (i.e. the State) but could not be invoked against another individual. Today it is increasingly accepted, especially in case law, that fundamental rights can be invoked both against the State (vertical effect) and between private individuals, including an employee and his or her employer (horizontal effect).[7]

Depending on each country, the length of the list of fundamental rights at work can vary. The same is true with regard to international covenants. The ILO Declaration on Fundamental Principles and Rights at Work, 1998, includes four major categories of fundamental rights, namely freedom of association and collective bargaining, non-discrimination, prohibition of forced labour and prohibition of child labour, which find their expression in the ILO fundamental Conventions, ratified by an overwhelming majority of ILO Members.[8] By contrast, the Charter of Fundamental Rights of the European Union considers that these rights include the prohibition of forced labour (Article 5), protection of privacy (Article 8), freedom of association (Article12), right to work in any Member State (Article 15), non-discrimination (Article 21), equality between men and women (Article 23), information

---

5 American Convention on Human Rights, 1969 (Covenant of San José) and its additional Protocol on Economic, Social and Cultural Rights, 1988 (Protocol of San Salvador).

6 This list is not exhaustive, and the HRA expressly states that reliance on an ECHR Convention right 'does not restrict any other rights or freedoms conferred by UK law'. Other rights commonly regarded as 'fundamental' are defined in specific legislation, such as legislation prohibiting discrimination on specific grounds, and legislation protecting information privacy and freedom of expression in specified circumstances.

7 See Fernando Valdés Dal-Ré, *Fundamental rights of the worker*, General Report submitted to the XVII World Congress of the International Society for Labour Law and Social Security (Montevideo, 2003), p. 75.

8 There have been 1,306 out of a total of 1,456 possible ratifications (data updated 21 November 2008). Regular updates are provided on the ILOLEX database, Ratifications of the Fundamental human rights Conventions by country, available at http://www.ilo.org.

and consultation of the workers at company level (Article 27), collective bargaining and industrial action, including the right to strike (Article 28), free access to employment services (Article 29), protection against unjustified dismissal in accordance with EC law and national law and practices (Article 30), fair conditions of work, that respect the health, security and dignity of the worker, including the limitation of the hours of work and daily and weekly rest, as well as annual vacations (Article 31), and prohibition of child work and the protection of young people at work (Article 32). However, the EU Charter[9] is not a binding international covenant.

There is no doubt that human rights concerns today occupy a place in labour law which is far more prominent than it was some 30 years ago. Apart from some precedents of historical value,[10] the subject of the respect of the fundamental rights of the person at the workplace has mainly developed from the 1960s onwards. Until then, everything pointed towards the idea that an enterprise was like a walled city within which workers were subjects rather than citizens, and gave away their rights during the time they were at the employer's disposal. It was only in 1958 that the ILO adopted the Discrimination (Employment and Occupation) Convention (No. 111), which committed ILO Members to 'declare and pursue a national policy designed to promote, by methods appropriate to national conditions and practice, equality of opportunity and treatment in respect of employment and occupation, with a view to eliminating any discrimination in respect thereof' (Article 2). It was then held that such a policy should aim at establishing certain limits on employers' discretionary powers when in conflict with employees' rights not to be discriminated against.

Compared to some national laws in force, Convention No. 111 might be perceived as being limited in its scope of application as, in addition to the catalogue of forbidden grounds of discrimination enumerated in its Article 1(a), it provides only for a facultative inclusion of further grounds of discrimination.[11] However, it represented an impressive breakthrough in 1958 and

---

9 The EU Charter was to be integrated in the Constitution of the European Union, thus becoming binding – but with an important qualification: the provisions of the Charter were addressed to the institutions, bodies, offices and agencies of the European Union with due regard for the principle of subsidiarity, and to the Member States only when they are implementing European Community law. In any event, the EU Constitution did not enter into force, following its rejection by popular referenda in France and the Netherlands.

10 Article VI of the Constitution of the United States of 1787 states that 'no religious Test shall ever be required as a Qualification to any Office or public Trust in the United States'.

11 Only discriminations on the basis of race, colour, sex, religion, political opinion, national extraction or social origin, are banned under Convention No. 111. Member States may add other grounds to this list but this is not mandatory. Age, disability, family responsi-

has been serving as a cornerstone for the promotion of work-related anti-discrimination policies since then. It was ahead of its time with respect to many countries, raising awareness about the need to provide for work-related anti-discrimination laws and not being limited to only one discrimination criterion. Some years after the adoption of this Convention, national case law and positive law started to develop and enrich the basic principle of non-discrimination: through the notion of indirect discrimination, for example, to which the principle of the shifting of the burden of proof was added. The United States Civil Rights Act, which is regarded as a landmark in the matter of the struggle against racial discrimination, was passed in 1964, and in a majority of countries it is difficult to find laws or judicial decisions that had addressed this problem effectively before that date. It was not until 1973 that apartheid became an international crime under the UN International Convention on the Suppression and Punishment of the Crime of Apartheid, which entered into force in 1976. Even within the European Union, between 1957 and 1976, only the principle of equal remuneration for men and women for equal work or work of equal value was addressed, and between 1976 and 2000 only equal treatment in employment for both men and women was dealt with under EC law.[12] It was necessary to wait almost another quarter of a century until the European Union adopted new EC law to address discrimination on grounds other than sex, namely those of racial or ethnic origin, religion or belief, disability, age and sexual orientation.[13] In France it was not until 1992 that a provision was included in the Labour Code to the effect that the restrictions that an employer could impose on the rights of his or her employees and their individual and collective liberties must always (a) be

bilities, language, matrimonial status, nationality, property, sexual orientation and state of health are commonly found grounds for discrimination that are prohibited under the national law of many countries as well as in a number of international instruments, but are not prohibited under Convention No. 111. However, discrimination on the grounds of trade union membership or participation on trade union activities is forbidden under the Protection of the Right to Organise and Collective Bargaining Convention, 1949 (No. 98), and discrimination on the grounds of family responsibilities is addressed under the Workers with Family Responsibilities Convention, 1981 (No. 156).

12 Council Directive 76/207/EEC of 9 February 1976 on the implementation of the principle of equal treatment for men and women as regards access to employment, vocational training and promotion, and working conditions, *Official Journal of the European Union*, L 039 (1976), pp. 40–2.

13 Council Directive 2000/43/EC of 29 June 2000, implementing the principle of equal treatment between persons irrespective of racial or ethnic origin, *Official Journal of the European Union*, L 180/22 (July, 2000); and Council Directive 2000/78/EC of 27 November 2000, establishing a general framework for equal treatment in employment and occupation, *Official Journal of the European Union*, L 303/16 (Dec. 2000).

justified by the nature of the task to be performed, and (b) be adapted to an aim that is in sight (which should of course be a legitimate aim). In the United Kingdom, formal recognition of the fundamental rights only took place with the adoption of the Human Rights Act of 1998, the purpose of which was to incorporate the ECHR into the English legal system, even though prior to or immediately after this several other statutes were adopted that also enshrined other fundamental rights.[14] This list serves to demonstrate how long it took for labour law to become aware of the importance of protecting fundamental human rights in relation to the workplace. As we will see in the following paragraphs, we now have good evidence that labour law seems to be on the right track.

Though they can encompass a relatively wide spectrum of topics, the fundamental rights share three common features: they reflect core values of a society; they cannot be waived; and when in conflict with other laws and rights they must be given priority, unless an exception based on reasonable and justified grounds can reverse that principle. In the light of numerous judicial decisions it would seem safe to add a fourth common feature: when claimants establish, before a court or other competent authority, facts from which it may be presumed that their fundamental rights have been violated, it is for the respondent to bear the burden of proving that such violations have not taken place or they are justified by a legitimate aim and that the means used have been appropriate. For example, in a judgment delivered in 2003, the Spanish Constitutional Tribunal held that when some factual elements are present, from which a presumption can be made that the dismissal of a worker is in breach of the worker's fundamental rights, it is up to the defendants to prove that their decision was based on grounds that are reasonable and unconnected to any intention to violate such rights. The Constitutional Tribunal added that there is a need to guarantee that the worker's fundamental rights are not left unprotected by making the excuse that the employer has simply been exercising managerial rights. In the case examined by the Tribunal, the worker had claimed that his dismissal, apparently justified by reorganization, was actually made in retaliation to his membership of a political party. While the claimant provided some evidence which purported to support his allegation, the employer offered no evidence to dismiss such a claim.[15]

---

14 These were the Sex Discrimination Act 1975, the Race Relations Act 1976, the Disability Discrimination Act 1995, the Data Protection Act 1984 and the Public Interest Disclosure Act 1998, protecting freedom of expression in certain circumstances.

15 Case *Garcia Ramírez*, judgment of the Constitutional Tribunal of Spain, TC 49/2003, 17 March 2003.

In addition, in recent years this shifting of the burden of proof has also been integrated into the law of many countries as well as into some international laws (see box 5.1). This is particularly important when a worker has been victim of indirect discrimination, which occurs when the effects of certain apparently objective requirements, conditions or practices imposed by an employer have a disproportionate impact on one group rather than other groups.[16] This is why equality legislation needs to address *both* direct and indirect discrimination.

Box 5.1 Understanding and proving discrimination[17]

With the recognition that discrimination is systemic came the need for the burden of proof in discrimination cases to reflect that recognition. The success of litigation strategies to advance gender equality rights depends to a significant degree on the burden of proof which applies to such litigation. Canada, with a substantial body of successful jurisprudence, shifts the burden of proof to employers once a complainant has shown a prima facie case of discriminatory effect. This is because it is understood that it is 'the employer who will be in possession of the necessary information to show undue hardship, and the employee will rarely, if ever, be in a position to show its absence'.[18] Italy's human rights law also takes this approach. Once a human rights seeker provides factual or statistical evidence that, for example, one sex is more favoured, directly or indirectly, than the other by a practice or policy (such as pay or hiring), the employer has the burden of disproving the evidence.[19] The EU has also followed this approach with its new Directives against Discrimination. However, this approach still leaves a burden on complainants which can be onerous. South Africa's Employment Equity Act, of 1998, specifically directs that the 'onus of instituting (and bearing the cost of) discrimination-related litigation rests on the individuals who complain of discrimination'. A noted South African expert acknowledges that 'bringing anti-discrimination litigation is extremely expensive

---

16 For example, when certain rights or benefits that are granted to full-time workers are denied to part-timers and it can be established that this affects proportionally more women than men.

17 Mary Cornish, *Securing sustainable human rights justice for workers*, unpublished paper prepared for this comparative overview (Geneva, ILO, 2007).

18 *Ontario (Human Rights Commission)* v. *Simpsons-Sears Ltd*, 23 DLR (4th) 321 at para. 28 [hereinafter *Simpsons-Sears*]; and F. Faraday et al. (eds), *Making equality rights real* (Toronto, Irwin Press, 2006).

19 ILO, *Promoting gender equality: A resource kit for trade unions, Booklet 3: The issues and guidelines for gender equality bargaining* (Geneva, 2002), p. 13.

and there are considerable difficulties in obtaining the evidence required to establish patterns of discrimination, particularly in the case of wage discrimination.'[20] Similarly in the United States, while the burden of proof shifts to the employer, the burden of persuasion that remains with the complainant is still high and often cannot be discharged. Given the widespread evidence of the societal systemic discrimination faced by vulnerable groups and the relative advantage employers have over such groups when it comes to resources and knowledge, employers should bear even more of the initial burden of proving that their employment practices do not have a discriminatory impact.

Here we will address a number of human rights that relate to the dignity of the human being at the workplace. These are known as *non-specific rights*, for they are meant to protect workers in their capacity as human beings. By contrast, rights such as freedom of association and collective bargaining are specifically addressed to workers. Non-specific workers' fundamental rights include, at least, the right not to be discriminated against, protection of privacy and private life, freedom of thought, freedom of religion and freedom of expression.

The problem to be addressed here relates to the possibility that some of the employees' fundamental rights will conflict with the employer's rights and prerogatives at the workplace. On the one hand, freedom to work, non-discrimination, protection of privacy, freedom of religion and of expression are fundamental rights of the person, which must be respected and protected both in general and at the workplace. On the other hand, property rights, freedom of trade and freedom to contract are crucial rights for an entrepreneur to be able to run a business. One of the consequences is that employers have the right to refuse a job applicant; they also have the right to assign work and tasks, to take management decisions which have a bearing on a worker's career and conditions of work, to organize work shifts, to monitor and supervise employees' work, to take care of the enterprise's image, to take measures to avoid misdemeanours and to impose disciplinary penalties, including dismissal. The question is whether such a power can be limited so that it does not undermine the employee's fundamental rights and, if it can, on what grounds and to what extent.

---

20 Paul Benjamin, 'Beyond 'lean' social democracy: Labour law and the challenge of social protection', in *Transformation: Critical Perspectives from Southern Africa* (2006), Vol. 60, p. 47.

In short, can an employer, before employing an individual, investigate a job applicant's private life, state of health or political or social opinions? Can an employer disregard a job application on the grounds of the applicant's sex or sexual orientation, family status, colour, national origin or religious belief? During employment, can an employer take decisions relating to the worker's job assignments and career, or dismiss a worker on the basis of factors belonging to the sphere of his or her private life? What kind of data can an employer request from a job applicant, or gather, process and store in respect of an employee before, during and after employment? Can an employer impose a given dress code or certain other obligations relating to the employee's physical appearance? Also, what kind of control can an employer exercise over the employee at the workplace? Can a worker be monitored by electronic devices at or outside the workplace? Can the employer intercept the workers' telephone communications or email? Can the use of the internet by the employee be restricted or monitored? On the other hand, can workers refuse instructions from their employer on the grounds that these affect the employees' beliefs or other fundamental liberties? Can workers use their freedom of speech to criticize their employer publicly? Can a worker, on the grounds that the employer has no rights over his or her private life, behave in such a manner that the enterprise's image may be tarnished?

Throughout the world, every day, employers and employees face these and other problems, many of which eventually come before the courts. The approach of the French law of 1992 – which is being shared by an increasing number of countries – has brought about a great change in the way that it has tried to redistribute the balance between, on the one hand, respect for the rights and liberties of the worker at the workplace, and on the other hand the supervision, control and disciplinary powers of the employer. The rule is now that the fundamental rights of the worker must be respected, and the exception is that the employer can restrict the exercise of those rights only with fair reasons and through appropriate means. Thus, only when the accommodation of the worker's fundamental freedom with the enterprise's needs is likely to impose undue, excessive or costly constraints on the latter, would it be acceptable for the employer's rights to be given priority over those of the employee. This may also imply (though this is not accepted everywhere) that the burden of the proof would fall on the employer, who must demonstrate that the restrictions that are imposed on the worker's fundamental freedoms and liberties are justified and adapted to the circumstances.

Yet, if this criterion seems simple, its application is much less so. It necessarily gives rise to very divergent positions in comparative law, particularly in case law. This is because the judge's subjectivity, let alone overall societal values and feelings, plays a substantial role when the time comes to determine what is to be considered just or suitable. What would be an acceptable exception to the above principle in France would perhaps not be acceptable in Canada, or vice versa. We will discuss these problems in the following sections.

Gender discrimination

Attitudes have changed a great deal since the times when women were not accepted in a number of areas of employment and certain occupations, both in the private and the public sectors. Yet this is still a fairly recent evolution: until the late 1970s it was still generally accepted, for example, that female workers could be prohibited from working night shifts in factories or that air hostesses could be grounded if they got married – something which would be unthinkable nowadays. Likewise, pay gaps between those jobs assumed to be female and those assumed to be male, as well as between male and female staff within the same occupational group, were the rule rather than the exception.

From a chronological viewpoint, the concept that men and women should be paid equally for equal work or work of equal value was addressed by international law before that of equal treatment in employment and occupation. Thus the ILO Equal Remuneration Convention (No. 100) was adopted in 1951 whereas the Discrimination (Employment and Occupation) Convention (No. 111) was adopted in 1958. Similarly, the equal pay rule was already included in the EC Treaty by 1957 (albeit on economic, not on social grounds), while it was not until 1976 that the EC adopted its first Directive on equal treatment for men and women as regards access to employment, vocational training and promotion, and working conditions. This may explain why national and international laws have traditionally dealt with equal pay and equal treatment issues under different rules, though they are in fact two aspects of the same problem; actually pay discrimination is just one aspect of discrimination. However, more recent instruments have started to address both equal pay and equal treatment, taking a more holistic approach. Most noteworthy in this respect is EC Directive 2006/54/EC, which embodies in a single instrument seven Directives adopted between 1975 and 2002, concerning equal treatment and equal pay between men and women.[21] This approach is

---

21 Directive 2006/54/EC of the European Parliament and of the Council of 5 July 2006, on the implementation of the principle of equal opportunities and equal treatment of men and women in matters of employment and occupation (recast), *Official Journal of the European Union*, L 204/23 (July 2006), pp. 23–36.

increasingly being followed in national law. For example, under s. 17 of the Swedish Act on Equality between Women and Men 1991, prohibitions against sex discrimination apply when the employer (1) decides on an employment issue, selects a job seeker for an employment interview or implements other measures during the employment procedure; (2) decides on promotion or selects an employee for training for promotion; (3) applies pay or other terms of employment for work which is regarded as equal or of equal value; (4) manages and distributes work; or (5) gives notice of termination, summarily dismisses, lays off or implements other significant measures against an employee.

Equal pay

Whereas most countries have adopted rules to guarantee equal pay for equal work, some of them have had difficulties in actually implementing equal pay rules and policies with respect to different work or jobs, even though they are of equal value. Other problems may arise in connection with the definition of 'pay', which may be more or less broad or narrow. A third type of problem can arise when acknowledged different pay rates are justified on given legal grounds; for instance, it might be argued that different pay is justified on objective reasons not related to the sex of the workers involved.

The most effective way to tackle the first problem consists in the development of job evaluation methods (box 5.2). Thus under Article 3 of Convention No. 100 it is provided that, where appropriate, 'measures shall be taken to promote objective appraisal of jobs on the basis of the work to be performed'. It further clarifies that 'differential rates between workers which correspond, without regard to sex, to differences, as determined by such objective appraisal, in the work to be performed shall not be considered as being contrary to the principle of equal remuneration for men and women workers for work of equal value'. The EC Equal Treatment and Opportunities Directive (2006) is still more explicit, for it provides that 'where a job classification system is used for determining pay, it shall be based on the same criteria for both men and women and so drawn up as to exclude any discrimination on grounds of sex'.

Box 5.2   Job evaluation methods free from gender bias: an effective tool to achieve pay equity[22]

Achieving pay equity requires comparing and establishing the relative value of two jobs that differ in content, by breaking jobs down into components or 'factors' and 'sub-factors' and assigning points to them. According to analytical job evaluation methods, such factors generally include skills/qualifications, responsibility, effort and working conditions.

Two jobs that are found to have the same numerical value are entitled to equal remuneration. Job evaluation is concerned with the content of the job and not with the characteristics or the performance of the persons doing the job.

To assess 'male' and 'female' jobs fairly, job evaluation must be free from gender bias, otherwise key requirements of women's jobs are either disregarded or scored lower than those of male jobs, thus reinforcing the undervaluation of women's jobs. The process whereby job evaluation methods are developed and applied is at least as important as these methods and their technical content. Possible and unintentional gender biases and prejudices may arise at any stage in its design and application.

Case law of the European Court of Justice (ECJ) has extensively developed this rule. Thus it is established ECJ doctrine that 'in order to determine whether employees perform the same work or work to which equal value can be attributed, it is necessary to ascertain whether, taking account of a number of factors such as the nature of the work, the training requirements and the working conditions, those persons can be considered to be in a comparable situation'.[23] For example, 'where an undertaking applies a system of pay with a mechanism for applying individual supplements to the basic salary, which is wholly lacking in transparency, it is for the employer to prove that his practice in the matter of wages is not discriminatory if a female worker establishes, in relation to a relatively large number of employees, that the average pay for women is less than that for men'. The Court has added that:

> under such a system, female employees are unable to compare the different components of their salary with those of the pay of their male colleagues

---

22 ILO, *Equality at work: Tackling the challenges: Global report under the follow-up to the ILO Declaration on Fundamental Principles and Rights at Work*, Report of the Director-General, International Labour Conference, 96th Session (Geneva, 2007), paras 283–5.

23 See Case C–309/97 *Angestelltenbetriebsrat der Wiener Gebietskrankenkasse* [1999] ECR I–2865, para. 17.

belonging to the same salary group and can establish differences only in average pay, so that in practice they would be deprived of any possibility of effectively examining whether the principle of equal pay was being complied with if the employer did not have to indicate how he applied the criteria concerning supplements.[24]

A further controversial issue relates to the definition of 'pay', as very often the workers' pay sheet is made up of different elements that top up basic pay. A practical and indeed quite frequent problem arises when either through regulation or by collective agreements the workers' take-home pay is increased by special allowances which are left out of the definition of salary or wage. The purpose in these cases is to avoid these bonuses being taken into consideration for the calculation of social security contributions or severance pay. From this viewpoint, a provision which states that a particular allowance is not included within the definition of 'pay' would not seem to be gender biased. However, it should be borne in mind that under Convention No. 100 the term 'remuneration' includes 'the ordinary, basic or minimum wage or salary and any additional emoluments whatsoever payable directly or indirectly, whether in cash or in kind, by the employer to the worker and arising out of the worker's employment'. The ILO Committee of Experts has further clarified that the term 'any additional emoluments whatsoever' brings within the ambit of the Convention elements as numerous as they are diverse. They include, for example, wage differentials or increments based on seniority or marital status, cost-of-living allowances, housing or residential allowances, and family allowances, paid by the employer, and benefits in kind such as the allotment and laundering of working clothes.[25] Similarly, entitlements under occupational or company-based pensions would also fall within the definition of *pay* as they are to be paid by reason of the employment relationship between the employee and his or her former employer.[26] The risk is that in these cases the criteria used to grant these allowances could be gender-biased – albeit in an indirect form – for example, when such allowances are granted only to workers who perform full-time work and it has been established that women workers are over-represented in the part-time workers' group.

---

24 Case 109/88 *Danfoss* [1989] ECR I–3199, para. 16.

25 ILO, *Equal remuneration, General Survey of the CEACR on the Equal Pay Convention, 1951 (No. 100) and Recommendation, 1951 (No. 90)*, Report III (Part 6B) International Labour Conference, 72nd Session, Geneva, 1986, paras 16 and 17.

26 Case C–147/95 *Dimosia Epicheirisi Ilektrismou (DEI)* v. *Evthimios Evrenopoulos*, judgment of the Court (Sixth Chamber) of 17 April 1997, [1997] ECR I–2057.

A number of landmark judgments by the European Court of Justice have clearly reacted against such rules or practices, which, though apparently objective, had actually put women workers at a disadvantage. For instance, the ECJ has taken the view that Article 141 of the EC Treaty (ex Article 119):

> must be interpreted as meaning that exclusion by a collective agreement from entitlement to a special annual bonus provided for by that collective agreement of persons in employment which involves a normal working week of less than 15 hours and normal pay not exceeding a fraction of the monthly baseline and is, on that basis, exempt from compulsory social insurance constitutes indirect discrimination based on sex, where that exclusion applies independently of the sex of the worker but actually affects a considerably higher percentage of women than men.[27]

More specifically it has held that, with respect to part-time workers, 'the members of the class of persons placed at a disadvantage, be they men or women, are entitled to have the same scheme applied to them as that applied to the other workers, on a basis proportional to their working hours'. Thus:

> Article 119 of the EEC Treaty [now Article 141 EC] is to be interpreted as precluding the application of a clause in a collective wage agreement applying to the national public service under which employers may exclude part-time employees from the payment of a severance grant on termination of their employment when in fact a considerably lower percentage of men than of women work part time, unless the employer shows that the exclusion is based on objectively justified factors unrelated to any discrimination on grounds of sex.[28]

The ECJ has also examined the bearing of the equal pay principle on the operation of occupational pension schemes, which provide for different retirement ages for men and women. In *Barber* v. *Guardian Royal Exchange Assurance Group*, the Court took the view that:

> unlike the benefits awarded by national statutory social security schemes, retirement pensions paid under private occupational schemes, which are characterized by the fact of being established either by an agreement between workers and employers or by a unilateral decision taken by the employer – whether financed by the employer alone or by both the

---

27 Case C–281/97 *Andrea Krüger* v. *Kreiskrankenhaus Ebersberg*, judgment of the Court (Sixth Chamber) of 9 September 1999.
28 Case C–33/89 *Maria Kowalska* v. *Freie und Hansestadt Hamburg*, judgment of the Court (Sixth Chamber) of 27 June 1990.

employer and the workers – which may by law with the employee's agreement operate in part as a substitute for the statutory scheme and which apply only to workers employed by certain undertakings, constitute consideration paid by the employer to the worker in respect of his employment and consequently fall within the scope of Article 119 of the Treaty (they are to be treated in the same way as remuneration). Accordingly, it is contrary to that provision to impose an age condition which differs according to sex for the purposes of entitlement to a pension under a private occupational scheme which operates in part as a substitute for the statutory scheme, even if the difference between the pensionable age for men and that for women is based on the one provided for by the national statutory scheme.[29]

In the case in question, Mr Barber was a participant in a private pension fund under which the normal pensionable age was fixed for the category of employees to which Mr Barber belonged at 62 years for men and at 57 years for women.

A similar approach was taken with respect to survivors' pensions. Thus in the case *DEI* v. *Efthimios Evrenopoulos* the Court held that:

a survivor's pension provided for by an occupational pension scheme is an advantage deriving from the survivor's spouse's membership of the scheme and accordingly falls within the scope of Article 119 EC. It follows that Article 119 EC [...] precludes the application of a provision of national law which makes the award of such a pension to a widower subject to special conditions which are not applied to widows, and there is no rule of Community law which could justify the maintenance in force of such a provision. [Thus] Article 119 of the Treaty requires that widowers discriminated against in breach of that provision be awarded a pension or other survivor's benefit under the same conditions as widows.[30]

In that case, the relevant regulation provided for a survivor's benefit to the widow of an insured person or a pensioner without restrictions, while the same benefit was granted to the widower only if he was without means and totally unfit for work and was maintained by the deceased throughout the five years preceding her death. The same reasoning has prevailed with respect to early retirement, when it is granted to female beneficiaries and denied to male applicants who nevertheless meet the same requirements.[31]

---

29 Case C–262/88 *Douglas Harvey Barber* v. *Guardian Royal Exchange Assurance Group*, judgment of the Court of 17 May 1990, [1990] ECR I–01889.

30 Case C–147/95 *DEI* v. *Evthimios Evrenopoulos*, judgment of the Court (Sixth Chamber) of 17 April 1997.

31 Case C–206/00 *Henri Mouflin* v. *Recteur de l'académie de Reims*, judgment of the Court (Second Chamber) of 13 December 2001.

Exceptions to the equal pay rule

Of course, the above does not mean that differences in pay between men and women are always deemed to be discriminatory. Both international and national law provide for a number of exceptions that permit deviations from this rule. It is accepted, for example, that the rule cannot be applied when two workers performing work of equal value are employed by two different employers, because the difference in pay cannot be attributed to a single source.[32] Certain conditions of the market, for example when an occupational group made up of a majority of men is more in demand than another occupational group made up of a majority of women, so that potential employers need to offer higher pay in order to attract potential workers with the required skills, may also explain, though not necessarily justify, different pay rates even if the work done by both groups is technically speaking of equal value.[33]

Equal treatment of men and women

A number of issues seem to have particularly attracted the attention of both legislation and case law within this topic, especially the admission of women or (much more rarely) of men to certain jobs, refusing to hire on the grounds of pregnancy, prohibition of night work by women, and the limits of affirmative action.

Access to certain jobs

The most obvious form of gender discrimination is to refuse employment to a female or (less frequently) to a male applicant on the sole grounds of her or his sex. In principle this is forbidden under both international and national

---

32 See the judgment of the ECJ in Case C–320/00 *A. G. Lawrence and Others* v. *Regent Office Care Ltd*, 17 September 2002.

33 See, with respect to this point, the reasoning followed by the ECJ in Case C-127/92 *Enderby* v. *Frenchay Health Authority and Secretary of State for Health*, judgment of the Court of 27 October 1993. The claimant, Ms Enderby, was employed as a speech therapist by the FHA (overwhelmingly a female profession). She considered that she was a victim of sex discrimination due to the fact that, at her level of seniority within the National Health Service, members of her profession were appreciably less well paid than principal pharmacists, a comparable profession in which, at an equivalent professional level, there are more men than women. The defendant alleged that part of the difference in pay was attributable to a shortage of candidates for one job, namely pharmacists, and to the need to attract them by higher salaries as, unlike speech therapists, who work almost exclusively in the public sector, pharmacists are also demanded by the private sector, which can offer them higher pay.

law, which nevertheless provide for a number of exceptions. Thus ILO Convention No. 111 specifies that: 'Any distinction, exclusion or preference in respect of a particular job based on the inherent requirements thereof shall not be deemed to be discrimination.' In the same way, under the EU Equal Opportunities and Treatment Directive (2006) Member States may provide:

> as regards access to employment including the training leading thereto, that a difference of treatment which is based on a characteristic related to sex shall not constitute discrimination where, by reason of the nature of the particular occupational activities concerned or of the context in which they are carried out, such a characteristic constitutes a genuine and determining occupational requirement, provided that its objective is legitimate and the requirement is proportionate.

This exception is indeed very narrow and subject to a relatively strong version of the principle of proportionality. A Member State wishing to use it must show that, for the occupation concerned, sex is a 'determining factor'; that is, a non-discriminatory policy in the occupation concerned would make it very difficult or impossible to carry out the activities required by that occupation. For instance, the sex of a person may be a determining factor with respect to certain employment activities in the arts, for example in dramatic perform-ances, or modelling for painters or sculptors, where the role to be fulfilled is one which could not be carried out authentically if undertaken by a person of the other sex. Decency and privacy may also justify certain posts being reserved for women or for men, depending upon the context in which the work is to be performed. For example, the ECJ has accepted the grounds of privacy as justification for sex segregation in various posts in the French prison service, such as warders whose job description includes the undertak-ing of physical searches of inmates.[34] A number of national laws also provide for exceptions on that basis.[35]

---

34 Case 318/86 *Commission* v. *France (Sex Discrimination in the Civil Service)* [1988] ECR 3559.
35 For example, under the United Kingdom's Sex Discrimination Act 1975, s. 7(2)(d), it is not discrimination if:

> The nature of the establishment, or of the part of it within which the work is done, requires the job to be held by a man because –
>   (i) it is, or is part of, a hospital, prison or other establishment for persons requiring special care, supervision or attention, and
>   (ii) those persons are all men (disregarding any woman whose presence is excep-tional), and
>   (iii) it is reasonable, having regard to the essential character of the establishment or that part, that the job should not be held by a woman.

In exceptional cases, cultural necessity may also justify employment of a person of a particular sex, in particular the employment of a man to work in a country in which it would be difficult, for religious and/or cultural reasons, for a woman to carry out the work, because women are excluded from the public sphere, or from business activity in that community.[36] In these circumstances, the sex of a person may constitute a genuine and determining occupational requirement, thus justifying an exception to the equal treatment principle.

By contrast, on many occasions the exclusion of female (or male) candidates from a given profession or position does no more than reflect stereotypical (and dated) attitudes to professions which are considered purely 'male' or 'female' domains. The most conspicuous example concerns jobs in military posts in the army or in the security forces, which until very recently were purely 'male' professions, and therefore closed to women. It was only in 2000 that a judgment of the ECJ held that an overall exclusion of women from military posts in the Bundeswehr was in breach of the equal treatment principle,[37] though in a different case the ECJ also admitted that some exceptions could meet the proportionality test.[38] The ECJ also considered discriminatory an Austrian regulation which established the absolute prohibition of employment of women in diving work. The Austrian government had tried to justify this prohibition on the grounds that, on average, women have less lung capacity and a lower blood cell count than men, which made them unsuitable for diving work. The ECJ dismissed this allegation, however, judging that it was too general, and reflected a stereotypical assumption. While it may be true that *on average* women have less respiratory capacity and a lower blood cell count than men, it should be borne in mind that an employer recruits a person, not just a statistical average (box 5.3).

---

36 This could be where the job involves work in a country whose laws or customs are such that the job can only be done, or can only be done effectively, by a man (or by a woman); for example, a job might involve driving a car in a country where women are forbidden to drive.

37 Case C–285/98 *Tanja Kreil* v. *Bundesrepublik Deutschland*, judgment of the Court of 11 January 2000.

38 Case C–273/97 *Angela Maria Sirdar* v. *The Army Board and Secretary of State for Defence*, judgment of the Court of 26 October 1999. The case concerned the selection of candidates for units of the Royal Marines.

> ### Box 5.3 An absolute prohibition on the employment of women in diving work infringes the equal treatment rule[39]
>
> The range of diving work is wide and includes, for instance, activity in the fields of biology, archaeology, tourism and police work.
>
> The absolute prohibition laid down in Article 31 of the regulation of 1973 excludes women even from work that does not involve significant physical stress and thus clearly goes beyond what is necessary to ensure that women are protected.
>
> In so far as the Austrian government claims that women have lesser respiratory capacity and a lower red blood cell count in order to justify such exclusion, it relies on an argument based on measured average values for women to compare them with those for men. However, as that government itself acknowledged during the pre-litigation procedure, as regards those variables there are significant areas of overlap of individual values for women and individual values for men.
>
> In those circumstances legislation that precludes any individual assessment and prohibits women from entering the employment in question, when that employment is not forbidden to men whose vital capacity and red blood cell count are equal to or lower than the average values of those variables measured for women, is not authorized by virtue of Article 2(3) of Directive 76/207 and constitutes discrimination on grounds of sex.

Though less frequently, men can also be discriminated against in access to certain jobs. This can be very obvious when job advertisements specify or are worded in such a manner that it is suggested that only female candidates will be considered, for example in respect to posts for secretaries, nurses, shop attendants, flight attendants or cashiers in supermarkets. Equal treatment and opportunities laws in most countries in the world specify that, as a rule, job advertisements must use gender-neutral wording; however it would seem that this legal requirement is often disregarded.

Further, laws or regulations may provide for qualifications for certain jobs which are more stringent for men than they are for women; for example, French law relating to public service fixed an age limit requirement for access to public employment, which did not apply to widows who had not remarried. Yet the same exemption did not benefit widowers who were in the same situation. Though the exemption from age limit was intended to facilitate the

---

39 Case C–203/03 *Commission of the European Communities* v. *Republic of Austria,* judgment of the Court (Grand Chamber) of 1 February 2005.

return of women to the labour market, the ECJ took the view that there was unequal treatment to the prejudice of men, which was contrary to EC law.[40]

On the other hand, an apparently neutral requirement for a job may be more difficult to meet for women that it is for men, resulting in indirect discrimination unless it could be demonstrated that the requirement was a genuine condition for the job. This did not seem to have been the case in the minimum height requirement of 170cm, which was required to apply to police academies in Greece. The ILO Committee of Experts considered that such a requirement was 'likely to be more difficult for women to comply with than men, and thus may amount to indirect discrimination on the grounds of sex, except if they could be justified under Article 1, paragraph 2, of the Convention which allows for certain distinctions, exclusions or preferences in respect of a particular job within the police force based on the inherent requirements thereof'.[41]

Pregnancy

Discrimination on account of pregnancy appears to be on the increase, even in countries that have long combated it and are facing plummeting fertility rates. In the United Kingdom, for example, a recent report by the Equal Opportunities Commission states that 30,000 women each year lose their jobs because of their pregnancy, and only 3 per cent of those who experience a problem lodge a claim at an employment tribunal. Discrimination also occurs when enterprises recruiting female workers require them to work for a certain period in the enterprise before becoming entitled to maternity benefits.[42] It is almost unnecessary to state that a refusal to hire or dismissal on the grounds of pregnancy, maternity leave or breastfeeding is tantamount to sex discrimination as only women can be pregnant, give birth or breastfeed.

It could, however, be said that a refusal to hire on the grounds of pregnancy could be admissible when a female worker applies for a position if the tasks she would have to undertake would be detrimental to her or her baby's health during pregnancy or while she is breastfeeding. National laws ought to prohibit female workers from being employed in such jobs during pregnancy or after childbirth while they are breastfeeding (for example, night work or work which is hazardous for their health or that of their babies). However,

---

40 Case C–319/03 *Serge Briheche* v. *Ministre de l'Intérieur, Ministre de l'Éducation nationale et Ministre de la Justice*, judgment of the Court (Second Chamber) of 30 September 2004.

41 See the individual observation concerning the Discrimination (Employment and Occupation) Convention, 1958 (No. 111) addressed to Greece in 2007 (available online at the ILOLEX database).

42 ILO, *Equality at work: Tackling the challenges*, op. cit., para. 28.

pregnancy is not a permanent condition. Thus it would be discriminatory for women workers to be refused a permanent job on such grounds. According to a ruling by the European Court of Justice, the right approach in this case would be that, during pregnancy, the employer temporarily adjusts the working conditions or hours or, if that is not possible, moves the worker to another job, or, as a last resort, grants the worker leave.[43]

It can be argued that a female worker who has been recently hired would not be able to take up the obligations arising out of her contract of employment if she is pregnant or breastfeeding. To take this reasoning further, pregnancy might be considered as a situation comparable to that of a man similarly incapable of performing work for medical or other reasons. However, it is an established doctrine in case law that the situation of a woman who finds herself incapable – by reason of pregnancy discovered very soon after signing her employment contract – of performing the task for which she was recruited *cannot* be compared with that of a man similarly incapable for medical or other reasons, since pregnancy is not in any way comparable with a pathological condition, and even less so with unavailability for work on non-medical grounds. Secondly, dismissal of a pregnant woman recruited for an indefinite period cannot be justified on grounds relating to her inability to fulfill a fundamental condition of her employment contract, even where the availability of the employee is necessarily, for the employer, a precondition for the proper performance of the employment contract.[44] It would also *not* be admissible to dismiss a female worker at any time during her pregnancy for absences caused by illness resulting from that pregnancy,[45] or to refuse to renew her fixed-term contract of employment when she had failed to inform the employer that she was pregnant, even though she was aware of this when the contract of employment was concluded, and because of her pregnancy she was unable to work during a substantial part of the term of that contract. Also, since the employer may not take the employee's pregnancy into consideration for the purpose of applying her working conditions, the employee is not obliged to inform the employer that she is pregnant.[46] It is for similar reasons that pre-employment pregnancy tests should be banned.

---

43 See Case C–177/88 *Dekker* v. *Stichting Vormingscentrum voor Jong Volwassenen (VJV-Centrum) Plus*, judgment of the ECJ of 8 November 1990.

44 See judgment of the ECJ in Case C–32/93 *Carole Louise Webb* v. *EMO Air Cargo (UK) Ltd*, judgment of the Court (Fifth Chamber) of 14 July 1994.

45 See judgment of the ECJ in Case C–394/96 *Mary Brown* v. *Rentokil Ltd*, judgment of the Court of 30 June 1998.

46 See judgment of the ECJ in Case C–109/00 *Tele Danmark A/S* v. *Handels-og Kontorfunktionærernes Forbund i Danmark (HK)*, judgment of the Court (Fifth Chamber) of 4 October 2001.

Night work, underground work and other jobs prohibited for women

The advent of night-time working in factories in the nineteenth century disrupted long-established social patterns predicated on working days and a weekly day of rest. Those concerned with improving the miserable circumstances of factory workers were struck by the particularly harsh impact of night work on women and children and thus made the adoption of measures to protect women and children from the harmful effects of night work a priority. Night work for women was first prohibited in England in 1844. More than 30 years later, England's approach was followed by Switzerland in 1877, New Zealand in 1881, Austria in 1885, the Netherlands in 1889 and France in 1892. At a time when women were viewed as physically weaker than men, as more susceptible to exploitation, and primarily as mothers and housekeepers, the legislators' articulated motivation in enacting this prohibition was concern for women's safety, moral integrity and health and for family welfare. For these reasons, legislators of that period viewed adult women and children as belonging to a special class of factory workers needing special protection, who were not in fact considered competent to make their own valid choices.[47] In 1906, well before the creation of the ILO, the first ever international labour Convention was adopted at a conference in Berne, and its purpose was precisely to ban night work by women.[48] When the ILO held its first Conference in Washington, DC, in 1919, it adopted six Conventions, one of which, Convention No. 4, provided for a general ban on night work by women in industry. This Convention was revised in 1934 by Convention No. 41 and again in 1948 by Convention No. 89. None of these revisions, however, provided for a lift of the general ban on night work by women, though they provided for some flexibility which was not allowed under the original Convention.

The fact is that what in the early twentieth century was generally considered as substantial social progress would seem nowadays to be sex discrimination, as a prohibition on night work by women obviously implies that they cannot be considered for a number of positions and jobs which may require tasks to be performed at night, thus impairing their access to employment.

---

47 ILO, *Night work of women in industry: General Survey of the Committee of Experts on the Application of Conventions and Recommendations on Conventions Nos 4, 41, 89 (and its protocol No. 98)*, Report III (Part 4B), International Labour Conference, 89th Session, Geneva, 2001, para. 3.

48 The International Convention of 26 September 1906, Respecting the Prohibition of Night Work for Women in Industrial Employment, entered into force in 1912. It was ratified by Austria, Belgium, France, Germany, Great Britain, Italy, Netherlands, Portugal, Spain, Sweden and Switzerland.

This perception is shared today by a great majority of countries in the world, though not by all of them. It remains the case that while both Conventions Nos 4 and 41 have been declared outdated by the ILO Governing Body and have been shelved, some countries have not formally denounced them, so they are legally bound to maintain a ban on night work by women in industry.

With regard to Convention No. 89, the situation is still more ambiguous. Out of a total number of 46 ratifications, Convention No. 89 has already been denounced by 21 countries, most of them from the European Union but also by some non-EU members, such as the Dominican Republic, Sri Lanka, Switzerland, Uruguay and Zambia. While in 1990 the ILO adopted the Night Work Convention (No. 171), which applies to night work of both men and women, it did not revise Convention No. 89, which remains open for new ratifications. However, Convention No. 171 has so far received only 11 ratifications. In addition to this Convention, the 1990 Conference adopted a Protocol that permits ratifying states to enlarge the scope of exceptions to night work by women under Convention No. 89; yet very few countries have so far used this and have preferred to denounce Convention No. 89 altogether.[49] In short, the overall approach to the prohibition of night work by women would seem to be outdated now, even though it is still in force in a number of countries.

Box 5.4 The prohibition of night work by women vis-à-vis EC law[50]

Alfred Stoeckel was a director of a French company which in 1988 fell into economic difficulties brought about by foreign competition, and needed to reorganize production. The enterprise considered laying off about 200 people at one of its plants. However, having calculated that the number and the effects of the redundancies could be limited if a continuous shift-work system were adopted, involving night work for the entire workforce, it undertook negotiations with the unions. These led to an agreement whereby night-work jobs were offered to all the staff. In view of the fact that the female workers in the company had the necessary skills for the posts that had been retained, the parties, wishing to ensure that women were given the same opportunities as men, agreed to make all posts available to

---

49 Only four countries have so far ratified the Protocol, of which two countries later denounced Convention No. 89 altogether.

50 Summary of the ECJ ruling in Case C–345/89 *Alfred Stoeckel*, judgment of the Court of 25 July 1991, [1991] ECR I–4047.

both men and women, subject to approval by a majority vote of the female workers. A majority voted in favour of the shift-work system and it was introduced with effect from 1 October 1988.

France had at the time ratified the ILO Night Work (Women) Convention (Revised), 1948 (No. 89), which prohibited night work by women in industry. French law therefore prohibited night work by women in industry, and a breach of this law was an offence. Alfred Stoeckel was thus prosecuted before the Tribunal de Police.

Stoeckel contended that the relevant French provision (Article L 213 of the Labour Code) was contrary to Article 5 of EC Directive 76/207 on the implementation of the principle of equal treatment for men and women as regards access to employment, vocational training and promotion, and working conditions, and to the judgment in Case 312/86 *Commission* v. *France* in which the ECJ held that, by failing to take all the necessary measures to eliminate inequalities prohibited by the Directive, the French Republic had failed to fulfil its obligations. In those circumstances, the French jurisdiction stayed the proceedings and referred the case to the European Court of Justice for a preliminary ruling on that question.

During the proceeding before the ECJ, the French and Italian governments submitted that the prohibition of night work by women, which in any case was subject to numerous exceptions, was in conformity with the general aims of protecting female workers and with particular considerations of a social nature relating, for example, to the risks of attack and the heavier domestic workload borne by women.

The ECJ recalled that the purpose of the Directive is to implement in the Member States the principle of equal treatment for men and women with regard, inter alia, to access to employment and working conditions. To that end, 'the Directive requires the abolition or the revision of national provisions that are contrary to that principle where the concern for protection which originally inspired them is no longer well founded'. It further considered that as far as the aims of protecting female workers are concerned, exceptions are valid only if, having regard to the equal treatment principle:

> [T]here is a justified need for a difference of treatment as between men and women. However, whatever the disadvantages of night work may be, it does not seem that, except in the case of pregnancy or maternity, the risks to which women are exposed when working at night are, in general, inherently different from those to which men are exposed. As regards the risks of attack, if it is assumed that they are greater at night than during the day, appropriate measures can be adopted to deal with them without undermining the fundamental principle of equal treatment for men and women. [...] Thus, the concern to provide protection, by which the general prohibition of

> nightwork by women was originally inspired, no longer appears to be well founded and the maintenance of that prohibition, by reason of risks that are not peculiar to women or preoccupations unconnected with the purpose of Directive 76/207, cannot be justified by the provisions of Article 2(3) of the Directive which are referred to in paragraph 3 of this judgment. [... It follows that] Article 5 of Directive 76/207/EEC is sufficiently precise to impose on the Member States the obligation not to lay down by legislation the principle that nightwork by women is prohibited, even if that obligation is subject to exceptions, where nightwork by men is not prohibited.

The same reasoning would apply to the prohibition of underground work, which is, however, provided for under the Underground Work (Women) Convention, 1935 (No. 45). This Convention has been ratified by 70 countries, of which 28 countries have already denounced it, many of which are EU Member States; in the light of a ruling by the European Court of Justice in 2005,[51] it is very likely that the rest of the EU Member States will follow suit. Similarly, certain labour codes, which still include protectionist-discriminatory provisions to the effect that women are treated in the same way as minors,[52] would need to be revisited and revised if necessary.

---

51 Case C–203/03 *Commission of the European Communities* v. *Republic of Austria*, cited above.
52 For example, under Article 248 of the Labour Code of Moldova:

> (1) Women's work is forbidden on heavy work and work in harmful working conditions, and also on underground work, with the exception of work on sanitary services and the work which does not demand physical effort.
> (2) It is forbidden for women to lift and carry weights, exceeding the limit rates established for them.
> (3) The list of heavy work, work in harmful conditions, on which women's work is forbidden, and also the limit rates of loading at lifting and carrying weights are approved by the Government after consultations with employers and trade unions.

> Analogous provisions existed in all of the Soviet-era Labour Codes and were maintained in some codes adopted immediately after the end of communist regime (for example, s. 75(1) of the Labour Code of Hungary, 1992, provided that women and minors must not be hired for jobs which may have detrimental consequences on their physical constitution or development. A similar provision existed in Article 168 of the Labour Code of Latvia. However, in most cases these provisions have now been removed.

Racial discrimination

The classic example of racial discrimination in recent history was the South African apartheid regime. On the basis of a racial classification system introduced by the Population Registration Act of 1950, which was the cornerstone of the policy of apartheid, a number of Acts organized the world of work in a discriminatory fashion. The abolition of the race laws and the political transformations accompanying the transition towards democracy have enabled South Africa to take its place in the international community and in the ILO in particular. Nowadays most, if not all, countries in the world have clearly put a ban on all forms of racial discrimination, including in employment and occupation. For example, the United States prohibited discrimination on the grounds of race in 1964 by means of the US Civil Rights Act, whose Title VII prohibits discrimination in employment 'based on race, color, religion, sex or national origin';[53] race discrimination is similarly addressed in the United Kingdom's Race Relations Act of 1976 (amended in 2000), as well as in many other countries. More recent developments have specifically targeted discriminatory practices in employment and occupation against the Roma people in several Central European countries and indigenous peoples in a number of Latin American countries. With respect to the latter, one should not fail to highlight the decisive breakthrough made by the ILO in 1989 through the adoption of the Indigenous and Tribal Peoples Convention, No. 169, which clearly banned discrimination against indigenous peoples while at the same time calling on the government to develop 'coordinated and systematic action' to protect the rights of these peoples and to guarantee respect for their cultural integrity. A further and no less worthwhile development in this area relates to regulations in respect of incitement to racial hatred.[54] Racial discrimination is also outlawed under a number of international instruments and covenants, which are amongst the most widely ratified instruments, such as the UN International Convention on the Elimination of All Forms of Racial Discrimination (ICERD), 1969[55] and the Discrimination (Employment and Occupation) Convention, 1958 (No. 111).[56] It is also addressed in EC law in

---

53 See a description of this law and its operation: U.S. Equal Employment Opportunity Commission: *Federal Equal Employment Opportunity (EEO) Laws*, available at: http://www.eeoc.gov.

54 ILO, *Equality in employment and occupation, General Survey by the Committee of Experts on the Application of Conventions and Recommendations*, Report III (Part 4B), International Labour Conference, 83rd Session, Geneva, 1996, para. 161.

55 There are 173 states who are parties to this Convention (data updated to 2 June 2008).

56 There have been 168 ratifications as of 21 November 2008.

EC Council Directive 2000/43/EC of 29 June 2000 implementing the principle of equal treatment between persons irrespective of racial or ethnic origin.

Yet this does not mean that anti-discrimination laws have done away with racism, which still persists in many behavioural patterns. While a first step has already been taken in the form of the adoption of laws and other regulations to ban race discrimination, the challenge consists nowadays in adopting and enforcing legislation with a view to actually eradicating racist forms of behaviour at the workplace. Thus, an employer would not only be prohibited from discriminating against a worker or a job applicant on the grounds of the latter's race, ethnic origin or colour of skin but would also be made liable for not taking the appropriate steps to avoid a worker being harassed or discriminated against by his or her fellow co-workers at the workplace on the aforesaid grounds.

Canadian rulings,[57] for example, have now established that the discriminatory psychological and emotional environments endured by vulnerable workers are just as much a term and condition of employment as the pay. As a result, racial slurs or jokes, demeaning comments, threats, racist graffiti, or physical assaults can constitute a form of racial harassment which contravenes anti-discrimination laws.[58] Managers who know or ought to know of the discrimination and do not stop it are also engaging in discriminatory conduct.[59] In an important Canadian systemic racism case, the following actions by management were found to have contributed to a 'poisoned work environment': (1) sporadic, inadequate and often grudging efforts to address the problem; (2) not seriously investigating racism allegations and failing to take measures to avoid their recurrence; (3) using inappropriate dispute resolution processes to address the concerns; (4) viewing the complainant's requests for action with suspicion, and either ignoring, mishandling or failing to take timely and unbiased investigation and resolution measures; (5) bullying the complainant and targeting him or her for reprisals and different treatment; and (6) doing nothing about racist graffiti, Nazi symbols, and inappropriate rumours about the complainant.[60]

---

57 Mary Cornish, *Securing sustainable human rights justice for workers*, op. cit. Canadian case law reported here is taken from Mary Cornish's paper.

58 *Dhillon* v. *F. W. Woolworth Co.* (1982), 3 C.H.R.R. D/743 (Ont. Bd. Inquiry); *Lee* v. *T. J. Applebee's Food Conglomeration* (1987), 9 C.H.R.R. D/4781 (Ont. Bd. Inquiry).

59 *Ghosh* v. *Domglas Inc. (No. 2)* (1992), 17 C.H.R.R. D/216 at D/227, para. 76.

60 See *McKinnon* v. *Ontario (Ministry of Correctional Services) (No. 3)* (1998), 32 C.H.R.R. D/1; *McKinnon* v. *Ontario (Ministry of Correctional Services) (No. 4)* (1999), 35 C.H.R.R. D/191; *Ministry of Correctional Services* v. *Ontario (Human Rights Comm.)* (2001), 39 C.H.R.R. D/308; *McKinnon* v. H.R.R. D/61; *Her Majesty the Queen in Right of Ontario, et al.* v. *Michael McKinnon, et al.* (unreported) 16 December 2003; *Ontario* v. *McKinnon* [2004] OJ No. 893;

Canadian tribunals have ordered a wide range of systemic remedies including:

- developing and implementing a comprehensive workplace harassment and discrimination policy, which includes a definition of harassing behaviour and an internal complaints process;[61]
- reviewing internal workplace standards or restrictions that adversely impact certain groups and bringing them into human rights compliance;[62]
- implementing 'special programmes' or plans to remedy past discrimination as well to prevent future discrimination;[63]
- changing hiring and/or recruitment practices in order to achieve proportional representation in the organization;[64]
- creating a workplace race relations committee (which may include external members) to set objectives and measures to improve workplace race relations;[65]
- establishing an internal review committee to monitor the implementation of human rights orders or plans, including periodic reports to senior management;[66]

and *McKinnon* v. *Ontario (Ministry of Correctional Services)* [2007] O.H.R.T.D. No. 5; *McKinnon and Ontario Human Rights Commission* v. *Ontario (Ministry of Correctional Services) et al.* [2002] O.H.R.B.I.D. No. 22.

61 *Curling* v. *Torimiro* (2000), 38 C.H.R.R. D/216, 4 C.C.E.L. (3d) 202 (Ont. Bd. Inq.); *Drummond* v. *Tempo Paint* (1999), 33 C.H.R.R. D/184 (Ont. Bd. of Inquiry) at D/190; *Moffatt* v. *Kinark Child and Family Services* (1999), 33 C.H.R.R. D/184 (Ont. Bd. of Inquiry) at D/360; *Miller* v. *Sam's Pizza House (No. 2)* [1995] N.S.H.R.B.I.D.

62 *Meiorin* v. *Ottawa (City) (No. 2)* (1990), 11 C.H.R.R. D/80 (Ont. Bd. of Inquiry) at D/93; *A* v. *Quality Inn* (1993), 20 C.H.R.R. D/230 (Ont. Bd. of Inquiry), which included revisions to harassment policy to clarify when discipline would result and what the discipline will be when the policy was not adhered to; *Gauthier* v. *Canada (Canadian Armed Forces) (No. 3)* [1989] C.H.R.D. (CHRT); *Gohm* v. *Domtar* (1992), 89 D.L.R. (4th) 305 (Ont. Div. Ct.); *Canada (A.G.)* v. *Green* [2000] F.C.J. No. 778 (F.C.T.D.)

63 *Canadian National Railway Co.* v. *Canada (Human Rights Comm.) and Action travail des femmes* (1987), 8 C.H.R.R. D/4210 (S.C.C.) [Eng./Fr. 24 pp.] S.C.C. Upholds Affirmative Action – Order of a Tribunal which requires that a company hire one woman in every four new hires for unskilled blue-collar jobs; *Canada (A.G.)* v. *Green*, op. cit., at 27; *Pitawanakwat* v. *Canada (Dept. of Secretary of State)* (1994), 21 C.H.R.R. D/355; *Gauthier* v. *Canada (Canadian Armed Forces)*, op. cit.

64 *Action travail des femmes*, op. cit.; *Pitawanakwat* v. *Canada (Department of Secretary of State)*, op. cit.; *National Capital Alliance on Race Relations* v. *Canada (Health and Welfare) (No. 3)* [1997] C.H.R.D. (CHRT).

65 *Dhillon* v. *F.W. Woolworth Ltd*, op. cit.; *Ahluwalia* v. *Metropolitan Toronto (Municipality) Commissioners of Police* (1983) 4 C.H.R.R. D/1757 (Ont. Bd. of Inquiry).

66 *National Capital Alliance on Race Relations* v. *Canada (Health and Welfare)*, op. cit.; and *McKinnon and Ontario Human Rights Commission* v. *Ontario (Ministry of Correctional Services) et al.*, op. cit.

- appointing a person responsible with full powers to ensure implementation orders are carried out;[67]
- requiring managers to attend a training programme to identify and address instances of harassment and inappropriate behaviour;[68]
- training management to mentor a cross-culturally diverse workforce;[69]
- requiring management to circulate to all employees information on available resources, complaint procedures and remedies for those with harassment concerns;[70]
- implementing annual performance assessments of managers which include evaluation of their compliance with human rights measures;[71]
- requiring attendance of all employees at human rights education programmes;[72]
- requiring the employer to state in all staffing notices and job postings and advertisements that the enterprise is an 'Equal Opportunity Employer';[73] and
- implementing individual career plans and training programs for visible minorities.[74]

In the United States, the Civil Rights Act of 1964 empowers the Equal Employment Opportunity Commission to investigate racial discrimination cases at the workplace, and where appropriate to initiate proceedings against employers that have violated the law, either by directly discriminating against a worker or indirectly by failing to take measures to stop a hostile work environment on the grounds of a worker's race or colour of skin. Proceedings can take the form of racial harassment lawsuits, the outcome of which could be the awarding of substantial financial compensation to workers who have been victimized on the grounds of their race or colour of skin (see box 5.5).

---

67 *National Capital Alliance on Race Relations* v. *Canada (Health and Welfare)*, op. cit.
68 *Curling* v. *Torimiro* (2000), 38 C.H.R.R. D/216, 4 C.C.E.L. (3d) 202 (Ont. Bd. Inq.) at p. 17; and *Chiswell* v. *Valdi Foods 1987 Inc.* (1995), 95 CLLC 230-004 (Ont. Bd. of Inq.).
69 *National Capital Alliance on Race Relations* v. *Canada (Health and Welfare)*, op. cit.
70 *Pitawanakwat* v. *Canada (Dept. of Secretary of State)*, op. cit.
71 *National Capital Alliance on Race Relations* v. *Canada (Health and Welfare)*, op. cit.
72 *Canada (A.G.)* v. *Green*, op. cit. at 27; *Pitawanakwat* v. *Canada (Dept. of Secretary of State)*, op. cit.
73 *National Capital Alliance on Race Relations* v. *Canada (Health and Welfare)*, op. cit.
74 *National Capital Alliance on Race Relations* v. *Canada (Health and Welfare)*, op. cit.

Box 5.5   Lockheed Martin to pay $2.5 million to settle racial harassment lawsuit[75]

HONOLULU – The U.S. Equal Employment Opportunity Commission (EEOC) today announced a major settlement of a race discrimination and retaliation lawsuit against Lockheed Martin, the world's largest military contractor, for $2,500,000 and other relief on behalf of an African American electrician who was subjected to a racially hostile work environment at several job sites nationwide – including threats of lynching and the 'N-word'.

The monetary relief for former Lockheed employee Charles Daniels is the largest amount ever obtained by the EEOC for a single person in a race discrimination case, and one of the largest amounts recovered for an individual in any litigation settlement by the agency. Additionally, the Bethesda, Md.-based company agreed to terminate the harassers and make significant policy changes to address any future discrimination, the EEOC said at a press conference in Hawaii.

The EEOC's suit, filed in August 2005, alleged that Daniels was subjected to severe racial harassment while working on military aircrafts as part of a field service team in Jacksonville, Fla., Whidbey Island, Wash., and Oah'u, Hawaii. The EEOC charged that Daniels was the target of persistent verbal abuse by co-workers and a supervisor whose racial slurs and offensive language included calling him the 'N-word' and saying 'we should do to blacks what Hitler did to the Jews' and 'if the South had won then this would be a better country.' Daniels was also subjected to multiple physical threats, such as lynching and other death threats after he reported the harassment. Despite its legal obligations, Lockheed failed to discipline the harassers and instead allowed the discrimination against Daniels to continue unabated – even though the company was aware of the unlawful conduct.

Commenting on the settlement, Daniels said: 'As an armed forces veteran who swore to defend the rights and interest of Americans around the globe, I find it sad that the U.S. government had to sue its largest defense contractor Lockheed Martin – whose slogan is 'We never forget who we're working for' – to protect my rights here at home!'

Daniels added, 'I am pleased that we stood up for justice, because it should help all hard-working Americans of every race and gender to know that we have rights and protections guaranteed under the laws of this nation.'

---

75 U.S. EEOC: 'Lockheed Martin to pay $2.5 million to settle racial harassment lawsuit', Press release, 2 Jan. available at: http://www.eeoc.gov.

> EEOC Regional Attorney William Tamayo said, 'This is a very good resolution because Lockheed Martin agreed to terminate and permanently bar Daniel's harassers from employment. It sends a powerful message that racism cannot and must not be tolerated.'
>
> Raymond Cheung, the EEOC attorney who led the government's litigation effort, added, 'To combat the harassment and threats faced by Mr. Daniels is at the heart of why the EEOC was created. Despite concerns of retaliation, this man had the courage to stand up and make public what happened to him, in an effort to ensure that it would not happen to anyone else. It has been a once-in-a-lifetime honor to work on this case.'
>
> The litigation and consent decree were filed by the EEOC under Title VII of the Civil Rights Act in the U.S. Court for the District of Hawaii (*U.S. Equal Employment Opportunity Commission* v. *Lockheed Martin*, CV-05-00479).

Religious belief

Jurisprudence has advanced a great deal in the matter of discrimination on the grounds of sex, but in many countries there is still hesitancy when cases relating to freedom of conscience and of religion come before the courts. In this respect it would seem that the tribunals of Canada or the United States are more open-minded than those of Europe when litigation relates to freedom of religion. Thus in *EEOC* v. *Townley Engineering and Manufacturing Corporation*, a US court considered that the obligation imposed on an agnostic employee to attend a religious service was incompatible with the religious freedom enshrined by the Civil Rights Act, even though this service was non-denominational. Similarly, the Supreme Court of Canada considered that the employer – a school – had to pay its Jewish teachers wages corresponding for the day on which they had not worked because they were observing Yom Kippur.[76] More generally, Canadian courts have held that freedom of religion 'includes the right to observe the essential practices demanded by the tenets of one's religion.'[77] Where an otherwise neutral employer rule or term in a collective agreement adversely affects an employee because of their religious beliefs, 'the employer and the union, to the extent of their respective responsibilities, will be required to accommodate that individual, short of undue

---

76 *Commission scolaire régionale de Chambly* v. *Bergevin,* available at http://scc.lexum.umontreal.ca.

77 *Re R. and Videoflicks Ltd* (1984), 9 C.R.R. 193 (Ont. C.A.), at p. 168 in M. Cornish and H. Simand, 'Religious accommodation in the workplace', in *Canadian Labour Law Journal*, Vol. 1, Nos 1 & 2, 1992.

hardship'.[78] By contrast, a Spanish court gave priority to the employer's interest as it considered acceptable a refusal to change a worker's work shift with
the sole purpose of allowing him to attend a religious service. In the same
way, the French Court of Cassation ruled that an employer was not obliged to
change the job assignments of a Muslim meat-cutter, who had been dismissed
on the grounds that he refused to cut pork. The Court held that the possibility of the meat-cutter refusing to cut pork should have been expressly
provided for in his contract of employment, something which had not been
done.[79]

The European Commission of Human Rights, meanwhile, has held that a
decision not to allow a Muslim schoolteacher to attend mosque on Friday
afternoons was *not* in breach of Article 9 of the ECHR on the basis that the
education authority had reached a fair balance between religious requirements and the need for an efficient school timetable.[80] Similarly, the
Commission held that dismissal of a Christian employee for refusing work on
Sundays was not in breach of Article 9, on the basis that the dismissal was for
failing to work her contractual hours rather than for her religious beliefs, and
she had the option of resigning in order to pursue those beliefs.[81] There is
therefore a tendency for the contractual and organizational needs of the
employer to be given priority over accommodation of religious beliefs within
the workplace.

By contrast, in Peru, a decision of the Constitutional Court held that an
employer is expected to accommodate a worker's religious beliefs while organizing his or her work, unless this is not possible because of higher ranked
organizational needs (box 5.6). This decision is comparable to one reached by
the Supreme Court of Canada in 1992, in the leading case *Central Okanagan
School District No. 23 v. Renaud*.[82]

---

78 M. Cornish and H. Simand, op. cit., p. 168 and *OPSEU (Kimmel/Leaf) and the Crown in right
    of Ontario (Ministry of Government Services)*, [1991] Grievance Settlement Board #1391/90
    (Kaplan) (unreported).

79 Cassation Sociale, 24 March 1998, num. 2056 PB, *Azad c. Chamsidine, Droit Social*, 1998,
    p. 614.

80 *Ahmad v. UK* (1981) 4 EHRR 126.

81 *Stedman v. UK* (1997) 23 EHRR 168.

82 *Central Okanagan School District No. 23 v. Renaud* [1992] 2 S.C.R. 970. This judgment is
    available online at http://scc.lexum.umontreal.ca.

> **Box 5.6 Discrimination on the grounds of religion. A decision by the Constitutional Court of Peru[83]**
>
> The plaintiff was a medical practitioner and worked in a publicly funded hospital. He was a member of the Seventh-day Adventist Church, a denomination which is distinguished by its observance of Saturday, the 'seventh day' of the week, as the Sabbath. Over the course of several years his working schedule did not include Saturdays. However, in 2001 a reorganization of the hours of work was introduced by his employer, which provided for work shifts on varying days, including Saturdays. The plaintiff then brought his case before the Constitutional Tribunal, alleging he had been discriminated against on the grounds of his religion.
>
> The defendant claimed that reorganization of the work shifts was due to 'institutional needs'. It alleged that religious observance and practices cannot oblige medical care institutions, having regard to their mission, to modify in a given way their working shifts, so as to benefit some workers to the detriment of other workers who would, however, be required to work on Saturdays. It suggested that such unequal treatment would be tantamount to discrimination against other physicians of different religious belief, who could not object to Saturday work shifts.
>
> The Constitutional Tribunal felt, however, that the defendant's allegations of 'institutional needs' were ambiguous and insufficient. They did not justify the employer's refusal to accommodate the claimant's religious beliefs. It observed that the equal treatment rights of co-workers would not appear to be affected by a decision to relieve some other workers from Saturday shifts, particularly as they would presumably not object to being assigned work on Sundays. Given the circumstances of the case, the Court concluded that the plaintiff's conscientious objection had a good cause, to the extent that the defendant had not brought objective evidence on the basis of which the Court could be satisfied that the change of working shifts was effectively due to the higher ranked interests of the institution, which – if they existed – might have justified that the claimant's rights be put aside.

No less thorny are the issues arising out of the hiring and firing practices of religious institutions. The question here consists in determining whether they can refuse a job applicant on the grounds that they do not share the same religious conviction, or whether they can dismiss employees because their private lives are in breach of the rules, principles or ethos of the institution. This question has been expressly addressed in EC Directive 2000/78/EC, of 27

---

83 Exp. no. 0895-2001-*Lucio Rosado Adanaque*, judgment of 19 August 2002.

November 2000, establishing a general framework for equal treatment in employment and occupation. Here it is provided that 'in very limited circumstances, a difference of treatment may be justified where a characteristic related to religion or belief, disability, age or sexual orientation constitutes a genuine and determining occupational requirement, when the objective is legitimate and the requirement is proportionate'. Thus it would be admissible for religious organizations to hire only their own members for jobs with responsibilities involving religious rituals and guidance. There would not seem to be any objection to a religious institution that operates a general educational programme hiring only members of its own congregation to teach religious courses. However, it is very likely that only hiring people who follow the same religion for teaching secular courses, or for performing other non-religious tasks such as washing dishes in the school cafeteria, would be considered as discrimination on the grounds of religious belief.

The dismissal of schoolteachers at Catholic schools on the grounds of their private life has given rise to a number of judicial decisions. In 1978 the French Court of Cassation took the view that the dismissal of a schoolteacher on the grounds of her divorce was justified, on the understanding that at the time of concluding the contract of employment the parties had implicitly taken in consideration the worker's religious convictions, and this element, which normally remains outside the employment relationship, had been incorporated in the intrinsic principles that a teacher at a Catholic school was expected to exemplify.[84] German case law has taken the same route in that it has maintained the lawfulness of dismissals caused by the workers' private life coming into conflict with the ideas professed by their employer, when that employer is an 'ideological organization' (*Tendenzbetrieb*). Nevertheless, Belgian jurisprudence, on the basis of Article 9 of the ECHR, held as unjustified the dismissal of a divorced schoolteacher in a Catholic school, who had maintained an adulterous relationship and entered into a second marriage while the first one – in the eyes of the Catholic faith – could not be dissolved.[85]

More recently, the ostensible use of certain religious symbols such as the Islamic headscarf (hijab) has been the subject of controversy, drawing the wide attention of the media and the general public alike. Two cases have been brought before the European Court of Human Rights, which held that in the

---

84 *Dame Roy* v. *Association pour l'éducation populaire Sainte-Marthe.* Mrs Roy, a teacher at a Catholic school subsidized by the State, was dismissed as a result of her divorce, something which was held by her employer as incompatible with the Catholic Church's fundamental values regarding marriage.

85 Judgments of the Cour du Travail of Brussels, dated 24 November 1977 and 4 May 1975.

particular circumstances that surrounded each case a prohibition on the wearing of the hijab was not in breach of Article 9 of the European Convention of Human Rights,[86] which provides under para. 2 that exceptions on the freedom of religion principle can be made where they are 'necessary in a democratic society in the interests of public safety, for the protection of public order, health or morals, or for the protection of the rights and freedoms of others'. In one of these cases,[87] the Court considered that the prohibition on wearing the hijab that the Department of Public Instruction of the Republic and Canton of Geneva, Switzerland, imposed on a female Muslim teacher was justifiable to preserve religious peace in the community, especially where the school had young students from diverse cultural traditions. In the second case, the Court dismissed an application by a student at the Medical School of the University of Istanbul who had been excluded from University because she insisted in wearing the hijab during her attendance at the University, where it was prohibited for reasons of laicism.[88]

However, as has been noted by Canadian legal scholar Mary Cornish, the balancing of interests in Europe appears to be weighted differently in a private sector context. A German court upheld the right of a female Muslim salesperson to wear a hijab. As the worker could not work without the headscarf, and the employer had not proved any loss of sales (just a fear of such loss), the court found that the employer should have used less drastic means than firing, such as transferring her from the perfume counter to another area.[89] We can also note that the ILO Committee of Experts on the Application of Conventions and Recommendations (CEACR) took a different view from that of the European Court of Human Rights. In an observation addressed in 2004 to the government of Turkey, relating to the application of the Discrimination (Employment and Occupation) Convention, 1958 (No. 111), and reiterated in

---

86 Article 9 – Freedom of thought, conscience and religion

    1. Everyone has the right to freedom of thought, conscience and religion; this right includes freedom to change his religion or belief and freedom, either alone or in community with others and in public or private, to manifest his religion or belief, in worship, teaching, practice and observance.

    2. Freedom to manifest one's religion or beliefs shall be subject only to such limitations as are prescribed by law and are necessary in a democratic society in the interests of public safety, for the protection of public order, health or morals, or for the protection of the rights and freedoms of others.

87 *Lucia Dahlab* v. *Switzerland,* 15 February 2001 (Application No. 42393/98).

88 *Leyla Şahin* v. *Turkey,* 29 June 2004 (Application No. 44774/98).

89 German Federal Labour Court (Bundesarbeitsgericht or BAG), 10 October 2002, 2 AZR 472/01; available online at http://lexetius.com.

2006, the CEACR expressed its concern that a ban on Muslim women wearing the hijab could deter women from entering higher education, thus having the effect of undermining their right to equal treatment in access to employment and occupation. An observation addressed in 2006 to France, which had imposed a ban on the use of ostensible religious symbols in public schools, was consistent with this approach.

Box 5.7 Discrimination on the grounds of religion

Observations made by the CEACR to the Governments of Turkey and France concerning the application of the ILO Discrimination (Employment and Occupation) Convention, 1958 (No. 111)[90]

Turkey
The Committee recalls that, in principle, where restrictions or exclusions based on a religious practice are made, which have the effect of nullifying or impairing equality of opportunity and treatment in employment and occupation, discrimination, as defined in the Convention, may have occurred. It maintains that restrictions on the wearing of head coverings may have the effect of nullifying or impairing the access to university education of women who feel obliged to or wish to wear, a headscarf out of religious obligation or conviction. The Committee trusts that the Government will keep the evolving situation under continuous review in order to determine whether such a general restriction is still necessary, and to ensure that the right of equal access to education and training at the university level of women who feel obliged to or wish to wear a headscarf out of religious conviction is not restricted, contrary to the Convention. The Committee remains concerned that the current restrictions may, in practice, keep women away from university education and training. In order to allow the Committee to obtain a better understanding of the situation, the Government is requested to provide in its next report its assessment of the impact of the current prohibition for university students to wear dress manifesting a religion on the participation of women in higher education, including an indication of the number of female students expelled from universities for wearing headscarves on university premises.

France
The Committee recalls the Act No. 65 of 17 March 2004 and its implementing circular of 18 May 2004 banning the wearing, in public schools, of any

---

90 Published in the CEACR Report, 2006 (ILO, Geneva, 2006).

conspicuous religious signs or apparel under penalty of disciplinary measures including expulsion. The Committee notes that for the school year 2003–04 initially about 600 pupils resisted complying with the Act, which after consultations held with parents and pupils, was reduced to about 100 pupils. It notes that, at the beginning of the school year 2004–05, a similar number of procedures were initiated before the disciplinary councils and that 47 definitive expulsions were pronounced. Against these, 39 appeals were filed to the rectors, who upheld the councils' decisions. Twenty-eight pupils requested the annulment of the rectors' decisions through the courts, which rejected 26 of these requests for annulment. While the Committee had noted in its previous observation that expulsion was applied only after extensive dialogue with the pupil and his or her parents, it nevertheless feared that in practice the Act might end up keeping some children, particularly girls, away from public schools for reasons associated with their religious convictions. This could diminish in future their capacity to find employment, contrary to the Convention. In order to assess whether Act No. 65 of 17 March 2004 and its implementing circular of 18 May 2004 is not diminishing the capacity of girls to find employment in future, contrary to the Convention, the Committee asks the Government to provide information on: (1) any judicial and administrative decisions with respect to the application of the abovementioned legislation; (2) the respective number of girls and boys that have been definitively expelled on the basis of the Act; and (3) the measures taken to ensure that the pupils who have been expelled nonetheless have proper opportunity to acquire education and training.

Other kinds of discrimination

Despite its wide acceptance, the right not to be discriminated against is not a positive right as such, as it has been formulated in the form of an exception. If one looks at the wording of Convention No. 111, ratifying States are required to prohibit discrimination on the basis of race, colour, sex, religion, political opinion, national extraction or social origin, but are not required to put a similar ban on other grounds of discrimination, such as age, disability, state of health or sexual orientation. Thus employers can treat differently two workers who are in the same situation: they can discriminate against one of them, provided the different treatment is not based on prohibited grounds. The same approach has been followed in EC law, though the list of prohibited grounds for discrimination is longer than it is under ILO Conventions. One of the problems arising out of this approach is that workers would have no case if they had been discriminated against on grounds which have not been expressly prohibited under national or international law. For example, in a 1998 judgment, the ECJ ruled that the refusal of travel concessions to same-sex partners – which had been granted to heterosexual couples – did not constitute sex discrimination and was therefore not prohibited under EC law[91] (discrimination on the grounds of sexual orientation was not prohibited under EC law until 2000). Similarly, workers in principle could not bring a case of discrimination if they had been refused employment or otherwise been prejudiced on the grounds of some aspects of their lifestyle, for example if they were smokers or overweight, if such grounds of discrimination have not been expressly forbidden.

However, it can be argued with some degree of confidence that workers could bring a complaint if they had been disciplined on the grounds of having contravened an employer's policy which conflicts with the employee's fundamental rights and appears not to be justified by the job's requirements. For example, an employer's rule that prescribes some forms of clothing (such as not wearing shorts) during working hours would be looked upon as being more reasonable than a rule that prohibits beards, which would affect employees' appearance during off-duty hours. The latter would require some business justification, which would need to be stronger than the rules that prescribed the clothing to be worn on duty.

In any event, though protection against discrimination is not a positive right, the list of prohibited grounds for discrimination is far longer today than it was some 30 or even 20 years ago. Historically, race, skin colour, trade union affiliation or activities, political opinion and sex were the most widely known grounds of prohibited discrimination. Today there is increasing awareness that workers can be discriminated against on a number of other grounds, and both international and national law are progressively reacting against such forms of discrimination.

Box 5.8　Discrimination on the grounds of employee lifestyle[92]

Employers sometimes attempt to impose their own lifestyle choices on their workers with respect to physical appearance. Federal law prohibiting employment discrimination forbids such intrusions if the effort affronts an

---

91　Case C–249/96 *Lisa Jacqueline Grant* v. *South-West Trains Ltd*, judgment of the Court of 17 February 1998, [1998] ECR I–621. In its judgment the Court explained that there would have been sex discrimination if the employer had refused to a female same-sex couple the concessions it had granted to a male same-sex couple, or vice versa.

92　International Society for Labour and Security Law, *Labour law and the fundamental rights of the person*, US Report to the XVII World Congress of the ISLSSL, Montevideo, 2000.

employee's religious practices or ethnic customs. If the worker is a government employee, federal constitutional standards of due process and equal protection further prohibit intrusions on employee lifestyles if the regulations are arbitrary; that is, the government employer must provide a rational job-related justification for the restriction. For example, employees who have beards can be required to shave them if their job responsibilities necessitate wearing a respirator mask and the beard will interfere with a proper seal between the mask and the worker's face. On the other hand, a beard could not be prohibited if the worker has no duties involving maintaining a particular public image and if the beard does not affect job performance.

Employees protected by a typical collective agreement with provisions against unjust discipline and unreasonable work rules cannot be disciplined for lifestyle-related choices that do not adversely affect job performance. In addition, some states have laws relating to specific types of lifestyle restrictions. For example, a Californian law adopted in 1994 protects the right of female employees to wear trousers (the state's and the federal laws prohibiting sex discrimination probably already provided that protection) and the District of Columbia has a law prohibiting employment discrimination based on physical appearance. In addition, some states prohibit an employer from interfering with any non-work activities of workers so long as the activities are legal. (One reason for the adoption of such laws has been to reject the policies of employers who, in order to reduce the cost of medical insurance, would no longer employ workers who use tobacco products off the job as well as at work.)

Family responsibilities

Both men and women can experience conflicts between work and their family life. This is why the ILO Workers with Family Responsibilities Convention, (No. 156) 1981, and its accompanying Recommendation (No. 165), apply to men and women with responsibilities to their dependent children and other members of their immediate family who clearly need their care and support. Similarly, EC Council Directive 96/34/EC of 3 June 1996 on the framework agreement on parental leave concluded by UNICE, CEEP and ETUC sought to facilitate the reconciliation of parental and professional responsibilities for working parents of either sex. Yet it is undisputed that the burden of family responsibilities is unequal as it places women at a disadvantage more often than it does men.

Discrimination on the grounds of family responsibilities can start as early as the recruitment stage, when job applicants can be refused a job, or certain jobs, if it appears that their family responsibilities would prevent them from adequately performing the work. Such a refusal may respond to a stereotypical attitude vis-à-vis persons with family responsibilities, but very often it will match reality. It cannot be denied that people with family responsibilities must accommodate two conflicting environments as the discharge of their responsibilities arising out of their employment may have a bearing on their family life and vice versa. For instance, conflict between work and family is associated with increased absenteeism, increased turnover of staff, decreased performance, and poorer physical and mental health. Workers with family responsibilities may also experience greater difficulties than other workers when they are taken on to do jobs that call for overtime, variable shifts, work at different worksites or frequent travel.

Family-friendly laws and regulations that provide for child care and parental leave are just some of the responses that can be promoted to help address this issue. However, most problems relating to the reconciliation of work and family responsibilities must be addressed at the workplace level. Typically these problems call for ad hoc arrangements that can be dealt with by collective bargaining or through labour–management consultations. Aside from child-care facilities, these may include parental leave, special leave, work from home and arrangement of working hours so as to make them more family-compatible. However, at a certain point, workers may be put under pressure to choose between their obligations arising out of employment, from which they earn their livelihood, and those arising out of their family responsibilities. This calls for a discussion about whether an employer can dismiss an employee on the grounds that the latter's family responsibilities render him or her incapable of fulfilling obligations arising out of employment.

As a rule, as stated in Article 8 of the Workers with Family Responsibilities Convention, 1981 (No. 156), 'family responsibilities shall not, as such, constitute a valid reason for termination of employment'. Similarly, Article 5(d) of the Termination of Employment Convention, 1982 (No. 158), provides that race, colour, sex, marital status, *family responsibilities*, pregnancy, religion, political opinion, national extraction or social origin shall not constitute valid reasons for termination of employment. In its General Survey of 1993, on Convention No. 156, the Committee of Experts acknowledged that the inclusion of this provision in the text of the Convention was decided only after some debate.[93] Besides, the wording used by the Convention suggests that the term 'as such' qualifies the word 'termination' in such a form that it does not rule out termination on the grounds of failure to fulfil obligations arising out of employment. Tribunals have been hesitant when called to

---

93 ILO, *Workers with family responsibilities, General Survey of the Committee of Experts on Convention (No. 156) and Recommendation (No. 165)*, Report III (Part 4B), International Labour Conference, 80th Session, Geneva, 1993, 118–21.

decide on the justification of a dismissal or other measures that have been decided by an employer on the grounds that a worker with family responsibilities has not fulfilled his or her obligations arising out of the contract of employment. For example, in a grievance procedure in the United States, an arbitrator was called on to judge whether the dismissal of a female worker who refused to work mandatory overtime on the grounds that it was impossible to find someone to look after her child during work was justified. The arbitrator found the mother technically guilty of insubordination but refused to uphold her dismissal on the grounds that 'no person should be forced to choose between his children or his livelihood'. However, in another case, an arbitrator dismissed a grievance by a worker who had been suspended because at the end of his shift he refused to work mandatory overtime on account of needing to pick up his child from school.[94]

Sexual harassment

Awareness of sexual harassment is relatively new. Most of the victims of sexual harassment are women, although cases of harassment of men by women and same-sex harassment have also been reported. Women have long been exposed to workplace harassment involving conduct of a sexual nature or simply harassment because of their sex. This kind of behaviour was not given a name until the 1970s, when women in the United States demanded that sexual harassment be recognized as sex discrimination under federal anti-discrimination legislation. This explains why the UN Convention on the Elimination of All Forms of Discrimination Against Women, 1979, did not contain a specific prohibition of sexual harassment. However, the Committee on the Elimination of Discrimination Against Women, set up under the Convention, has since explicitly addressed the problem. The Committee's General Recommendation of 1989 recognized sexual harassment as a form of violence against women.[95]

The designation 'sexual harassment' has since been adopted in many other countries. It covers any unwanted sexual attention that is explicitly or implicitly made a condition for favourable decisions affecting a person's employment or that creates an intimidating, hostile or offensive work environment. It is a specific form of violence that affects primarily, but not exclusively, women. More explicitly, the ILO Committee of Experts has considered that the terms 'sexual harassment' and 'unsolicited sexual attention':

---

94 National Academy of Arbitrators, 2005 Annual Meeting, Program Materials.
95 Deirdre McCann, *Sexual harassment at work: National and international response,* Conditions of Work and Employment Series No. 2 (Geneva, ILO, 2005).

include any insult or inappropriate remark, joke, insinuation and comment on a person's dress, physique, age, family situation, etc; a condescending or paternalistic attitude with sexual implications undermining dignity; any unwelcome invitation or request, implicit or explicit, whether or not accompanied by threats; any lascivious look or other gesture associated with sexuality; and any unnecessary physical contact such as touching, caresses, pinching or assault. In order to constitute sexual harassment in employment, an act of this type must, in addition, be justly perceived as a condition of employment or precondition for employment, or influence decisions taken in this field, and/or affect job performance.[96]

During the last two decades, legislation, court decisions, awareness-raising initiatives, and workplace programmes and policies have recognized and reacted to this problem. In the last decade in particular, advances have been made in both industrialized and developing countries, including those in which there had previously been little public recognition of the problem. At the international level too, sexual harassment has been recognized and addressed by a number of bodies, including the ILO. While the Discrimination (Employment and Occupation) Convention, 1958 (No. 111) does not specifically mention sexual harassment as a form of discrimination, the Committee of Experts has taken the view that it is implied in Article 2, which provides that 'ratifying states are to undertake and pursue [...] a national policy designed to promote, by methods appropriate to national conditions and practice, equality of opportunity and treatment in respect of employment and occupation, with a view to eliminating any discrimination in respect thereof'. EC law is still more explicit as both harassment and sexual harassment have been expressly included within the meaning of discrimination.

Sexual harassment differs from other forms of discrimination in that the worker can be victimized by acts not only by his or her employer but also by supervisors and co-workers. This is why national laws that aim to prevent sexual harassment normally oblige employers to investigate the circumstances surrounding the events which have been reported by employees as constituting harassment. In such cases, employers are expected to take measures that may be required to prevent continuation of the sexual harassment, and could be made liable for damages if they fail to adopt such measures.[97]

---

96 ILO, *Equality in employment and occupation, General Survey of the Committee of Experts on Convention No. 111*, Report III (Part 4B), International Labour Conference, 83rd Session , Geneva, 1996, para. 39.

97 See, for example, the Swedish Equal Opportunities Act 1991, ss. 27, 27A.

Some laws or regulations go beyond this, and extend the employer's responsibility for unwanted acts of a sexual nature which have been committed by 'a client, customer or other business contact of the victim's employer and the circumstances of the harassment are such that the employer ought reasonably to have taken steps to prevent it'.[98] For example, under Canada's Labour Code, an employer's sexual harassment policy must contain a statement that the employer will take appropriate disciplinary action against any person under its direction who subjects any employee to sexual harassment; a statement outlining how complaints of sexual harassment may be brought to the attention of the employer; and finally a statement that the confidentiality of the complaint will be maintained except where disclosure of the complainant's name is necessary for purposes of investigating the complaint or taking disciplinary action. Also, once an employer has been informed of sexual harassment in the workplace, there is a duty on the employer to ensure that the practice ceases. A similar approach exists in the United States, where the enforcement agency, the Equal Employment Opportunity Commission, is entitled to file lawsuits against offenders.

Box 5.9 United States: Fines imposed on employers who have failed to take measures to stop sexual harassment[99]

LAS VEGAS – Caesars Palace will pay $850,000 to settle a sexual harassment and retaliation lawsuit filed by the U.S. Equal Employment Opportunity Commission (EEOC), the agency announced today. The EEOC had charged that the Las Vegas resort/casino's Latina kitchen workers were subjected to repeated and sometimes severe sexual harassment.

In its 2005 lawsuit against Desert Palace, Inc., doing business as Caesars Palace, the EEOC asserted that male supervisors would demand and/or force female workers to perform sex with them under threat of being fired. Women, predominantly monolingual Spanish speakers, were forced to have sex in makeshift sex rooms. In addition, EEOC claimed that supervisors performed other lewd acts on or in front of women, including unwanted sexual touching. The EEOC also charged that management failed to address and correct the unlawful conduct, even though women complained about it. Further, the EEOC said, when workers complained about the unlawful conduct, they were retaliated against in the form of demotions, loss of wages, further harassment, discipline or discharge.

---

98 See Ireland's Equality Act 2004, s. 14A.
99 U.S. EEOC, 'Caesar's Palace to pay $850,000 for sexual harassment and retaliation', Press Release, 20 Aug. 2007.

> Sexual harassment and retaliation for complaining about it violate Title VII of the Civil Rights Act of 1964. The EEOC filed suit after first attempting to reach a voluntary settlement.
>
> 'In a case like this where many of the workers were monolingual Spanish speakers, victims of sexual harassment often feel further isolated, marginalized and unable to vindicate their rights,' said Anna Park, Regional Attorney for the EEOC's Los Angeles District. 'This case also illustrates that employers need to ensure their policies and procedures provide adequate avenues for complaint and redress to non-English speakers.'
>
> Under the three-year consent decree resolving the case, Caesars Palace agreed to pay $850,000 to the employees identified by the EEOC to have been sexually harassed or retaliated against. As part of the injunctive relief, Caesars Palace further agreed: (1) to provide training to all employees in English or Spanish; (2) to provide semi-annual reports to the EEOC regarding its employment practices for a period of three years; and (3) to revise its employment policies and procedures to conform to its obligations under Title VII. The EEOC filed the suit and consent decree in U.S. District Court for the District of Nevada (*EEOC* v. *Caesars Entertainment, Inc., et al.*, 2:05-CV-0427-LRH-PAL).

Sexual orientation

Recognition that discrimination on the grounds of sexual orientation is also an offence against human dignity is even more recent. As pointed out in the ILO Global Report under the Declaration of 2007 concerning Equality at Work, sensitivity towards discrimination and willingness to tackle it varies over time and according to the grounds of discrimination. In the EU Member States, for instance, the least progress has been achieved up to now on the grounds of sexual orientation, compared to the other recently recognized grounds of discrimination. In a number of countries there is a cultural refusal to acknowledge this problem, and in some others homosexuality is still a crime. Yet the number of countries that have adopted legislation to outlaw discrimination on the grounds of sexual orientation is on the increase, particularly in the EU in the past three years following the adoption of Directive 2000/78/EC of 27 November 2000, which established a general framework for equal treatment in employment and occupation.[100] Some shortcomings have nonetheless been observed with regard to the implementation of the Directive.[101]

---

[100] Council Directive 2000/78/EC of 27 November 2000, establishing a general framework for equal treatment in employment and occupation, *Official Journal of the European Union*, L 303/16 (Dec. 2000).

[101] ILO, *Equality at work: Tackling the challenges*, op. cit., para. 157.

Case law has also been instrumental in the move towards outlawing discrimination on the grounds of sexual orientation. In Canada, for example, provincial tribunals have confirmed the position taken by the Federal Department of Justice, according to which the Canadian Human Rights Act should be interpreted and applied as expressly prohibiting all discrimination based on sexual orientation on the grounds contained in s. 3 of the Act. In addition the Canadian Supreme Court has ruled that sexual orientation falls within the prohibited grounds of discrimination under s. 15 of the Canadian Charter of Rights and Freedoms, under which every individual is equal before and under the law and has the right to the equal protection and equal bene-fit of the law without discrimination and, in particular, without discrimina-tion based on a number of criteria: race, national or ethnic origin, colour, religion, sex, age or mental or physical disability. This jurisprudence has been instrumental in granting same-sex couples equal rights to those of heterosex-ual families with respect to medical care, pensions and other allowances. In the United States a number of states have adopted legislation to ban employ-ment discrimination on the grounds of sexual orientation, and a Bill was introduced in 2007 (the Employment Non-Discrimination Act (ENDA)) which sets out the same rule at the federal level.

In France, the prohibition of discrimination on the grounds of sexual orientation is included within the more general concept of discrimination on the grounds of personal lifestyle. As early as 1991, the Court of Cassation delivered a judgment in the famous case of *Painsecq*, a sacristan who performed his functions at the Church of Saint-Nicolas-du-Chardonnet.[102] Mr Painsecq had been performing the duties of sacristan to the full satisfac-tion of his parish. Nonetheless, his employer, the ultraconservative Catholic association of the Fraternity of Saint Pio X, found out about his homosexual inclinations and dismissed him. The Cassation Court, based on the funda-mental principle of the right to privacy (*vie privée*), ruled that his dismissal was null and void.

Age

Though discrimination on the grounds of age was not prohibited as such under ILO Convention No. 111, adopted in 1958, it has been addressed in a special part of the Older Workers Recommendation (No. 162), adopted in 1980. The Recommendation applies to 'all workers who are liable to

---

102 *P. Painsecq* c. *Association Fraternité Saint-Pie X*, Cass. Soc., 17 April 1991. See *Droit Social*, 1991, p. 489, with a note by J. Savatier.

encounter difficulties in employment and occupation because of advance-
ment in age'. It defines, in terms comparable to those of Convention No. 111,
the measures to be taken to prevent any discrimination in employment
against older workers, having regard to the special nature of their situation
due to age, the need for the adjustment of working conditions and the problems of access to retirement.

In recent years, many countries have adopted legislation to outlaw
discrimination on the grounds of age. Thus the US Age Discrimination in
Employment Act of 1967 (ADEA) provides that:

> it shall be unlawful for an employer (1) to fail or refuse to hire or to
> discharge any individual or otherwise discriminate against any individual
> with respect to his compensation, terms, conditions or privileges of employ-
> ment, because of such individual's age; (2) to limit, segregate, or classify his
> employees in any way which would deprive or tend to deprive any individ-
> ual of employment opportunities or otherwise adversely affect his status as
> an employee, because of such individual's age.

More recently, in 2000, EC Directive 2000/78/EC establishing a general framework for equal treatment in employment and occupation included age in the
list of prohibited grounds for discrimination.

This does not mean, however, that an age requirement for a job-seeker
would be unlawful in all circumstances. In certain occupations it could be
reasonable to fix an age limit, which would be justified – particularly for
reasons involving the safety or health of workers or third parties – in jobs
where risk is a factor, such as those of airline pilots, police officers, fire-fight-
ers, bus drivers. Thus, under EC Directive 2000/78/EC, Member States can
provide that the Directive, in so far as it relates to discrimination on the
grounds of disability and age, shall not apply to the armed forces.
Furthermore, the Directive allows Member States to provide that differences
of treatment on grounds of age shall not constitute discrimination if, 'within
the context of national law, they are objectively and reasonably justified by a
legitimate aim, including legitimate employment policy, labour market and
vocational training objectives, and if the means of achieving that aim are
appropriate and necessary'. For example, the fixing of a maximum age for
recruitment which is based on the training requirements of the post in question or the need for a reasonable period of employment before retirement
would not be deemed discrimination on the grounds of age. Also, courts
would be inclined to consider age as a bona fide occupational requirement for
jobs where safety considerations were paramount or an age limitation was
required in the interests of the adequate performance of the work.[103]

However, it is very likely that the courts would require that employers bear the burden of proving that age is a bona fide occupational requirement. According to the Supreme Court of Canada:

> A bona fide occupational qualification must be imposed honestly, in good faith, and in the sincerely held belief that it is imposed in the interests of adequate performance of the work involved with reasonable dispatch, safety and economy and not for ulterior or extraneous reasons that could defeat the Code's purpose. The qualification must be objectively related to the employment concerned, ensuring its efficient and economical performance without endangering the employee or others. Evidence as to the duties to be performed and the relationship between the ageing process and the safe, efficient performance of those duties is imperative, with statistical and medical evidence being of more weight than the impressions of persons experienced in the field.[104]

Does the setting of a mandatory retirement age constitute discrimination based on age? It is interesting to note that Recommendation No. 162 addresses this question somewhat cautiously. It recommends adoption of the principle that retirement should be on a voluntary basis and that the age of entitlement to old-age benefits should be made more flexible. It also recommends that legislative and other provisions making mandatory the termination of employment at a specified age should be examined in the light of the principle of non-discrimination. Nowadays an increasing number of countries tend to prohibit employers from forcing employees to retire merely because they have reached retirement age. This prohibition may also apply when such a mandatory separation age has been established in a collective agreement. Thus the French Court of Cassation ruled in 1989 that an employer terminating a contract of employment of a worker who has reached the normal age of retirement set by collective agreement, for no reason other than age, must compensate the worker and treat the dismissal as being without real and serious cause.[105] In *Mangold*, the ECJ followed a comparable approach (box 5.10).

---

103 *Large* v. *Stratford (City)* [1995] 3 S.C.R. 733, Decision of the Supreme Court of Canada of 19 October 1995; available online at http://scc.lexum.umontreal.ca. In this case, Mr Large, a police officer in the City of Stratford, Ontario, Canada, had challenged a mandatory retirement policy which had been introduced by the City as a result of demands by the Police Association, and was later on expressly included in the relevant collective agreement.

104 *Ontario Human Rights Commission* v. *Etobicoke* [1982] 1 S.C.R. 202; available online at http://csc.lexum.umontreal.ca.

105 ILO, *Equality in employment and occupation,*1996, op. cit., para. 251.

Box 5.10 Age discrimination: *Werner Mangold v. Rüdiger Helm*[106]

The German law on part-time work and fixed-term contracts (Gesetz über Teilzeitarbeit und befristete Arbeitsverträge, 'the TzBfG') of 2000 authorizes, without restriction (except in specific cases of a continuous employment relationship), the conclusion of fixed-term contracts of employment once the worker has reached the age of 52. The German Government considered that the purpose of this law was to promote the integration into working life of unemployed older workers, in so far as they encounter considerable difficulties in finding work. In its opinion, an objective of that kind justifies 'objectively and reasonably' a difference of treatment on grounds of age, which is otherwise outlawed under European Community law (Council Directive 2000/78/EC of 27 November 2000 establishing a general framework for equal treatment in employment and occupation (*OJ*, 2000, L 303, p. 16)).

In June 2003 Mr Mangold, then 56 years old, concluded with Mr H. a fixed-term contract of employment that took effect on 1 July 2003. It was recognized that the sole reason for this contract being agreed upon for a specified duration was the said law's provision. Mr Mangold further challenged before a German labour court the validity of the clause specifying his engagement for a limited duration. The German court then referred the case to the European Court of Justice for a preliminary ruling on the compatibility of that provision with EC law.

The ECJ acknowledged that the EU Member States enjoy broad discretion in their choice of the measures capable of attaining their objectives in the field of social and employment policy. However, it also took the view that a provision of national law such as that contained in the TzBfG 'goes beyond what is appropriate and necessary to attain the legitimate objective pursued'. According to the ECJ:

> [the] application of the national legislation at issue leads to a situation in which all workers who have reached the age of 52, without distinction, whether or not they were unemployed before the contract was concluded and whatever the duration of any period of unemployment, may lawfully, until their retirement, be offered fixed-term contracts of employment which may be renewed an indefinite number of times. This significant body of workers, determined solely on the basis of age, is thus in danger, during a substantial part of its members' working life, of being excluded from the benefit of stable

---

106 Case C–144/04 *Werner Mangold* v. *Rüdiger Helm*, judgment of the European Court of Justice of 22 November 2005.

> employment which, however, constitutes a major element in the protection of workers. In this case, it has not been shown that fixing an age threshold, as such, regardless of any other consideration linked to the structure of the labour market in question or the personal situation of the person concerned, is objectively necessary to the attainment of the objective which is the integration into working life of unemployed older workers.

Disability

Disability was not included as grounds for prohibited discrimination in ILO Convention No. 111 in 1958. It is only since the 1970s that the disadvantages faced by disabled people, their social exclusion and discrimination against them, have increasingly come to be regarded as human rights issues. The shift from a social-welfare approach to one based on human rights is reflected in explicit references to persons with disabilities in human rights charters, Conventions and initiatives adopted since the 1980s and in an increasing number of instruments adopted by such organizations as the United Nations and the Council of Europe. These instruments include the Council of Europe Coherent Policy for the Rehabilitation of People with Disabilities, 1992, and the UN Standard Rules on the Equalization of Opportunities for Persons with Disabilities, 1993. In 1983 the ILO adopted Convention No. 159 and Recommendation No. 168 concerning Vocational Rehabilitation and Employment (Disabled Persons). Convention No. 159 requires ratifying States to introduce a national policy based on the principle of equality of opportunity between disabled workers and workers generally, respecting equality of opportunity and treatment for disabled women and men and providing for special positive measures aimed at effective implementation of these principles. The emphasis on full participation is reflected in the definition of vocational rehabilitation as 'being to enable a disabled person to secure, retain and advance in suitable employment and thereby to further such a person's integration or reintegration into society'.

Since then, an increasing number of States have prohibited discrimination on the grounds of disability, particularly in the field of employment, either through comprehensive laws applying to different groups in the population as a whole or disability-specific laws. This reflects an acknowledgement that disability is frequently used as a reason to exclude people with disabilities and to deny them equal employment opportunities, when this is not justified in the given circumstances. The objective of such laws is thus to combat such exclusion and denial of equal opportunities to people because of particular characteristics, such as disability. By making disability one of the protected grounds, the law extends protection against discriminatory behaviour and punishes those people who violate the non-discrimination norm.[107]

Thus the Canadian Charter of Rights and Freedoms 1982, s. 15, provides that 'every individual is equal before and under the law and has the right to the equal protection and equal benefit of the law without discrimination, and in particular, without discrimination based on race, national or ethnic origin, colour, religion, sex, age *or mental or physical disability* [emphasis added]'. In Ireland, the Employment Equality Act 1998 outlaws discrimination on the basis of gender, marital status, family status, sexual orientation, religious belief, age, *disability*, race and membership of the traveller community. In Namibia, the Affirmative Action Act 1998 applies to racially disadvantaged persons, women irrespective of race *and persons with disabilities (physical or mental limitations, irrespective of race or gender)*. Some other countries have adopted legislation specifically aimed at protecting people with disabilities, including Costa Rica (Law 7600 on Equal Opportunities for People with Disabilities 1996), Ghana (Disabled Persons Act 1993), Malta (Equal Opportunities (Persons with Disability) Act 2000) and the United States of America (Rehabilitation Act 1973; Americans with Disabilities Act 1990). Many of these laws require employers to take account of an individual's disability and to make efforts to cater for the needs of a disabled worker or job applicant, and to overcome the barriers erected by the physical and social environment. This obligation is known as the requirement to make a *reasonable accommodation*, that is any modification or adjustment to a job or the work environment that will enable a qualified applicant or employee with a disability to apply for a given job or to perform essential job functions. Failure to provide a reasonable accommodation for workers and job applicants who face obstacles in the labour market is not merely a bad employment practice but is increasingly perceived as an unacceptable form of employment discrimination.

However, an employer is not required to make an accommodation if it would impose an 'undue hardship' on the operation of the employer's business. 'Undue hardship' is defined as an 'action requiring significant difficulty or expense' when considered in light of a number of factors. These factors include the nature and cost of the accommodation in relation to the size, resources, nature and structure of the employer's operation. Undue hardship is determined on a case-by-case basis. This rule is, for instance, acknowledged

---

107 ILO, *Achieving equal employment opportunities for people with disabilities through legislation: Guidelines* (Geneva, 2004).

in EC Directive 2000/78/EC establishing a general framework for equal treatment in employment and occupation.

Box 5.11 Reasonable accommodation for disabled persons

EC Directive 2000/78/EC establishing a general framework for equal treatment in employment and occupation

Article 5
In order to guarantee compliance with the principle of equal treatment in relation to persons with disabilities, reasonable accommodation shall be provided. This means that employers shall take appropriate measures, where needed in a particular case, to enable a person with a disability to have access to, participate in, or advance in employment, or to undergo training, unless such measures would impose a disproportionate burden on the employer. This burden shall not be disproportionate when it is sufficiently remedied by measures existing within the framework of the disability policy of the Member State concerned.

State of health and HIV/AIDS

A worker's state of health has not been mentioned as such in Convention No. 111 within the list of expressly forbidden grounds for discrimination. However, in its General Survey of 1996, the ILO Committee of Experts considered that:

> A worker's state of health should only be taken into consideration by employers with regard to the specific requirements of a particular job, and not be considered automatically as affecting the right to access to employment, or conditions of work within the employment relationship. Taking into account the past or present physical or mental state of health of an individual could be a major barrier to applying the principle of equal access to employment. Unless there is a very close link between a worker's current state of health and the normal occupational requirements of a particular job, using state of health as a reason to deny or continue employment contravenes the spirit of the Convention.[108]

Prohibition of discrimination on the grounds of state of health generally falls within the scope of the prohibition of all discrimination based on disability. However, it is actually different from disability since a worker who suffers

---

108 ILO, *Equality in employment and occupation*, 1996, op. cit., para. 255.

from a physical or mental disability may be unfit to work or to perform certain tasks. By contrast, a worker's state of health as such would not make him or her unfit to work, though a number of activities or work-related tasks might be unsuitable in view of vulnerability to certain illnesses or risks. Yet workers can be and in fact are frequently discriminated against on the grounds of their state of health because of a perception that they are unfit to work – rather than on their actual working capacity. Quite often, a refusal to hire workers on the grounds of their state of health is because of the cost considerations which would result from the workers' possible absences from work, or from medical care or medical insurance premiums that the employer would be called upon to bear, either directly or indirectly, should the worker actually become ill. On other occasions, discrimination can be the result of a popular stigma associated with certain illnesses, notably those associated with the HIV virus or AIDS.

Discriminatory practices against people with HIV or with AIDS may take many forms, which are often hidden. For example, workers may be questioned about their HIV status, or be required to submit to AIDS screening (for example, blood samples may be taken), often without realizing the tests include those for HIV. They can also be dismissed solely on the ground of their HIV status. Such practices constitute discrimination. Although there are occupations in which HIV status needs to be taken into account, they are few. While HIV-positive status is an unacceptable ground of discrimination, there are occupations in which such status should be taken into account when fitness for a job is being assessed: for example, nurses, doctors or dentists whose field of specialization (such as surgery or the administration of injections) involves a risk of contact that could transmit the virus could be considered as unfit for their job. In such instances, absence of HIV infection could be considered as a necessary occupational requirement. However, this is not the case for a large number of jobs and occupations, in which having AIDS or being HIV-infected would not be legitimate grounds for refusing employment or for dismissing a worker.

But the harshest kind of discrimination to which HIV-positive workers may be subjected can occur in the workplace among fellow workers who might reject these people because of ignorance, prejudice or fear of the illness. In anticipation of such situations, by 2006 some 73 countries had included HIV/AIDS-related provisions in their labour legislation or anti-discrimination laws. In 1996 the United Nations adopted International Guidelines on HIV/AIDS and Human Rights; this was followed in 2001 by an ILO code of practice on HIV/AIDS and the world of work,[109] which covers the following

---

109 ILO, *HIV/AIDS and the world of work* (Geneva, 2001).

key areas of action: (1) prevention of HIV/AIDS; (2) management and mitigation of the impact of HIV/AIDS on the world of work; (3) care and support of workers infected and affected by HIV/AIDS; (4) elimination of stigma and discrimination on the basis of real or perceived HIV status. Case law from a number of countries also provides highly pertinent examples of how to combat discrimination on the grounds of HIV/AIDS.[110]

Box 5.12 Refusal to hire a job applicant on the grounds of HIV-positive status constitutes discrimination[111]

In South Africa, the 2000 decision in *Hoffmann* v. *South African Airways* demonstrated that the judiciary was aware of the progressive nature of the disease and the circumstances of transmission. Mr Hoffmann was refused a job as a cabin attendant at South African Airways (SAA) because he was HIV-positive. SAA argued that its decision was based on medical, safety and operational grounds. It stated that harm would be done to its commercial interest if it were known that HIV-positive people were in its employ. The Constitutional Court was asked to determine the constitutionality of excluding a job applicant solely on the basis of his HIV status. The Court found that:

> An asymptomatic HIV-positive person can perform the work of a cabin attendant competently. Any hazards to which an immunocompetent cabin attendant may be exposed can be managed by counselling, monitoring, vaccination and the administration of the appropriate antibiotic prophylaxis if necessary. Similarly, the risks to passengers and other third parties arising from an asymptomatic HIV-positive cabin crew member are therefore inconsequential and, if necessary, well-established universal precautions can be utilized.

Concerning SAA allegations that hiring HIV-positive persons would negatively impact on public opinion and favour its competitors, the Court sent a clear message about presumptions concerning public image:

> Legitimate commercial requirements are, of course, an important consideration in determining whether to employ an individual. However, we must guard against allowing stereotyping and prejudice

---

110 See, for example, Jane Hodges, *Guidelines on addressing HIV/AIDS in the workplace through employment and labour law*, InFocus Programme on Social Dialogue, Labour Law and Labour Administration Paper No. 3 (Geneva, ILO, 2004).

111 Cited by Hodges, ibid., p. 12.

to creep in under the guise of commercial interests. The greater interests of society require the recognition of the inherent dignity of every
human being, and the elimination of all forms of discrimination. Our
Constitution protects the weak, the marginalized, the socially outcast,
and the victims of prejudice and stereotyping. It is only when these
groups are protected that we can be secured that our own rights are
protected [...].

The Court ruled in favour of the applicant and ordered SAA to employ him.

Affirmative (or positive) action

The adoption of affirmative action stems from the observation that the legal
banning of discrimination is not enough to eliminate it in practice. Use of
this term indicates that specific measures can be taken to eliminate, prevent
or remedy past discrimination. It goes beyond legislation on equal treatment
by promoting substantive equality (equality of outcomes), for example, by
addressing structural disadvantages rather than merely aiming for equality of
opportunity or prohibitions on discrimination. Affirmative action measures
aim at remedying past discrimination on the grounds of sex as well as on
other grounds such as colour, race or national origin, which have led to the
employment and training opportunities of certain groups of persons being
impaired. Such measures are authorized under Article 5 of ILO Convention
No. 111,[112] as well as under the Treaty of Amsterdam (in respect to gender
equality).[113] They are further contemplated in Article 3 of the Equal

---

112 Convention No. 111, Article 5:

> 1. Special measures of protection or assistance provided for in other Conventions
> or Recommendations adopted by the International Labour Conference shall not be
> deemed to be discrimination.
> 2. Any Member may, after consultation with representative employers' and workers'
> organizations, where such exist, determine that other special measures designed to
> meet the particular requirements of persons who, for reasons such as sex, age, disable-
> ment, family responsibilities or social or cultural status, are generally recognised to
> require special protection or assistance, shall not be deemed to be discrimination.

113 Under Article 141(4) EC, '[T]he principle of equal treatment shall not prevent any
Member State from maintaining or adopting measures providing for specific advantages
in order to make it easier for the under-represented sex to pursue a vocational activity
or to prevent or compensate for disadvantages in professional careers.'

Opportunities and Equal Treatment Directive 2006/54/EC,[114] Article 7 of Directive 2000/78/EC establishing a general framework for equal treatment in employment and occupation (discrimination on the grounds of religion or belief, disability, age or sexual orientation), and Article 5 of Directive 2000/43/EC of 29 June 2000, implementing the principle of equal treatment between persons irrespective of racial or ethnic origin.

Laws on affirmative action in employment usually target specific groups, which commonly include women, minorities (linguistic or ethnic, for example) and people with disabilities. The Canadian federal jurisdiction was one of the first to adopt an employment equity law, aimed at correcting the disadvantage in employment experienced by four specified groups: women, aboriginal people, people with disabilities and those who are in a visible minority in Canada because of their race or colour. In a relatively brief text, the legislator laid down the obligation of employers to consult with representatives of their employees on ways to implement employment equity. This pattern, however, is not universal, as affirmative action is generally used against forms of discrimination which are the most visible or the most politically sensitive in a given national context. For example, race discrimination would be a major political issue in countries with significant ethnic minorities,[115] but less important in other countries. Similarly, discrimination on the grounds of caste (or social origin, in the terminology of Convention No. 111) is a core issue in countries such as India or Nepal, while it is not in other countries where the caste system does not exist.

Affirmative action is frequently associated with quotas, that is, a system where a number of positions are reserved for people belonging to a designated group, and for which other people, perhaps with higher qualifications,

---

114 Directive 2006/54/EC, Article 3:

> *Positive action:* Member States may maintain or adopt measures within the meaning of Article 141(4) of the Treaty with a view to ensuring full equality in practice between men and women in working life. Positive action is also envisaged in Article 5 of Council Directive 2000/43 which implements the principle of equal treatment between persons, irrespective of racial or ethnic origin and in Article 7 of Council Directive 2000/78 which establishes a general framework for equal treatment in employment and occupation. In the latter case, specific provision is made for disabled persons.

115 Race discrimination is also a major political issue in countries where the majority group has, for historical or other reasons, been impaired in terms of their overall rights, including in employment, in comparison with a minority which has held the political or economic power (or both) for a long time, for example the black majority in South Africa, or the Malay majority in Malaysia.

cannot apply because they do not belong to that group. The quota system is very controversial and has been challenged on various grounds: first, that quotas may conflict with the equal treatment principle when they give preferential treatment to groups that historically have been disadvantaged but may act to the detriment of other groups that historically have not been, thus creating a reverse discrimination. This problem would seem to have been at the root of a provision in the US Civil Rights Act 1964, which stated that:

> Nothing contained in this title [Title VII] shall be interpreted to require any employer [...] to grant preferential treatment to any individual or to any group because of race, color, religion, sex or national origin of such individual or group on account of an imbalance which may exist with respect to the total number or percentage of persons of any race, color, religion, sex or national origin employed by an employer [...]

Yet this did not prevent the United States from implementing affirmative action programmes a few years later, which included quotas in the access to high-level teaching and training institutions. Further challenges to the quota system point to the stigma possibly inflicted on the intended beneficiaries, because people who have benefited from the preference may fall under the suspicion that they are not really qualified for such positions.

Rejection of the quota system, at least in its more rigid forms, would seem to be the position of the European Court of Justice, which has taken the view that an affirmative action provision like the quota system constitutes direct discrimination on the grounds of sex. However, the ECJ has accepted that some preference may be given to the under-represented sex, provided some conditions are met. Thus, in *Kalanke*[116] it considered that EC law on equality precludes national laws or regulations which give automatic preference to the under-represented sex when two candidates, equally qualified, apply for the same post. Later, in *Abrahamsson*,[117] it took the view that EC law precludes national rules whereby:

> a candidate from the under-represented sex must be chosen in preference to a candidate of the opposite sex who would otherwise have been appointed, where this is necessary to secure the appointment of a candidate of the under-represented sex and the difference between the respective merits of the candidates is not so great as to give rise to a breach of the requirement of objectivity in making appointments.

---

116 Case C-450/93 *Eckhard Kalanke* v. *Freie Hansestadt Bremen*, judgment of the Court of 17 October 1995, [1995] ECR I–3051.
117 Case C–407/98 *Katarina Abrahamsson*, judgment of the Court (Fifth Chamber), 6 July 2000.

However, in *Badeck* it accepted that:

> in sectors of the public service where women are under-represented, national laws or regulations can give priority, where male and female candidates have equal qualifications, to female candidates where that proves necessary for ensuring compliance with the objectives of the women's advancement plan, if no reasons of greater legal weight are opposed, *provided that that rule guarantees that candidatures are the subject of an objective assessment which takes account of the specific personal situations of all candidates* [emphasis added].[118]

This was certainly not the position taken by an Argentinian tribunal which, on the basis of evidence produced by an NGO (and not denied by the defendant), was satisfied that a well-known ice-cream parlour chain refused to take on female staff. As a remedy, the tribunal ordered that the defendant recruit only female staff 'until an equitable and reasonable sex distribution of its staff is achieved'.[119]

However, promotion of equality can be pursued by means other than quotas. A good alternative is offered by the Italian Act No. 125 of 10 April 1991, providing for affirmative action to achieve equal treatment of men and women in employment (box 5.13).

Box 5.13 Affirmative action policies in Italy[120]

Section 17
(1) For the purposes of this Act 'affirmative action' means a set of affirmative action measures designed to ensure that persons in designated groups enjoy equal employment opportunities at all levels of employment and are equitably represented in the workforce of a relevant employer.
(2) Without limiting the generality of the definition in subsection (1), an affirmative action measure referred to in that subsection includes, but is not limited to –

---

118 Case C–158/97 *Georg Badeck and Others, interveners: Hessische Ministerpräsident and Landesanwalt beim Staatsgerichtshof des Landes Hessen,* judgment of the Court of 28 March 2000, [2000] ECR I–1875.

119 *Fundación de Mujeres en Igualdad y otro c/Freddo SA s/amparo,* Cámara Nacional de Apelaciones en lo Civil, Sala H, judgment of 16 December 2002.

120 Italy's Act No. 125 of 10 April 1991 providing for affirmative action to achieve equal treatment of men and women in employment.

> (a) identification and elimination of employment barriers against persons in designated groups;
> (b) making reasonable efforts in the workplace to accommodate, physically or otherwise, persons with disabilities; and
> (c) instituting positive measures to further the employment opportunities for persons in designated groups, which may include measures such as –
> – ensuring that existing training programmes contribute to furthering the objects of this Act;
> – establishing new training programmes aimed at furthering the objects of this Act; and
> – giving preferential treatment in employment decisions to suitably qualified persons from designated groups to ensure that such persons are equitably represented in the workforce of a relevant employer.
> (3) To determine whether a designated group is equitably represented in the various positions of employment offered by a relevant employer, the Commission shall take into account, in addition to such other factors as it may determine –
> (a) the availability of suitably qualified persons in that designated group for such positions of employment; and
> (b) the availability of persons in designated groups who are able and willing, through appropriate training programmes, to acquire the necessary skills and qualifications for such positions of employment.

Protection of privacy

The right to privacy is acknowledged as a basic human right in many countries around the world. The protection of a worker's privacy at the workplace is not a new issue, as many earlier laws addressed this question in relation to body-searches that employers could undertake on their workers in order to protect their property. For example, Article 18 of the Spanish Worker's Charter 1980 provided that the dignity and privacy of the worker must be respected while undertaking a body-search. Many other laws contained analogous provisions. Nevertheless, most national laws did not go much beyond such provisions, partly because there was no need and partly because of a widespread feeling that human rights concerns were not an issue at the workplace.

Looking for comparative precedents, it seems to be difficult to find judicial decisions on workers' rights to privacy before the 1960s or the early 1970s: for example, in Japan, a Supreme Court decision in *Nishi-Nikon Railway*, which is regarded as a leading case on workers' privacy, was reached in 1968. In that case the plaintiff was a train conductor who refused to take off his shoes during a body-search, which was required after he had sold tickets and collected money from ticket sales. He was dismissed for disobedience and subsequently took his case to the courts. The Supreme Court set out four requirements: that there be reasonable grounds for such an examination; that the examination be carried out in a proper manner and within appropriate limits; that the examination be applied uniformly to all relevant employees without discrimination; and that the examination procedure should be clearly stipulated in writing.[121]

Two new developments, however, changed this situation. First, new information and communication technologies have made it easier for the employer to intrude into workers' private lives and to exercise control both at and outside the workplace, thus exposing workers to intrusions for a very large part of their daily lives. Secondly, the concept of 'private life' has enlarged significantly, to the extent that the scope of protection for private life goes beyond that of a person's home. In this respect a landmark judgment by the European Court of Human Rights in 1992 held that 'it would be too restrictive to limit the notion (home and private life) to an "inner circle" in which the individual may live his own personal life as he chooses and to exclude therefrom entirely the outside world not encompassed within that circle. Respect for private life must also comprise to a certain degree the right to establish and develop relationships with other human beings'.[122] Widespread acceptance of this reasoning led to the extension of human rights and protection of privacy concerns to the workplace.

A number of international rules and guidelines have been adopted in the last decade to address the general question of the protection of privacy. Article 17 of the UN International Covenant on Civil and Political Rights deals, inter alia, with the right to privacy. From the European perspective, the most important legal instruments are the Personal Data Protection Directive 95/46/EC, the Privacy and Electronic Communications Directive 2002/58/EC and the Council of Europe Convention for the Protection of Individuals with regard to Automatic Processing of Personal Data, 1981. Article 8 of the European Convention on Human Rights can also be invoked and has actually provided the legal basis for several landmark decisions both by the European Courts of Human Rights and national courts. Similarly, Article 11 of the American Convention on Human Rights enshrines the right to privacy. While none of these rules specifically address workplace issues, they can all be

---

121 Quoted in Tadashi Hanami, Introductory Remarks, in 'On-line rights for employees in the Information Society', in *Bulletin of Comparative Labor Relations* (The Hague/London/New York, Kluwer Law International, 2002), No. 40, p. xvii.

122 *Niemitz v. Germany* (1992) 16 EHRR 97 (16 December 1992).

invoked for a court case on the grounds that a worker's right to privacy has been infringed at the workplace.

Several non-binding international instruments may be added to this list, including Article 12 of the Universal Declaration of Human Rights and Article 7 of the Charter of Fundamental Rights of the European Union. With regard to the specific aspect of the protection of workers' privacy, so far only the ILO has adopted rules, namely Article 6 of the Private Employment Agencies Convention, 1997 (No. 181), which applies to job-seekers rather than to workers actually in an employment relationship.[123] Non-binding international rules on the same subject include para. 12 of the ILO Private Employment Agencies Recommendation, 1997 (No. 188), the Council of Europe Recommendation No. R (89) 2 on the protection of personal data used for employment purposes, the ILO code of practice on Protection of Workers' Personal Data (1996) (see box 5.14) and the OECD Guidelines on the Protection of Privacy and Transborder Flows of Personal Data (1980).

A growing number of countries have fairly recently adopted general rules to protect privacy against breaches by third parties, which can be used, inter alia, at the workplace level: the United Kingdom has put in place the Data Protection Act 1988; Denmark has the Processing of Personal Data Act 2000. Other countries such as France and the Russian Federation have addressed this question in their labour codes, which contain provisions dealing specifically with the protection of workers' personal data that can be read and used alongside more general rules on the protection of privacy. But so far it would seem that only Finland has adopted a comprehensive law on the Protection of Privacy in Working Life. This law, enacted in 2004, lays down provisions on the processing of personal data about employees, the performance of tests and examinations on employees and the related requirements, technical surveillance in the workplace, and retrieving and opening employees' electronic mail messages. In Belgium this topic has been addressed by two national collective agreements signed within the National Labour Council. These have been extended to all workers, in the form of National Collective Agreement No. 81 on the protection of workers' privacy with respect to controls on electronic on-line communications data and National Collective Agreement No. 68 concerning the protection of the workers' private life with regard to the surveillance by video cameras at the workplace.

---

123 Article 6 of Convention No. 181 reads as follows: 'The processing of personal data of workers by private employment agencies shall be: (a) done in a manner that protects this data and ensures respect for workers privacy in accordance with national law and practice; (b) limited to matters related to the qualifications and professional experience of the workers concerned and any other directly relevant information.'

In many other countries the protection of workers' privacy at the work-place is derived from general constitutional principles relating to the protection of human dignity, which have been further developed by case law. In the United States a federal law that protects employee privacy is the Employee Polygraph Protection Act 1988,[124] which substantially limits the situations in which employees or job applicants can be required to take lie-detector tests and regulates the manner in which such tests are administered. Another federal law that protects employee privacy is the Electronic Communications Privacy Act 1986, which protects oral, electronically transmitted communications from interception when the speaker, including an employee, has a reasonable expectation that it will not be intercepted through electrical, mechanical or other devices. Violations of both statutes can result in the award of civil damages as well as criminal prosecution.

Amongst the different issues which could now be considered in this regard, the following deserve particular attention, both in the legislation and case law of many countries:

- the collection, retrieval, storage processing, use and possible disclosure of data relating to a worker's or a job applicant's private life;
- the private use by the worker of the internet, intranet and email provided by the employer;
- the monitoring of the worker's telephone communications, including those made from his or her own home;
- the use of electronic devices to monitor the worker's activities, both at the workplace and outside the workplace;
- post-9/11 insecurity: in some countries employers may be required by government security agencies to monitor workers and disclose information about them as part of government action against terrorism.

Some of these issues can be raised even before a worker is taken on by an employer, as job-seekers are usually required to provide information on their professional profile. Unless such a right is legally limited, an employer could request information which goes far beyond the strict minimum in order to consider an applicant's job profile, for example, relating to their state of health, political opinions, religious beliefs, sex life or other elements of their private life. While nobody denies that an employer has the right to ascertain the qualifications and aptitudes of a job applicant, there is a risk that after

---

124 See U.S. Dept. of Labor, *The Employee Polygraph Protection Act (EPPA)* (Washington, D.C., 2008); available at: http://www.dol.gov.

having conducted such enquiries the employer might dismiss an application for reasons relating to the applicant's private life which are unrelated to the qualifications required for the job. This could constitute discrimination on prohibited grounds. For that reason, a logical consequence of the right not to be discriminated against has been the development of rules and principles under legislation or case law, with a view to limiting the type of information that an applicant could be required to disclose, as well as the means which could be used to obtain, gather, process, store and disclose that information. The right of access by workers to their personal files and that of requesting a correction to inaccurate data has also been addressed. In France, for example, the law provides that job applicants or employees can be required to provide only such information which is relevant to the assessment of their qualifications or skills in order to fill the post. Furthermore, no personal information can be gathered by methods that have not been brought to the attention of the concerned employee or job applicant.[125]

Box 5.14 Protection of workers' personal data: an ILO code of practice[126]

3. Definitions
3.1. The term 'personal data' means any information related to an identified or identifiable worker.
3.2. The term 'processing' includes the collection, storage, combination, communication or any other use of personal data.
3.3. The term 'monitoring' includes, but is not limited to, the use of devices such as computers, cameras, video equipment, sound devices, telephones and other communication equipment, various methods of establishing identity and location, or any other method of surveillance.
3.4. The term 'worker' includes any current or former worker or applicant for employment

5. General principles
[...]
5.2. Personal data should, in principle, be used only for the purposes for which they were originally collected. [...]
5.4. Personal data collected in connection with technical or organizational measures to ensure the security and proper operation of auto-

---

125 Labour Code, Article L. 121-6.
126 Excerpts from ILO, *Protection of worker's personal data* (Geneva, 1997).

mated information systems should not be used to control the behaviour of workers. [...]

5.7. Employers should regularly assess their data processing practices:

(a) to reduce as far as possible the kind and amount of personal data collected; and

(b) to improve ways of protecting the privacy of workers.

5.8. Workers and their representatives should be kept informed of any data collection process, the rules that govern that process, and their rights. [...]

5.12. All persons, including employers, workers' representatives, employment agencies and workers, who have access to personal data, should be bound to a rule of confidentiality consistent with the performance of their duties and the principles in this code.

5.13. Workers may not waive their privacy rights.

6. Collection of personal data

[...]

6.5 (1) An employer should not collect personal data concerning a worker's:

(a) sex life;

(b) political, religious or other beliefs;

(c) criminal convictions.

(2) In exceptional circumstances, an employer may collect personal data concerning those in (1) above, if the data are directly relevant to an employment decision and in conformity with national legislation. [...]

6.7. Medical personal data should not be collected except in conformity with national legislation, medical confidentiality and the general principles of occupational health and safety, and only as needed:

(a) to determine whether the worker is fit for a particular employment;

(b) to fulfil the requirements of occupational health and safety; and

(c) to determine entitlement to, and to grant, social benefits.

6.8. If a worker is asked questions that are inconsistent with principles 5.1, 5.10, 6.5, 6.6 and 6.7 of this code and the worker gives an inaccurate or incomplete answer, the worker should not be subject to termination of the employment relationship or any other disciplinary measure. [...]

6.10. Polygraphs, truth-verification equipment or any other similar testing procedure should not be used. [...]

6.12 Genetic screening should be prohibited or limited to cases explicitly authorized by national legislation. [...]

6.14. (1) If workers are monitored they should be informed in advance of the reasons for monitoring, the time schedule, the methods and techniques used and the data to be collected, and the employer must minimize the intrusion on the privacy of workers. [...]

7. Security of personal data
7.1. Employers should ensure that personal data are protected by such security safeguards as are reasonable in the circumstances to guard against loss and unauthorized access, use, modification or disclosure.

8. Storage of personal data
8.1. The storage of personal data should be limited to data gathered consistent with the principles on the collection of personal data in this Code.

8.2. Personal data covered by medical confidentiality should be stored only by personnel bound by rules on medical secrecy and should be maintained apart from all other personal data. [...]

8.5. Personal data should be stored only for so long as it is justified by the specific purposes for which they have been collected unless:

(a) a worker wishes to be on a list of potential job candidates for a specific period;

(b) the personal data are required to be kept by national legislation; or

(c) the personal data are required by an employer or a worker for any legal proceedings to prove any matter to do with an existing or former employment relationship. [...]

10. Communication of personal data
[...]

10.6. Personal data should be internally available only to specifically authorized users, who should have access only to such personal data as are needed for the fulfilment of their particular tasks. [...]

11. Individual rights
11.1. Workers should have the right to be regularly notified of the personal data held about them and the processing of that personal data.

11.2. Workers should have access to all their personal data, irrespective of whether the personal data are processed by automated systems or are kept in a particular manual file regarding the individual worker or in any other file which includes workers' personal data.

11.3. The workers' right to know about the processing of their personal data should include the right to examine and obtain a copy of any records to the extent that the data contained in the record includes that worker's personal data. [...]

11.6. Workers should have the right to have access to medical data concerning them through a medical professional of their choice. [...]

11.8. Employers should, in the event of a security investigation, have the right to deny the worker access to that worker's personal data until the close of the investigation and to the extent that the purposes of the investigation would be threatened. No decision concerning the employment relationship should be taken, however, before the worker has had access to all the worker's personal data. [...]

11.13. In any legislation, regulation, collective agreement, work rules or policy developed consistent with the provisions of this code, there should be specified an avenue of redress for workers to challenge the employer's compliance with the instrument. Procedures should be established to receive and respond to any complaint lodged by workers. The complaint process should be easily accessible to workers and be simple to use.

12. Collective rights

[...]

12.2. The workers' representatives, where they exist, and in conformity with national law and practice, should be informed and consulted:

(a) concerning the introduction or modification of automated systems that process worker's personal data;

(b) before the introduction of any electronic monitoring of workers' behaviour in the workplace;

(c) about the purpose, contents and the manner of administering and interpreting any questionnaires and tests concerning the personal data of the workers.

Video and telephone surveillance

The monitoring of workers during working hours, and sometimes also outside them, is an extremely delicate issue. Unquestionably employers have the right and sometimes also the obligation to establish systems of control and monitoring in their companies, with a view to avoiding damage to their interests, just as they do for security reasons. Nevertheless, protection of the dignity and the private life of the worker require that these controls be limited. In France, a Court of Appeal has disregarded evidence obtained by hidden surveillance, stating that such monitoring offends the dignity of employees and creates a climate of distrust, contrary to the duties of loyalty and good faith implied in the contract of employment. In another case, the Court of Cassation held that evidence collected by a private investigator could not be used in litigation when the employee concerned was not aware of this means of investigation. However, use of hidden surveillance could be admitted where the purpose was to determine whether an employee was committing a criminal act, rather than just a breach of contract, as ruled by the Italian Court of Cassation.[127] Courts in Belgium have taken the view that it is not permissible to spy on employees during their work activities with a video camera as this constitutes a violation of the privacy to which an employee is entitled, even during working hours; these methods violate Article 16 of the law on contracts of employment, which provides that employers and employees have a duty of mutual respect.[128] A similar criterion was followed in the Netherlands where it was considered that the installation of video surveillance cameras constituted in principle a violation of the workers' rights to privacy, which could only be justified by urgent necessity.[129]

In Chile in 2006, in a case brought by two unions, the Supreme Court decided that surveillance of workers by video cameras was illegal when its purpose was to monitor when and how the employees work, as this affected their right to privacy and their dignity.[130] The Court admitted that the employer had the right to take measures with a view to protecting his property and workers' safety, including if necessary video cameras. However, given the nature of that device, use must be kept within a legal framework, which was provided by both the labour code and overall protection of the fundamental rights of the workers, including that of respect for privacy, private life and dignity guaranteed by the Constitution. It further recalled that in keeping with the labour code, video surveillance must be expressly provided for in the enterprise's internal regulations; it must be brought to the workers' attention; and must be used only with the specific purpose for which it has been envisaged, that is, to survey a place, not an individual.

Labour courts in a number of other Latin American countries, for example Argentina, have reached similar conclusions.[131] In Canada also, an arbitration

---

127 Cases cited by Menachem Goldberg, 'Privacy of the employee as a human right', in R. Blanpain and R. Ben-Israel (eds), *Labour law, human rights and social justice* (The Hague, Kluwer Law International, 2001).

128 Case Soc. Kron., Labour Court of Brussels, decision of 26 March 1990, cited by F. Hendrickx, 'Belgian Law', in R. Blanpain (ed.), op. cit., p. 68.

129 See Taufan C.B. Homan, 'Dutch Law', in R. Blanpain (ed.), op. cit., p. 103.

130 Writ of Protection Case 5234-2005, Supreme Court, 24 October 2005.

131 See, for example, in Argentina, a decision by the National Court of Appeal on Labour, VI Chamber, 15 July 2002, Figueroa, *Sergio A.* v. *Compañía de Servicios Hoteleros S.A.*, in *Jurisprudencia Argentina*, DT 2003-A, 818.

award held that a decision to dismiss a worker because he was moving house at a time when he refused to work as a driver on the grounds of back pain (evidence for which was provided by illegal videotaping) should be annulled as the evidence was obtained illegally (see box 5.15). Yet some exceptions are admitted. In Belgium, a decision of the Court of Cassation considered that Article 8 of the ECHR did not prevent an employer from installing a secret video camera when suspicion of robberies in their establishment existed. However, it should be noted that in Belgium monitoring by cameras has been regulated by a national collective agreement that establishes a limited list of instances in which video surveillance can be authorized, for example when such a measure is necessary to protect the company's assets.[132]

The decisions cited above imply that video cameras, or other means of electronic surveillance of the workers, are not forbidden as such; but they must meet specified and legally admitted purposes, and take due account of the workers' fundamental rights, including the right to privacy.

Box 5.15 Canada: Video surveillance not admissible under federal privacy legislation[133]

M.R., a driver with RTL, was dismissed after the employer's private investigator video-taped him moving his household's furniture when he was supposed to be injured.

In February 2002 M.R., a truck driver with RTL had sustained a lower back injury on the job. He missed four days work, for which he collected compensation benefits. M.R.'s doctor further advised that as a result of his back injuries he should not return to work as a truck driver. He was then assigned clerical and administrative duties. At some point his supervisor felt that M.R. was malingering in order to delay return to work as a driver, and hired a private investigator to put him under surveillance at his residence. In April 2002 M.R. was videotaped loading furniture into a pickup truck and was subsequently dismissed from his job on the grounds that he had lied when he had maintained that he had back pain. M.R. brought a complaint against his dismissal, which in accordance with Federal Canadian Law was heard by an adjudicator.

---

132 Collective Agreement No. 68 of 16 June 1998 concerning the protection of workers' private life in relation to the monitoring by means of cameras at the workplace; available online at http://www.cnt-nar.be.

133 *Lancaster's Federal Labour & Employment Law Reporter* (Toronto, Ontario, Lancaster House, 2003), Vol. 3, No. 7/8, July/August.

> The adjudicator ruled that the videotape surveillance involved the collection of information within the meaning of the federal Personal Information Protection and Electronic Documents Act (PIPEDA). Under this law the collection of personal information without the knowledge and consent of the individual is permitted only 'if it is reasonable to expect that the collection with the knowledge or consent of the individual would compromise the availability or the accuracy of the information and the collection is reasonable for purposes relating to investigating a breach of an agreement or the contraventions of the laws of Canada or a province'. The arbitrator noted that M.R. had no disciplinary record, and the employer had a doctor's note confirming his impairment. He further considered that if the employer really thought that M.R. was malingering he could have required an independent medical examination. In the arbitrator's view, 'the collection of this personal information in the form of video surveillance tape was not reasonable for any purpose related to the investigation of a breach of the employment agreement'.
>
> Without the tape the employer did not have a case. The arbitrator ruled that M.R. had been unjustly dismissed. Accordingly, M.R. was awarded 58 weeks' salary, plus a portion of his legal costs.

A similar reasoning would seem to apply to the monitoring of telephone conversations and the use of email by employees. In 1997 a decision of the European Court of Human Rights, in *Halford* v. *United Kingdom*, considered that the monitoring of private telephone calls made from the workplace by an English police officer, without the employee's consent, was a breach of Article 8 of the European Convention on Human Rights. In 2001, in the famous *Nikon* case, the French Supreme Court overturned a decision by a Court of Appeal, saying that an employee has a right to privacy at the workplace during working hours and that the employer does not have the right to access an employee's personal email, even when employees are forbidden to use the computer at work for personal use.

Some qualification to this approach was, however, made in a recent decision by the Brazilian Superior Labour Court, which upheld the employer's right to obtain evidence to discharge an employee by monitoring the latter's professional email. In that case the monitoring of email was undertaken by an insurance company after it was brought to its attention that the corporate email system was being used by the employee to send pornography to his colleagues.[134] The Brazilian labour courts now understand that employers

---

134 A similar case was reported in the Netherlands, where an employee working at the

may, on a 'moderate, general and impersonal basis', monitor incoming and outgoing messages sent and received in the company's email system for the strict purpose of avoiding misuse, and to the extent that such misuse may result in losses to the company. In short, while monitoring and surveillance of workers might constitute an intrusion on their right to privacy, there are some situations where the courts may be ready to accept that an employer *can* use such means to gather evidence of a worker's dishonesty.

Box 5.16 The interception of telephone conversations made from an employee's workplace: *Halford* v. *United Kingdom*[135]

Ms Halford was appointed to the rank of Assistant Chief Constable with the Merseyside Police. Following a refusal to promote her, Ms Halford commenced proceedings in the Industrial Tribunal claiming that she had been discriminated against on grounds of sex. She alleged that certain members of the Merseyside Police Authority had launched a 'campaign' against her in response to her complaint to the Industrial Tribunal. This took the form of leaks to the press and interception of her home and her office telephone calls for the purposes of obtaining information to be used against her in the discrimination proceedings. She claimed a breach of Article 8 of the European Convention on Human Rights (ECHR).[136]

The Government of the United Kingdom submitted that telephone calls made by Ms Halford from her workplace fell outside the protection of Article 8 of the ECHR because she could have had no reasonable expectation of privacy in relation to them. At the hearing before the Court, counsel for the Government expressed the view that an employer should in principle, without the prior knowledge of the employee, be able to monitor calls made by the latter on telephones provided by the employer.

Department of Justice was dismissed in 1998 after it was discovered that he collected pornography from the internet and used the email account provided by his employer to distribute the material (see T.C.B. Homan, 'Dutch Law', in R. Blanpain (ed.), op. cit., p. 96).

135 *Halford* v. *United Kingdom* (1997) EHRR 523 (25 June 1997).
136 Article 8 of the ECHR provides:

1. Everyone has the right to respect for his private and family life, his home and his correspondence. 2. There shall be no interference by a public authority with the exercise of this right except such as is in accordance with the law and is necessary in a democratic society in the interests of national security, public safety or the economic well-being of the country, for the prevention of disorder or crime, for the protection of health or morals, or for the protection of the rights and freedoms of others.

The Court held, however, that telephone calls made from business premises as well as from the home may be covered by the notions of 'private life' and 'correspondence' within the meaning of para. 1 of Article 8 of the ECHR. It considered that:

> There is no evidence of any warning having been given to Ms Halford, as a user of the internal telecommunications system operated at the Merseyside police headquarters, that calls made on that system would be liable to interception. She would, the Court considers, have had a reasonable expectation of privacy for such calls, which expectation was moreover reinforced by a number of factors. As Assistant Chief Constable she had sole use of her office where there were two telephones, one of which was specifically designated for her private use. Furthermore, she had been given the assurance, in response to a memorandum, that she could use her office telephones for the purposes of her sex-discrimination case.

For these reasons, the Court concluded that the conversations held by Ms Halford on her office telephones fell within the scope of the notions of 'private life' and 'correspondence' and that Article 8 was therefore applicable to that part of her complaint. Furthermore, it held that the evidence justified the conclusion that there was a reasonable likelihood that calls made by Ms Halford from her office were intercepted by the Merseyside police with the primary aim of gathering material to assist in the defence of the sex-discrimination proceedings brought against them. This interception constituted an 'interference by a public authority', within the meaning of Article 8, para. 2, with the exercise of Ms Halford's right to respect for her private life and correspondence.

The Court also discussed whether that interference was 'in accordance with the law'. It considered that:

> this expression does not only necessitate compliance with domestic law, but also relates to the quality of that law, requiring it to be compatible with the rule of law. In the context of secret measures of surveillance or interception of communications by public authorities, because of the lack of public scrutiny and the risk of misuse of power, the domestic law must provide some protection to the individual against arbitrary interference with Article 8 rights. Thus, the domestic law must be sufficiently clear in its terms to give citizens an adequate indication as to the circumstances in and conditions on which public authorities are empowered to resort to any such secret measures.

Freedom of thought and expression

Advances in the matter of protection of freedom of expression at the workplace have also been recorded. While it is a fundamental right, it is also true that its use by the worker, inside or outside the workplace, can conflict with a duty of loyalty towards the employer, which is implicit in all contracts of employment. Yet, as observed by eminent German scholar Manfred Weiss, 'the recourse to the freedom of expression has led to a very interesting trend. The huge amount of case law in this area clearly shows that, compared to the 1950s, more weight is given to freedom of expression, at the same time reducing the relevance of the duty of loyalty and the duty not to disturb the 'peace' in the establishment.'[137] This remark, which has been made specifically in respect to German statute law and case law, would also seem to be applicable to many other countries.

Perhaps the greatest problems in this respect arise when workers make use of that right to criticize their company or denounce illicit facts or reprehensible practices of the company, knowledge of which they have gained by virtue of their employment. Known as *whistle-blowing*, legal protection of this right has been the subject of considerable legislative development, for example in Australia[138] and the United Kingdom.[139]

Less controversial is the right to make public declarations, even though they affect a company's public image. The French Court of Cassation has confirmed that freedom of expression can be fully exerted outside the scope of an enterprise, even though measures can still be taken to prevent or sanction abuses.[140] However, it would seem somewhat more difficult to protect freedom of expression in respect to declarations made within the scope of an enterprise; this would explain why France has considered it necessary to address this question in the laws introduced by Minister of Labour Jean Auroux in 4 August 1982, which, inter alia, confer immunity on wage-earners for their declarations formulated within a meeting concerning their conditions of work. This right was acknowledged in the case of *Clavaud*. In an interview with a local newspaper, Mr Clavaud, a worker in a chemical factory, had talked about the working conditions in the firm in which he worked, describing one of his nightshifts. He was then dismissed by his employer on

---

137 Manfred Weiss, 'The interface between constitution and labour law in Germany', in *Comparative Labor Law and Policy Journal* (2005), Vol. 26, No. 2, p. 197.

138 Protected Disclosures Act 1994 (New South Wales); Whistleblowers Protection Act 1994 (Queensland); Whistleblowers Protection Act 1993 (South Australia).

139 Public Interest Disclosure Act 1998; available online at http://www.opsi.gov.uk.

140 Court of Cassation, decision of 28 April 1988, *Droit Social*, p. 428.

the grounds he had discredited the firm, something that was not compatible with obligations arising out of his contract of employment. The Court of Cassation held, however, that this dismissal was null and void as it considered that the worker had been victim of retaliation because he had exercised his constitutional right to freedom of expression.[141]

By contrast it would seem that the courts have taken a more restrictive position in the United States. In the cases *Pavolini* v. *Bard-Air Corporation*[142] and *United States* v. *Robel*[143] it was held that the First Amendment, which guarantees freedom of speech, does not apply in labour relations, so that the dismissal of a worker for having carried out certain acts of a political nature does *not* violate the Constitution. In *Rendell-Baker* v. *Kohn*,[144] the Supreme Court held that the decision of a private school to dismiss a group of teachers, hired by virtue of public subsidies, as a consequence of their sending a letter to a local newspaper criticizing the people responsible for the centre, did not violate their constitutional right to freedom of speech.[145] More generally, the courts have accepted a number of restrictions on freedom of speech and the participation in political activities by civil servants. For example, the US Supreme Court has upheld the constitutionality of a law that prohibits most federal and many state employees from taking an active part in political campaigns or the management of political parties, even though they have undertaken political activities during off-duty hours and they have not identified themselves as government employees.[146] Similarly, some decisions imply that a government employee's freedom of expression can be limited to the extent of subjecting the employee to removal from office for public statements critical of a superior's policy decisions if the statements reasonably result in diminished personal confidence in the worker on the part of the person to whom the worker reports, especially if the affected employee has policy-making or advisory responsibilities.[147]

---

141 Cass. Soc., 28 February 1988, *SA Dunlop France* c. *Clavaud, V. Droit Social,* 1988, p. 428, with note by Couturier.

142 *Pavolini* v. *Bard-Air Corporation.,* 352 U.S. 292 (1956).

143 *United States* v. *Robel,* 389 U.S. 258 (1967). Mr Robel was a member of the Communist Party. He had been dismissed by virtue of the provisions held in the 1950 Subversive Activities Control Act. The right in conflict was that of the freedom of expression.

144 *Rendell-Baker* v. *Kohn,* 457 U.S. 830 (1982).

145 This judgment contrasts with the solution in *Millonas* v. *Williams,* adopted by a federal court (691 F. 2e 931, 1982), which considered the decision of a private school to expel a group of students who had complained that the centre was using polygraphs to detect lies and censoring their mail, which constituted a breach of their constitutional liberties.

146 5 U.S.C. §§ 1501–1503; *U.S. Civil Service Commission* v. *National Association of Letter Carriers,* 413 U.S. 548 (1973).

147 *Rutan* v. *Republican Party,* 497 U.S. 62 (1990); *Rankin* v. *McPherson,* 483 U.S. 378 (1987); *Branti* v. *Finkel,* 445 U.S. 507 at n.14 (1980).

Chapter 6

Regional perspectives

The European Union

The emergence of a supranational labour law

Until the late 1970s, international labour law was made up almost exclusively of ILO standards. While this is still so in many countries, it is no longer the case in the European region, because European Community (EC) law in the field of labour and employment nowadays has a significant bearing on the shaping of domestic law in the 27 European Union Member States[1] and beyond. EC law is also relevant for three of the four European Free Trade Area (EFTA) members that have agreed to set up the European Economic Area (EEA)[2] with the EU. It is also widely used by several other States in Europe, who – though not EU Members – refer to the *acquis communautaire* when they review and revise their domestic law, including labour law. This is certainly the case for EU candidate countries Croatia, Turkey and the former Yugoslav Republic of Macedonia, as well as for Albania, both entities of Bosnia-Herzegovina,[3] Montenegro and Serbia, whose labour laws draw inspiration from EC law in many respects. Therefore, when one talks about international labour law, it is now essential to give due consideration to international legislation and overall social and labour policies adopted within the framework of the European Union (see box 6.1), as well as to ILO standards. It is equally indispensable to be acquainted with an increasingly important number of landmark decisions by the European Court of Justice (ECJ).

---

1 Since 1 January 2007, the EU Member States are Austria, Belgium, Bulgaria, Czech Republic, Cyprus, Denmark, Estonia, Finland, France, Germany, Greece, Hungary, Ireland, Italy, Latvia, Lithuania, Luxembourg, Malta, the Netherlands, Poland, Portugal, Romania, Slovakia, Slovenia, Spain, Sweden and the United Kingdom.
2 Iceland, Liechtenstein and Norway. Although a member of EFTA, Switzerland has not joined the EEA.
3 The Muslim-Croat Federation of Bosnia and Herzegovina (BiH) and the Republika Srpska. Both entities have a distinct competence to legislate on most issues, and indeed have formally distinct labour laws, though the respective contents are very similar.

Box 6.1 Other relevant European standards in the field of labour law

Apart from EC law, attention should be drawn to a number of international instruments that have been adopted within the framework of the Council of Europe. The most well known of these is the European Social Charter[4] of 1961, which was revised in 1996. The Charter sets out a list of fundamental social rights that are to be respected by all of the Council of Europe members. The legal position of the Charter vis-à-vis national law is comparable to that of ILO standards, that is, it supersedes any domestic legislation stipulating otherwise, in the case of a monist state, and it calls for implementation through national law or regulations in a dualist system. Its follow-up procedures have very largely drawn inspiration from the ILO supervisory machinery, as monitoring is based on national annual reports, which are examined by an independent European Committee of Social Rights (ECSR). The Committee decides whether or not the situation in the countries concerned is in conformity with the Charter. Its decisions, known as 'conclusions', are published every year. If a State takes no action on a Committee's decision that it does not comply with the Charter, a Committee of Ministers addresses a recommendation to that State, asking it to change the situation in law and/or in practice. In addition, under a protocol opened for signature in 1995, which came into force in 1998, complaints about violations of the Charter may be lodged with the European Committee of Social Rights.[5] Though not enforceable before a court, the conclusions of the ECSR and follow-up procedures have doubtless been influential in recent changes to the labour laws of a number of Council of Europe members.

Another important international source is the European Convention on Human Rights, especially Articles 6, 8, 11 and 14, which has provided the legal basis for some important decisions by the European Court on Human Rights relating to the respect for the fundamental human rights of workers at the workplace, in particular freedom of religion, non-discrimination, especially on the ground of religion and political opinion, freedom of association and protection of privacy.[6]

Yet there is nothing to suggest that labour and social issues were in the minds of the founding fathers of the European Union when the Treaty of Rome[7] was

---

4 Detailed information about the European Social Charter is available at http://www.coe.int.
5 At present 47 states have joined the Council of Europe. Thirty-nine states have ratified the Social Charter, of which 14 states have accepted the collective complaints procedures.
6 Detailed information on the ECHR is available at http://www.echr.coe.int.
7 The EC Treaty.

signed in 1957. On the contrary, in its original formulation the Treaty of Rome was meant to create a common market, within which goods, services, capital and labour were to circulate freely. Apart from Article 39 of the Treaty of the European Community (hereafter EC) (ex Article 48 EC) which provides for freedom of movement for workers, and Article 141 EC (ex Article 119 EC) on the principle of equal pay for male and female workers for equal work or work of equal value, the EC Treaty did not include any other provisions with social value. So it was not easy to reach today's situation where the existence of a European Social Model can no longer be seriously challenged, even though the content of that model is controversial. Indeed, there is heated discussion between those who hold that the social glass is half empty, those who consider that it is half full, those who feel that it is already completely full, and still others who argue that it is now overflowing.

When the Treaty of Rome was signed, it was understood that some of its provisions that did possess a social value, such as the clauses on free movement and equal pay above, were intended to provide a better governance of the Common Market rather than to protect the workers. It was not until 1976 that the European Court of Justice recalled that the equal pay principle had both economic and social substance in the *Defrenne II*[8] case (Chapter 4, box 4.1). Similarly, the principle of freedom of movement for workers was, in a way, an extension of the overall principle of free movement of goods and capital, rather than a positive workers' right.

Nevertheless, from the 1970s on, the European Community began to adopt legislation in matters such as collective dismissals (1975), equal pay (1975) and equal treatment between men and women (1976), protection of the workers' rights in the case of transfer of enterprises or part thereof (1977), and the protection of workers in the case of the insolvency of the employer (1980). It is true that with perhaps the sole exception of the Equal Treatment Directive of 1976, all the other Directives were adopted in accordance with Article 94 EC (ex Article 100), which confers competence on the European Community to adopt legislation for better governance of the Common Market. Yet the fact is that all these rules had the effect of offering legal protection to workers in areas which, in many cases, were not addressed under their own domestic law.

A further step was taken with the adoption of the Community Charter of Fundamental Social Rights of Workers on 9 December 1989, despite tough opposition from the United Kingdom, who feared that the European Community was trying to expand its field of action beyond the limits set out

---

8 *Defrenne v. Société Anonyme Belge de Navigation Aérienne* [1976] ECR 455. See Chapter 4, Box 4.1.

by the EC Treaty. With the adoption of the Charter, the Community's concern about the protection of workers took on a political, if not a legal, basis, which was different from strictly Common Market concerns. The Charter set out 19 key principles, on which the European Social Model was to be developed.[9] Though the Charter does *not* have a legally binding effect, it expresses a political will to develop those rights, either at the national or the Community level, or both, in keeping with the subsidiarity principle (box 6.2).

Box 6.2 The principle of subsidiarity in EC law

The principle of subsidiarity is a fundamental rule in European Community law. It is based on Article 5 EC (ex Article 3b EC), which provides for the following:

> The Community shall act within the limits of the powers conferred upon it by this Treaty and of the objectives assigned to it therein.
>
> In areas which do not fall within its exclusive competence, the Community shall take action, in accordance with the principle of subsidiarity, only if and insofar as the objectives of the proposed action cannot be sufficiently achieved by the Member States and can therefore, by reason of the scale or effects of the proposed action, be better achieved by the Community.
>
> Any action by the Community shall not go beyond what is necessary to achieve the objectives of this Treaty.

The next step was taken in the Inter-Government Conference of 1992 on political union, in which an agreement was adopted on social policy. Again it was opposed by the United Kingdom Government, and so took the form of a Social Protocol annexed to the Treaty on European Union, or Treaty of Maastricht, binding on 11 of the then 12 EC Member States. Later on, when the New Labour Party came to power in the United Kingdom, both the Charter and the Social Protocol were accepted by the UK Government. They were subsequently introduced in the Treaty of Amsterdam, 1997, whose most

---

9 The Charter contains sections relating to free movement of workers, employment and wages, improvement of working and living conditions, social protection, freedom of association and collective bargaining, training, equality of treatment of men and women, information, consultation and participation of the workers, health and safety protection at work, protection of children, protection of older workers and of disabled workers.

important innovation was new Title VIII, which called for 'a coordinated strategy for employment and particularly for promoting a skilled, trained and adaptable workforce and labour markets responsive to economic change with a view to achieving the objectives defined in Article 2 of the Treaty on European Union and in Article 2 of this Treaty' (Article 125 EC). Later, the Charter of Fundamental Rights of the European Union, signed by the Members of the EU in Nice in February 2001, also included an important chapter on the rights of workers, which to a very large extent was drawn from the 1989 Charter. Though not legally binding, the Charter can be used as an important interpretative source when applying EC law.[10]

Box 6.3 The Charter of Fundamental Rights of the European Union[11]

[...]

Article 5
Prohibition of slavery and forced labour
1. No one shall be held in slavery or servitude.
2. No one shall be required to perform forced or compulsory labour.
3. Trafficking in human beings is prohibited.
[...]

Article 7
Respect for private and family life
Everyone has the right to respect for his or her private and family life, home and communications.

Article 8
Protection of personal data
1. Everyone has the right to the protection of personal data concerning him or her.
2. Such data must be processed fairly for specified purposes and on

---

10 The Charter was to be given binding effect under the EU Constitution, adopted in 2004, but only in relation to the Community institutions and national States *when they were implementing EC law* (emphasis added). It was thus not intended to have 'horizontal' effect. However, the Constitution was rejected by popular referenda in France and the Netherlands, and did not come into force.

11 Excerpts from the Charter of Fundamental Rights of the European Union, *Official Journal of the European Communities*, C 364/01 (Luxembourg, 2000). Available http://www.europarl.europa.eu [21 Nov. 2008].

the basis of the consent of the person concerned or some other legitimate basis laid down by law. Everyone has the right of access to data which has been collected concerning him or her, and the right to have it rectified.

3. Compliance with these rules shall be subject to control by an independent authority. [...]

Article 12
Freedom of assembly and of association
1. Everyone has the right to freedom of peaceful assembly and to freedom of association at all levels, in particular in political, trade union and civic matters, which implies the right of everyone to form and to join trade unions for the protection of his or her interests. [...]

Article 15
Freedom to choose an occupation and right to engage in work
1. Everyone has the right to engage in work and to pursue a freely chosen or accepted occupation.
2. Every citizen of the Union has the freedom to seek employment, to work, to exercise the right of establishment and to provide services in any Member State. [...]

Article 21
Non-discrimination
1. Any discrimination based on any ground such as sex, race, colour, ethnic or social origin, genetic features, language, religion or belief, political or any other opinion, membership of a national minority, property, birth, disability, age or sexual orientation shall be prohibited.
2. Within the scope of application of the Treaty establishing the European Community and of the Treaty on European Union, and without prejudice to the special provisions of those Treaties, any discrimination on grounds of nationality shall be prohibited. [...]

Article 23
Equality between men and women
Equality between men and women must be ensured in all areas, including employment, work and pay.
The principle of equality shall not prevent the maintenance or adoption of measures providing for specific advantages in favour of the under-represented sex. [...]

Article 27
Workers' right to information and consultation within the undertaking
Workers or their representatives must, at the appropriate levels, be guaranteed information and consultation in good time in the cases and under the conditions provided for by Community law and national laws and practices.

Article 28
Right of collective bargaining and action
Workers and employers, or their respective organisations, have, in accordance with Community law and national laws and practices, the right to negotiate and conclude collective agreements at the appropriate levels and, in cases of conflicts of interest, to take collective action to defend their interests, including strike action.

Article 29
Right of access to placement services
Everyone has the right of access to a free placement service.

Article 30
Protection in the event of unjustified dismissal
Every worker has the right to protection against unjustified dismissal, in accordance with Community law and national laws and practices.

Article 31
Fair and just working conditions
1. Every worker has the right to working conditions which respect his or her health, safety and dignity.
2. Every worker has the right to limitation of maximum working hours, to daily and weekly rest periods and to an annual period of paid leave.

Article 32
Prohibition of child labour and protection of young people at work
The employment of children is prohibited. The minimum age of admission to employment may not be lower than the minimum school-leaving age, without prejudice to such rules as may be more favourable to young people and except for limited derogations.
Young people admitted to work must have working conditions appropriate to their age and be protected against economic exploitation and any work likely to harm their safety, health or physical, mental, moral or social development or to interfere with their education. [...]

Article 33
Family and professional life
1. The family shall enjoy legal, economic and social protection.
2. To reconcile family and professional life, everyone shall have the right to protection from dismissal for a reason connected with maternity and the right to paid maternity leave and to parental leave following the birth or adoption of a child.

Article 34
Social security and social assistance
1. The Union recognises and respects the entitlement to social security benefits and social services providing protection in cases such as maternity, illness, industrial accidents, dependency or old age, and in the case of loss of employment, in accordance with the rules laid down by Community law and national laws and practices.
2. Everyone residing and moving legally within the European Union is entitled to social security benefits and social advantages in accordance with Community law and national laws and practices.
3. In order to combat social exclusion and poverty, the Union recognises and respects the right to social and housing assistance so as to ensure a decent existence for all those who lack sufficient resources, in accordance with the rules laid down by Community law and national laws and practices. [. . .]

Article 51
Scope
1. The provisions of this Charter are addressed to the institutions and bodies of the Union with due regard for the principle of subsidiarity and to the Member States only when they are implementing Union law. They shall therefore respect the rights, observe the principles and promote the application thereof in accordance with their respective powers.
2. This Charter does not establish any new power or task for the Community or the Union, or modify powers and tasks defined by the Treaties.

The contribution of EC law to the body of labour law has been both political and legal. It is political in the sense that what was originally just an economic area – the Common Market – later expanded to include social values and labour regulations. This suggests that it is technically possible for countries which share a common market to formulate and adopt fair rules for labour and social issues, so that none of the stakeholders of that common market benefit from trade advantages obtained from sub-standard labour. Certainly, nobody would deny that it is much more difficult to do this on a worldwide scale than on a regional one, but the difficulty stems from a lack of political will rather than from technical and legal hurdles. In addition, it is probably thanks to the same political will that while workers' rights have suffered some erosion (or even significant setbacks), almost everywhere in the world such erosion has not been as serious in the European Union as it has been elsewhere.

Similarly, while collective bargaining has suffered recurrent attrition in most parts of the world, it has benefited from both institutional and political support within the European Union. Indeed, under the Treaty of the European Community, collective bargaining was singled out as both a means of implementing (Article 137 EC) and of creating (Article 138 EC) European Community law. In effect, the Treaty has provided that Member States may entrust management and labour, at their joint request, with the implementation of Directives adopted in the field of labour. Under Article 138 EC (ex Article 118b EC), a legal base was granted for the collective negotiation by the social partners at the European level of Community-wide framework agreements, which would eventually take the form of EC Directives addressed to the Member States. This procedure has already led to the adoption of three Community Directives of general character[12] and two of sectoral reach.[13] In addition, the European-level social partners have agreed on a number of framework agreements that, unlike the previous ones, have not been transposed into EC Directives addressed to EU Member States. Instead, these agreements are to be implemented in each EU Member State through national collective bargaining or by other means that rely on social dialogue.[14]

---

12 Namely Council Directive 96/34/EC of 3 June 1996 on the framework agreement on parental leave concluded by UNICE, CEEP and ETUC, *OJ*, L 145, 19 June 1996, pp. 4–9 ; Council Directive 97/81/EC on the framework agreement on part-time work, *OJ*, L 014 of 20 January 1998; Council Directive 1999/70/EC of 28 June 1999 concerning the framework agreement on fixed-term work concluded by ETUC, UNICE and CEEP, *OJ*, L 175, 10 July 1999, pp. 43–48.

13 Council Directive 2000/79/EC of 27 November 2000 concerning the European Agreement on the Organisation of Working Time of Mobile Workers in Civil Aviation concluded by the Association of European Airlines (AEA), the European Transport Workers' Federation (ETF), the European Cockpit Association (ECA), the European Regions Airline Association (ERA) and the International Air Carrier Association (IACA), *OJ*, L 302/57 of 1 December 2000, and Council Directive 2005/47/EC of 18 July 2005 on the Agreement between the Community of European Railways (CER) and the European Transport Workers' Federation (ETF) on certain aspects of the working conditions of mobile workers engaged in interoperable cross-border services in the railway sector, *OJ*, L 195, 27 July 2005, pp. 15–17.

14 Namely, *Framework agreement on telework* (Brussels, 2002); *Framework agreement on work-related stress* (Brussels, 2004); and *Framework agreement on harassment and violence at work* (Brussels, 2007). All available at: http://www.ec.europa.eu [21 Nov. 2008].

A further political impact of the European Union's social policy can be traced in the overall evolution of labour law in the former communist States of Central and Eastern Europe. Since 1989, when these countries repudiated the communist system, they have had to review and revise their overall legal systems, including their labour law, so as to build a new institutional framework consistent with political pluralism and a market economy. At that time an ideological choice was left open for them, so that they could either reformulate their labour laws and labour relations systems in keeping with a neoliberal model (that is, a model based on the individual contract of employment), such as the one prevailing in North America, or reformulate it on the prevailing patterns in Western Europe, thus bringing them closer to EC law and values. Though these countries were put under strong pressure to adopt the first of these models, they all finally decided to bring their labour laws and labour relations closer to the second.

The legal contribution of EC law comes as much from the content of the EC norms as from its supranational nature, to which one should add the interpretative work done by the European Court of Justice. It is true that, in general, EC law does not offer a catalogue of subjects as comprehensive as that of the ILO. Also, the EC Treaty has left a number of matters, such as pay, the right of association, the right to strike or the right to impose lock-outs, out of the scope of EC law (though these issues are addressed by the ILO). Yet EC law covers an ample range of topics in the field of individual employment relations, such as contracts of employment, equal pay, non-discrimination, duration of work, protection of minors and of pregnant women, collective dismissals, and protection of workers' claims in the event of the insolvency of the employer, just as it does in the fields of occupational safety and health and information and consultation of the workers' representatives, where EC law is indeed more comprehensive than ILO standards.

Still more important is the effect of EC law on the national law of each of the EU Member States. Apart from the Treaties, which require ratification, EC law (the Regulations and Directives adopted by the EC legislative bodies) is directly binding on EU Member States, so that the traditional distinction between dualist and monist legal systems is irrelevant in respect to the relationship between EC law and the national laws of the EU Member States. Thus once an EC Regulation is adopted, a Member State has to apply it in the same way as national laws; for example, an individual can sue another individual on the basis of an EC Regulation.

The position of EC Directives is somewhat different from EC Regulations as Directives are addressed to the EU Member States, not to individuals. The EC Treaty specifies that an EC Directive 'shall be binding, as to the result to be achieved, upon each Member State to which it is addressed, but shall leave to the national authorities the choice of form and methods' (Article 249 EC, ex Article 189 EC). Nonetheless, under EC law a number of legal means exist to ensure that a Directive is applied even when a Member State has not taken measures to transpose it into national law. The European Commission can summon a State to enforce a Directive and, if it does not, can bring a complaint against that State before the European Court of Justice for failure to fulfil obligations arising out of the EC Treaty. If the Court finds that a country has failed to adequately transpose[15] an EC Directive, it can order that the State remedy this without delay, and if necessary impose on it a fixed or periodic financial penalty.

Furthermore, the EC Treaty has introduced a procedure of preliminary ruling by the ECJ, under Article 234 EC (ex Article 177 EC), which is unique in international law. This procedure is an instrument of cooperation between the ECJ and national courts, by which the ECJ provides an interpretation of Community law to the national courts to enable them to deliver judgment in cases they are hearing.[16] The preliminary ruling procedure can be started by a request from a national court or a tribunal to the ECJ to give a binding opinion on the compatibility of a national rule (including a collective agreement and even a practice) with EC law. It can be raised in any kind of litigation, for instance between an individual or a legal entity and a public authority (vertical effect) or between private individuals or legal entities (horizontal). Though the parties to the procedure may not approach the ECJ directly, they are allowed to make submissions. Similarly, the European Commission and any Member State can also intervene in the procedure.

A preliminary ruling by the ECJ is not strictly speaking a judgment (though it is called a judgment in ECJ terminology) because it is up to the national courts, not the ECJ, to adjudicate the dispute. But it directly determines the outcome of a case for which a reference for a preliminary ruling has been made, because the judge in the Member State must interpret national law, as far as possible, in the light of the opinion delivered by the ECJ.

Case law developed through this procedure has been instrumental in achieving considerable progress in the law of EU Member States in many

---

15 In accordance with the EC Treaty, Directives are binding, as to the result to be achieved, upon each Member State to whom they are addressed. However, the national authorities are left the choice of form and methods to achieve their objectives. This process is called 'transposition' in EC law. While Directives are normally transposed by national law, they may also be transposed by collective agreements, provided they are generally binding and cover all the workers and employers who were covered by the original Directive.

16 See, inter alia, Case C–112/00 *Schmidberger* [2003] ECR I–5659, para. 30, and the case law cited there.

sensitive areas, such as freedom of work and movement, equality of remuneration of men and women, and equality of treatment in employment and
occupation.[17] Some landmark decisions by the ECJ in the field of equal pay
and non-discrimination have already been referred to in Chapter 5. It was
within the context of a labour-related Directive of 1980 (EC Directive 80/987
on the protection of employees in the event of the insolvency of their
employer) that the ECJ established the principle that EU Member States are
liable for the damages caused to individuals when they have failed to
adequately implement EC law. Furthermore, it is established ECJ doctrine that
when a Directive is belatedly transposed, the date on which the national
implementing measures actually enter into force in the Member State does
not constitute the relevant point in time for assessing damages. Thus, in
Adeneler the Court ruled that:

> Such a solution would be liable seriously to jeopardize the full effectiveness
> of Community law and its uniform application by means, in particular, of
> directives [...]. It follows that a directive produces legal effects for a Member
> State to which it is addressed – and, therefore, for all the national authori-
> ties – following its publication or from the date of its notification, as the case
> may be.[18]

In the case *Francovich and Bonifaci*, the ECJ has taken the view that countries
can be made liable vis-à-vis their citizens for prejudices arising out of failure
to transpose EC directives into national law:

> The full effectiveness of Community rules would be impaired and the
> protection of the rights which they grant would be weakened if individuals
> were unable to obtain reparation when their rights are infringed by a breach
> of Community law for which a Member State can be held responsible. Such
> a possibility of reparation by the Member States is particularly indispensable
> where the full effectiveness of Community rules is subject to prior action on
> the part of the State and where, consequently, in the absence of such
> action, individuals cannot enforce before the national courts the rights
> conferred upon them by Community law.

---

17 See Tamara K. Hervey, *EC law on justifications for sex discrimination in working life*, in
    Proceedings of the VII European Congress of Labour Law of the International Society of
    Labour Law and Social Security (Geneva, ISLLSS, 2002).
18 See Case C–212/04 *Konstantinos Adeneler and Others* v. *Ellinikos Organismos Galaktos
    (ELOG)*, judgment of the Court, 4 July 2006.

It follows that the principle whereby a State must be liable for loss and damage caused to individuals by breaches of Community law for which the State can be held responsible is inherent in the system of the Treaty.[19]

The impact of certain recent ECJ rulings on labour relations in the European Union

In two recent decisions, the European Court of Justice (ECJ) has strongly qualified workers' rights to undertake collective action in an EU Member State when such action would conflict with Article 43 EC (ex Article 52 EC) that provides for freedom of establishment.[20] The first of these cases, known as the *Viking* case, arose when FSU, a Finnish-based seafarers' union, supported by the London-based International Transport Workers' Federation (ITF), threatened to undertake collective action against Viking Line ABP, a Finnish-based shipowner that intended to reflag as Estonian a Finnish-registered vessel (the *Rosella*) with a view to running the vessel with an Estonian crew, paid at Estonian, not Finnish rates. On 18 August 2004, Viking Line ABP brought an action before the High Court of Justice of England and Wales, requesting it to declare that the action taken by the ITF and FSU was contrary to Article 43 EC. It also requested an order for the withdrawal of a circular from the ITF to its affiliates, asking them to refrain from entering into negotiations with Viking or Viking Eesti, and to order FSU not to infringe the rights which Viking enjoys under Community law. By a decision of 16 June 2005, the court granted the form of order sought by Viking, on the grounds that the actual and threatened collective action by the ITF and FSU imposed restrictions on freedom of establishment contrary to Article 43 EC and, in the alternative, constituted unlawful restrictions on freedom of movement for workers and

---

19 Joined Cases C–6/90 and C–9/90 *Andrea Francovich and Danila Bonifaci and Others* v. *Italian Republic*, judgment of the Court, 19 November 1991, [1991] ECR I–5537.
20 Article 43 EC (ex Article 52 EC) provides the following:

> Within the framework of the provisions set out below, restrictions on the freedom of establishment of nationals of a Member State in the territory of another Member State shall be prohibited. Such prohibition shall also apply to restrictions on the setting up of agencies, branches or subsidiaries by nationals of any Member State established in the territory of any Member State.
> Freedom of establishment shall include the right to take up and pursue activities as self-employed persons and to set up and manage undertakings, in particular companies or firms within the meaning of the second paragraph of Article 48, under the conditions laid down for its own nationals by the law of the country where such establishment is effected, subject to the provisions of the Chapter relating to capital.

freedom to provide services under Articles 39 EC and 49 EC. Both FSU and ITF brought an appeal against this decision before the Court of Appeal, which referred the case to the ECJ for a preliminary ruling.

In its judgment of 11 December 2007, the ECJ ruled that the right to take collective action, including the right to strike, is a fundamental right which forms an integral part of the general principle of Community law. The Court, however, noted that these are not absolute rights, and may therefore be subject to certain restrictions and in particular must be reconciled with the requirements relating to rights protected under the EC Treaty. In concrete terms, the Court took the view that collective action:

> which seeks to induce a private undertaking whose registered office is in a given Member State to enter into a collective work agreement with a trade union established in that State and to apply the terms set out in that agreement to the employees of a subsidiary of that undertaking established in another Member State, constitutes a restriction within the meaning of Article 43 EC. That restriction may, in principle, be justified by an overriding reason of public interest, such as the protection of workers, provided that it is established that the restriction is suitable for ensuring the attainment of the legitimate objective pursued and does not go beyond what is necessary to achieve that objective.[21]

The Court considered that it is for the national court, not the ECJ, to assess whether collective action, such as that undertaken by the interested unions, pursued a legitimate objective and did not go beyond what is necessary to achieve that objective. In this respect it held that:

> as regards the collective action taken by FSU, even if that action – aimed at protecting the jobs and conditions of employment of the members of that union liable to be adversely affected by the reflagging of the *Rosella* – could reasonably be considered to fall, at first sight, within the objective of protecting workers, such a view would no longer be tenable if it were established that the jobs or conditions of employment at issue were not jeopardized or under serious threat.

The second case, known as the *Laval* case, arose when Bygettan, a Swedish-based union, undertook industrial action against Laval, a Latvian-based enterprise that had posted to Sweden a number of Latvian workers to work for a

---

21 Case 438/05 *International Transport Workers' Federation, Finnish Seamen's Union* v. *Viking Line ABP, OÜ Viking Line Eesti*, Decision of the Court (Grand Chamber) of 11 December 2007; available online at http://curia.europa.eu.

subsidiary company incorporated under Swedish law at a number of building sites.[22] Bygettan demanded that Laval, first, sign the collective agreement for the building sector in respect of one of the building sites, and secondly, guarantee that the Latvian workers would receive an hourly wage that was comparable to the prevailing rates in Sweden for similar workers. Byggettan declared that it was prepared to take collective action in the event that Laval failed to agree to this. Since negotiations were not successful, the union initiated a blockade of the building site in November 2004. In December 2004, the Swedish electricians' trade union commenced solidarity action which stopped all electrical work on the site. On 7 December 2004, Laval commenced proceedings before the Labour Court with a view to seeking a declaration that the industrial action undertaken against it was illegal and an order that such action should cease. It also sought an order that the trade unions pay compensation for the damage suffered. By a decision of 22 December 2004, the national court dismissed Laval's application for an interim order that the collective action should be brought to an end. However, since it wished to ascertain whether Articles 12 EC and 49 EC and Directive 96/71 precluded

---

22 Posting of workers is, in EC law, addressed by Directive 96/71/EC (*Official Journal*, L 018, 21 January 1997, pp. 1–6). This Directive applies to undertakings established in a Member State which, in the framework of the transnational provision of services, post workers to the territory of a Member State. In Article 2, this Directive defines a posted worker as 'a worker who, for a limited period, carries out his work in the territory of a Member State other than the State in which he normally works'. The Directive provides that Member States shall ensure that, whatever the law applicable to the employment relationship, the undertakings to which the Directive applies guarantee workers posted to their territory the terms and conditions of employment covering the following matters which, in the Member State where the work is carried out, are laid down:
– by law, regulation or administrative provision, and/or
– by collective agreements or arbitration awards which have been declared universally applicable within the meaning of paragraph 8, insofar as they concern the activities referred to in the Annex:
  (a) maximum work periods and minimum rest periods;
  (b) minimum paid annual holidays;
  (c) the minimum rates of pay, including overtime rates; this point does not apply to supplementary occupational retirement pension schemes;
  (d) the conditions of hiring-out of workers, in particular the supply of workers by temporary employment undertakings;
  (e) health, safety and hygiene at work;
  (f) protective measures with regard to the terms and conditions of employment of pregnant women or women who have recently given birth, of children and of young people;
  (g) equality of treatment between men and women and other provisions on non-discrimination.

trade unions from attempting, by means of collective action, to force a foreign undertaking which posts workers to Sweden to apply a Swedish collective agreement, it decided on 29 April 2005 to make a reference to the ECJ for a preliminary ruling. In its decision of 18 December 2007 the ECJ ruled that:

> Article 49 EC and Article 3 of Directive 96/71/EC of the European Parliament and of the Council of 16 December 1996[23] concerning the posting of workers in the framework of the provision of services are to be interpreted as precluding a trade union, in a Member State in which the terms and conditions of employment covering the matters referred to in Article 3(1), first subparagraph, (a) to (g) of that directive are contained in legislative provisions, save for minimum rates of pay, from attempting, by means of collective action in the form of a blockade of sites such as that at issue in the main proceedings, to force a provider of services established in another Member State to enter into negotiations with it on the rates of pay for posted workers and to sign a collective agreement the terms of which lay down, as regards some of those matters, more favourable conditions than those resulting from the relevant legislative provisions, while other terms relate to matters not referred to in Article 3 of the directive.[24]

In the Court's view, collective action such as that undertaken in the *Laval* case encompasses restrictions to Article 49 EC, which would be admissible only if the action: (a) had a legitimate aim that was compatible with the EC Treaty and was justified by overriding reasons of public interest; (b) was suitable for securing the objective pursued; and (c) did not go beyond what was necessary to achieve that objective.[25]

A third, and perhaps more far-reaching decision of the ECJ was taken in *Rüffert v. Land Niedersachsen*.[26] The dispute here related to the application of a local rule in Lower Saxony which required contracting authorities to allocate contracts for public works only to contractors who, when submitting their tenders, agreed in writing to pay their employees, in return for performance of the required services, at least the wages provided for in the collective agreement in force at the place where those services were to be performed. In this case, a German enterprise had been awarded a public works contract for

---

23 *Official Journal*, L 018, 21 January 1997, pp. 1–6.
24 C–341/05 *Laval un Partneri Ltd* v. *Svenska Byggnadsarbetareförbundet, Svenska Byggnadsarbetareförbundets avd. 1, Byggettan, Svenska Elektrikerförbundet*, judgment of the Court of 18 December 2007; available online at:http://curia.europa.eu.
25 See the *Laval* judgment, para. 101.
26 Case 346/06, judgment of the Court (Second Chamber) of 3 April 2008; available online at http://curia.europa.eu.

the structural work involved in building a prison in the Niedersachsen (Lower Saxony) *Land*. The contractor subcontracted work to an undertaking established in Poland. In summer 2004 this undertaking came under suspicion of having employed workers on the building site at wages below those provided for in the 'buildings and public works' collective agreement. After investigations began, the contract was terminated. Land Niedersachsen justified the cancellation of the contract, inter alia, on the fact that the contractor had failed to fulfill its contractual obligation to comply with the (German) collective agreement. When the case came before the courts, it was argued that the obligation to comply with the collective agreements meant that construction firms from other Member States must adapt the remuneration they pay to their workers to the higher levels in force in the area of the Federal Republic of Germany where the contract was to be performed. It was argued that such a requirement caused those undertakings to lose the competitive advantage which they enjoyed by reason of their lower wage costs, so that the obligation to comply with the collective agreements would constitute an impediment to market access for persons or undertakings from Member States other than the Federal Republic of Germany. Having regard to this question, the national court decided to stay the proceedings and refer the following question to the ECJ for a preliminary ruling:

> Does it amount to an unjustified restriction on the freedom to provide services under the EC Treaty if a public contracting authority is required by statute to award contracts for building services only to undertakings which, when lodging a tender, undertake in writing to pay their employees, when performing those services, at least the remuneration prescribed by the collective agreement in force at the place where those services are performed?

In its judgment of 3 April 2008 the Court delivered the following opinion:

> Directive 96/71/EC of the European Parliament and of the Council of 16 December 1996 concerning the posting of workers in the framework of the provision of services, interpreted in the light of Article 49 EC, precludes an authority of a Member State, in a situation such as that at issue in the main proceedings, from adopting a measure of a legislative nature requiring the contracting authority to designate as contractors for public works contracts only those undertakings which, when submitting their tenders, agree in writing to pay their employees, in return for performance of the services concerned, at least the remuneration prescribed by the collective agreement the minimum wage in force at the place where those services are performed.

All of the cases above have concerned the balance between social protection of workers and EU rules on freedom to provide services, and it cannot be denied that the ECJ rulings have in principle put freedom to provide services above the right to undertake collective action to protect the workers' interests, in the *Viking* and *Laval* cases, and above the right of EU Member States to take measures to avoid wage dumping, in the *Rüffert* case. However, it is still too early to assess the actual impact that these decisions will have on the labour law and labour relations systems of EU Member States.

Labour law in former communist countries

From a comparative perspective, the most far-reaching changes in the field of labour law are undoubtedly those that have taken place in the old Soviet Union and the countries of Central and Eastern Europe in the aftermath of the downfall of communism. Before the end of communism, all of these countries (apart from those which became independent by secession from 1990 onwards)[27] were already Members of the ILO and had ratified an important number of ILO Conventions and built up comprehensive labour law systems. However, in all cases, their labour law was based on political and economic assumptions completely different from those that prevailed in market economy democracies. Their key features could be summarized as follows.

First, it was assumed that most workers performed work or provided services in conditions of legal subordination to the State as, aside from a few exceptions, private entrepreneurship, let alone ownership of the means of production, was not compatible with the communist system. It followed that the employer's paradigm was either the great State-owned company, or a large central or local administration, which were always subordinated to the State. Hence there was barely any difference between private and public employment.

Secondly, all individuals were granted a job by the State, so that unemployment did not exist, though it did not mean that all workers had truly produc-

---

27 Fifteen new States gained independence as a result of the demise of the Soviet Union, six new States became independent after the dissolution of Yugoslavia, and former Czechoslovakia was split into two new States in 1993. Some time before, in 1990, the German Democratic Republic was dissolved and became part of the Federal Republic of Germany. It should be noted that before the dissolution of the Soviet Union, Belarus and Ukraine (but not Russia) had international Statehood and were members of both the United Nations and the ILO.

tive employment. Furthermore, the recruitment and the dismissal of workers, just like functional mobility, were subject to rigid rules. Workers could be dismissed only with the consent of the trade union, something which was in principle very difficult to obtain. In the case of unjustified dismissal, workers were entitled to reinstatement and back pay. On the other hand, workers' freedom to choose jobs was limited by both the principle of centralized management of the workforce and the fact that the State was the sole employer, so that it had coercive power to decide the type and kind of job which was to be assigned to each worker. Notoriously, the State could, and in many cases did, use this power to punish political deviants, would-be emigrants and other 'undesirables', by assigning them to the worst possible jobs. Persons evading socially useful work and leading a parasitic way of life were also liable to prosecution.[28]

Nevertheless, the most remarkable differences from labour law in market economy democracies were to be found in the field of collective labour relations. Trade unions certainly existed in the communist system and, indeed, were endowed with far-reaching powers at the enterprise and State levels, but their core role was to support the building of the socialist society under the 'enlightened' guidance of the Communist Party, as emphasized in the Brezhnevian Soviet Constitution of 1977. From the moment capitalism was abolished, there could no longer be any conflict between the interests of managers and those of the workers, let alone between the workers and the State – which was, by definition, the State of the workers and peasants under the leadership of the (single) Communist Party. Trade unions were thus intended to function as conveyor belts between the authority of the State – that is, the Party – and the workers. Although they were ostensibly elected by the rank and file, union leaders were actually bureaucrats in the administration of the State or the Party, on secondment to the trade unions. Their election was a mere formality whereby the voters rubber-stamped appointments made at the top. Instead of representing class interests, trade unions in the communist system were to represent workers' interests with regard to production, labour, welfare, living conditions and culture. In short, they were supposed to serve three purposes. The first one related to their educational and mobilization function, which made them responsible for enforcing

---

28 See, for example, the observations made by the ILO Committee of Experts on the Application of Conventions and Recommendations in respect to the application by the Soviet Union of the Forced Labour Convention, 1930 (No. 29) in ILO, Report III (Part 4A), International Labour Conference, 58th Session, Geneva, 1973, pp. 79–80; ILO, Report III (Part 4A), International Labour Conference, 59th Session, Geneva, 1974, pp. 88–89; ILO, Report III (Part 4A), International Labour Conference, 61st Session, Geneva, 1976, p. 79.

labour discipline with a view to attaining and exceeding planned production targets at the plant level – hence their efforts to organize 'socialist emulation'. Their second function was to act as administrators of social well-being by managing an extensive network of sanatoria, rest homes, housing, children's holiday camps, cultural centres and sports facilities for workers, all of which played a crucial part in everyday life, even more essential than money. Undoubtedly this is one of the reasons why practically all workers were trade union members even though there was no mandatory unionization.[29] The single union structure was the rule, even though no formal prohibition on establishing non-official unions existed.[30]

Nor could collective bargaining in communist countries be compared with that carried out in market economy democracies. In communist regimes the collective bargaining agenda was fixed by decree, and collective agreements were essentially written documents in which management and labour established their respective commitments in the context of the achievement of the enterprise's production plan. Collective agreements included other provi-

---

29 For example, in the early stages of *perestroika*, Soviet trade unions organized virtually the entire adult population of the Soviet Union, including pensioners and high school and technical school students, into 31 mega-unions at the industry level (the biggest being that of the agro-industrial sector, with 37.4 million members) to which some 713,000 primary-level unions were affiliated. The trade unions employed 7,500 occupational health and safety inspectors (in addition to over 4.6 million members who were also involved in inspection work on a voluntary basis or who served on workplace health and safety commissions). The trade unions' network of health and recreational facilities included some 1,000 sanatoria, 900 tourist resorts, 23,000 cultural clubs and centres, 19,000 libraries, some 100,000 'pioneer' camps and 25,000 sports centres. In addition, the trade unions were housed in grand and prestigious buildings in Moscow and in all of the regional capitals. The trade union daily, *Trud*, had a circulation of 20 million copies; see S. Ashwin and S. Clarke, *Russian trade unions and industrial relations in transition* (New York, Palgrave Macmillan, 2003), p. 30.

30 It is worthwhile noting that freedom of association complaints brought against the Soviet Union because of persecution suffered by people who intended to set up independent trade unions had not been challenged by the Soviet Government on the ground that pluralism was not legally permitted. Instead, the Government claimed that the people alleged to have been persecuted for trying to set up independent unions were in fact not workers at all, but ex-convicts, social dropouts, sexual harassers or individuals suffering from mental disorders. See, for example, Case No. 905, complaint against the Government of the Soviet Union presented by the International Confederation of Free Trade Unions and the World Confederation of Labour on 9 May 1978. The relevant reports are available in *Official Bulletin* (Geneva), Vol. 62, 1979, Series B, No. 1, for Interim Report No. 190 (paras 361–388); Vol. 62, 1979, Series B, No. 3, for Interim Report No. 197 (paras 592–640); Vol. 63, 1980, Series B, No. 3 and Vol. 64, 1981, Series B, No. 1, for Final Report No. 207 (paras 100–130).

sions, relating, for example, to the development of 'socialist emulation', professional improvement and labour discipline (which was very poor in socialist enterprises), but did not deal with pay issues as wages were centrally fixed by the State. With the exception of Poland, collective agreements were exclusively negotiated at the enterprise level and were so closely linked to the State plan that in most communist countries no collective agreement existed at all in non-productive sectors such as education and health. Last but certainly not least, though strikes were not ruled out, in terms of communist principles, the absence of capitalism rendered the reason for striking redundant; furthermore, strikes could be regarded as a form of sabotage against socialist property, and strikers could be made liable to prosecution.[31]

Labour law and transition

Some changes had already taken place during the last few years of the communist regimes, mainly in countries such as Hungary and Poland, just as in the Soviet Union after the arrival of Gorbachev in 1985.[32] None of this was, however, comparable to the changes that followed the fall of the communist regimes in Central Europe after 1989 and the dissolution of the Soviet Union in December 1991. In general these changes took place in two stages. During the first stage, pluralist democracy was introduced; at the same time the transition towards a market economy was put on track. It is against this framework that the former communist countries did away with the single-union and communist-dominated trade union structure; they also introduced free collective bargaining and recognized the right to strike.

Largely, these new regulatory frameworks drew inspiration from ILO standards (namely Conventions Nos. 87 and 98) and the doctrine of the ILO supervisory bodies on freedom of association and collective bargaining. Thus former Czechoslovakia granted freedom of association in 1990 and adopted a law on collective bargaining in 1991. In Estonia, a new trade union law was adopted in 1989; in 1993 another law was enacted, on collective conflicts. Hungary passed a law in 1989 on the right to strike. Lithuania promulgated legislation on collective agreements and strikes, respectively in 1991 and

---

31 The reach of the Soviet Union's law of December 1958 relating to criminal responsibility for crimes against the State has never been clear: under that law, all facts or abstentions with the intention of undermining industry, transport or agriculture with the purpose of weakening the Soviet State would be considered criminal acts.

32 The situation was also different in Titoist Yugoslavia, where far-reaching administrative decentralization, especially in Croatia and Slovenia, existed alongside strong political centralization.

1992. Similarly, Poland adopted legislation in 1991, regulating, respectively, the right of association of workers and of employers. In Slovenia, a 1993 law established criteria for the determination of union representativeness. In the former Soviet Union a law on labour conflicts was enacted in 1989; it was replaced in 1991, and applied to the Russian Federation. It was further amended in 1995 and later on in 2001, by the new Labour Code. In 1992 a law was adopted on collective bargaining; it was further modified by the Labour Code of 2001, which also underwent further reforms in 2006. In Ukraine, shortly before the disintegration of the Soviet Union, a Declaration was adopted, which paved the way for the establishment of independent trade unions. This was followed in 1992 by an Act on Public Associations and in 1993 by an Act on Collective Agreements and Accords, later amended in 1995.

The second wave of reforms addressed the individual employment relationship. Before the change of regime, all these countries, apart from the former Yugoslavia, had detailed Labour Codes, which had nevertheless become dated when communist rule came to an end. New Labour Codes were therefore adopted, as early as 1992 in Hungary, but in general from 1995 onwards (for instance, in Albania and Croatia) in most of the other countries, though partial reforms had been made in some countries from 1993. Nowadays, apart from Bulgaria, Poland and Ukraine,[33] all former communist countries have adopted entirely new Labour Codes or comprehensive new labour laws.

A further third wave of reforms took place in the 10 countries[34] which were invited to join the European Union in 1993. At its meeting in Copenhagen that year, the Council of the European Union decided to welcome their candidatures provided that the EU was satisfied that the applicant countries fulfilled the following accession criteria (commonly referred to as the Copenhagen criteria): (a) *political*: stability of institutions guaranteeing democracy, the rule of law, human rights and respect for and protection of minorities; (b) *economic*: a functioning market economy as well as the capacity to cope with competitive pressure and market forces within the Union; and (c) *institutional*: the ability to take on the obligations of membership including adherence to the aims of political, economic and monetary union, and the transposition of the *acquis communautaire* into national law. In subsequent years these countries undertook far-reaching revisions of their overall

---

33 The Labour Codes of Poland (1974) and Bulgaria (1986) have also been comprehensively amended and revised.

34 Bulgaria, Czech Republic, Estonia, Hungary, Latvia, Lithuania, Poland, Romania, Slovakia and Slovenia.

institutional and legislative frameworks, including their labour law, so as to bring their laws and institutions in line with the *acquis communautaire*. Eight of these countries joined the European Union in 2004 and the remaining two countries became EU members in January 2007.

Very broadly, both economic and political change and the reform of labour laws in the former communist countries have shared the following patterns: (a) the scope of application of labour law has become narrower; (b) the content of labour law has been largely enriched; and (c) attempts have been made to bring the industrial relations system closer to the prevailing Western European legal frameworks and practices.

The narrowing of the scope of labour law stems from the emergence of diverse employment relations practices and patterns of employment which were all but unknown under the old regimes. When the economy was essentially in the hands of the State, and operated under a central planning system, there was no real need to make any distinction between the status of civil servants in the public administration and workers in the private production sectors. However, the introduction of a market economy and the overall reform of the State led to the recognition of diverse kinds of employment. In market economies, employees may work for a private-sector employer, or in government administration, or in public law agencies or organizations that do not perform government functions. It follows that labour law applies to the first category of workers only, while public law governs the relations between the State and civil servants, or at least certain categories of government employees (though it is also true that an increasing number of public administrations and government agencies now apply private law to their employees). This needed to be taken into account when redrafting labour laws in the former communist countries. Furthermore, the passage to a market economy led to the closure of many State-owned enterprises as well as to massive staff cuts. Self-employment and the use of civil law arrangements for the performance of work or the provision of services have also been on the increase. When put together, these factors have resulted in a sharp decrease in the coverage of labour law.

Nevertheless, while the scope has narrowed, the content of labour legislation has become qualitatively richer as a result of the introduction of concepts which were unknown under the communist regimes. Some of them belong to the field of collective labour relations: they relate to the need to define rules in systems where trade unions are private law associations, pluralism is possible (and has in fact become the rule in most former communist countries), trade union representation can be challenged, collective bargaining is bilateral and voluntary, and labour conflicts and strikes are a reality which call for some form of regulation. As former communist countries were unfamiliar with these situations, it became necessary to review labour laws in order to provide them with a regulatory frame.

Other changes were focused on individual employment relations. Concepts were introduced that were either unknown or simply had not been used under the old regime because they had much less importance than in a market economy. These changes regulated issues such as alternative forms of the contract of employment, hiring and dismissal procedures, protection against unjustified dismissal, transfer of enterprises, variations in the terms and conditions of employment during the life of a contract of employment, protection of wages, including in cases of the insolvency of the employer.

However, all these reforms were undertaken within an extremely short time-frame. It would therefore be reasonable to raise some questions concerning the capacity of these countries to apply and administer their new labour laws. No less important is a discussion of the extent to which the new rules have led to changes in a culture that had been formed over several decades of communist regime; it would be naive to assume that they could be modified by a mere change to the law. This explains why legislators considered it advisable to retain a number of elements from previous laws.

Amongst these elements is the fact that most of the labour laws recently adopted in Central and Eastern Europe are based on the assumption that large companies still set the prevailing patterns of work organization. It follows that little space is allowed for the treatment of employment relationships in small firms. For example, remedies in cases of unfair dismissal almost always feature the reinstatement of workers in their old positions, something which is often not feasible in small enterprises.[35] In some cases, as in Bulgaria, Estonia and Lithuania, labour laws include rules relating to the appointment or promotion of employees by competition or popular election, which would seem misplaced in a private-law labour code. The worker's workbook, disciplinary procedures and the contractual liability of workers are other issues that were frequently addressed in the old labour codes and which, unlike those of Western economies, are still very visible in the labour legislation of the former communist countries. Still more surprising is the retention of provisions, for example in the Labour Code of the Russian Federation, that advocate the giving of rewards by the employer to deserving employees – though these could be compared to 'employee of the month' awards that are common practice in the United States.

---

35 In order to escape this rule, the Labour Codes of Slovakia and the Russian Federation allow small and medium-sized enterprises (SMEs) to hire their entire workforce under fixed-term contracts of employment, that is without any objective reason to justify the recourse to fixed-term employment. This is an unusual provision in comparative labour law.

Box 6.4 Rewards to 'deserving employees' in the Russian Federation

Labour Code

Article 191
Labour incentives
The employer motivates employees who perform their work duties diligently (by thanking them officially, paying them a merit bonus, giving them valuable gifts, certificates, or putting them forward for the title 'Best in Profession').

Other kinds of awards for employees' good work are specified in the collective agreement or in the organization's internal labour regulations, as well as in the charters and discipline regulations. For special services to society, state employees can be put forward for state awards.

Social dialogue in the post-communist states

Industrial relations practices, including workers' representation and the coverage of collective bargaining, still lag well behind those prevailing in Western Europe,[36] though important differences can be observed among these countries. Unionization rates have sharply decreased in almost all countries, with rates that can be as low as 15 per cent, while they were closer to 100 per cent before the collapse of communism.[37] Rates are particularly low in small and medium-sized enterprises, which cannot fail to have an impact on the coverage of collective bargaining: in most new EU Member States the prevailing bargaining level is the enterprise, there are relatively few sectoral-level agreements and still fewer of them are extended. It should also be noted that private employers' associations have all come into existence fairly recently, so that frequently they are not strong enough to engage in collective bargaining, and their representativeness can easily be challenged by individual enterprises.

Above all, the major difficulty at present stems from the fact that the practice of collective bargaining presupposes the existence of certain behavioural patterns and of a culture of collective bargaining that has not had sufficient

---

36 Or EU-15 as the pre-enlargement EU Member States are currently referred to.
37 See Eurofound, 'Industrial relations in the candidate countries', in *EIROnline* database (Dublin, 2002).

time to take root since the downfall of communism. Such difficulties should, however, be weighed against the political will to support collective bargaining, both as a means of promoting and implementing EC social and labour policy (in the case of the new EU Member States), and as a tool for achieving social stability at national, sectoral or enterprise levels. This explains why in many countries the State has promoted social dialogue at a national level, and even encouraged national collective bargaining. General Collective Agreements have been concluded, for example, in Serbia, Macedonia, Montenegro and both entities of Bosnia-Herzegovina. Recent data would suggest that more sectoral agreements are being concluded in some countries, and the overall rate of coverage would also seem to be on the increase, with, however, a pronounced gap still existing with respect to EU-15 countries.[38]

Finally, it would seem worthwhile reviewing how the political changes arising out of the disintegration of the Soviet Union and downfall of communism in Central and Eastern Europe and Central Asia have a bearing on the position of the relevant countries vis-à-vis international law. This is explained in box 6.5.

Box 6.5 The position of the former Central and Eastern European countries vis-à-vis international law

The disintegration of the Soviet Union and of former Yugoslavia and the split of former Czechoslovakia into two new States have had a bearing on the application of ILO Conventions ratified by the pre-existing States. The present position of the new countries vis-à-vis international law, and more particularly in terms of the application of ILO Conventions, can be summarized as follows.

Former Soviet Union
Before the disintegration of the Soviet Union, the Ukraine and Belarus (but not the Russian Federation) had international Statehood and were members of both the UN and the ILO, and the international obligations of these countries did not change with the extinction of the Soviet Union. On the other hand, the Russian Federation was admitted to the UN and the ILO as a successor State and confirmed the application of all of the ILO Conventions that had been ratified by the former Soviet Union and applied on its territory. Some of the former Soviet republics did the same while some others tackled this question on a case-by-case basis. This was most notably the approach followed by the three Baltic States (Estonia, Latvia and Lithuania),

---

38 Eurofound, *Industrial relations development in Europe,* 2006 (Luxembourg, 2007).

which had been members of the ILO until they were occupied and annexed by the Soviet Union in 1940. When they regained independence in 1989, they did not consider themselves bound by the Conventions that had been ratified by the former Soviet Union and had applied in their territory under the occupation. Instead, they confirmed the application of the Conventions they had ratified before the Soviet occupation, and examined all the other Conventions on a case-by-case basis. Similarly, two Central Asian former Soviet republics, namely Kyrgyzstan and Tajikistan, but not Kazakhstan, Turkmenistan and Uzbekistan, declared that they remained bound by the ILO Conventions once ratified by the Soviet Union. With regard to the Caucasian republics, Azerbaijan, but not Armenia and Georgia, confirmed the application of the Conventions that had been ratified by the Soviet Union. Moldova also followed the case-by-case approach.

Former Czechoslovakia
Czechoslovakia was split into two new countries, the Czech Republic and the Republic of Slovakia. Both confirmed the validity of the international obligations that had applied in their respective territories before the new States were created.

Former Federal Republic of Yugoslavia
A more complex situation applies to the countries of the former Federal Republic of Yugoslavia. On the one hand, Bosnia-Herzegovina, Macedonia and Slovenia confirmed the ratification of the ILO Conventions which were applicable in their respective territories at the time of independence. Serbia and Montenegro, which at the time formed the Federal Republic of Yugoslavia, later renamed Serbia-Montenegro, was accepted as the successor State to the former Socialist Republic of Yugoslavia, and continued to be bound by all the pre-existing international obligations. When Montenegro declared independence in 2006, it also accepted the ILO Conventions that had once applied to Serbia-Montenegro. On the other hand, Croatia accepted most, but not all, of the ILO Conventions previously applying in its territory; notoriously, it did not confirm the ratification of the Termination of Employment Convention, 1982 (No. 158). To complete the picture, it should be noted that the status of the former Serbian province of Kosovo remained unsettled at the end of 2007.

Former German Democratic Republic
When the German Democratic Republic (GDR) joined the Federal Republic of Germany in 1990, all the ratifications so far in force in that country were cancelled, and all the Conventions that had been ratified by the FRG were also made applicable in the territory of the former GDR.

Latin America

The development of labour law in Latin America

The Latin American region is far from being homogeneous. Nevertheless a large number of countries in Latin America share common patterns that have had a deep impact on the evolution of their labour law and industrial relations practices. First, while most countries have been independent since the early decades of the nineteenth century,[39] they have inherited a tradition of bureaucracy and State intervention from their former colonial powers – Portugal, in the case of Brazil, and Spain in that of the other countries. Secondly, whereas most Latin American constitutional systems have largely drawn inspiration from the US Constitution of 1787, civil and private law in general have taken the Napoleonic French Civil Code of 1804 as their model. Thirdly, Western European labour law, in particular that of France, and more recently Spain, have had strong influence in the framing of labour laws in all of Latin America, though some minor influence of the US National Labor Relations Act 1935 can also be traced in a handful of countries.[40] Furthermore, Western European influence is apparent not only in the shaping of Latin American labour law but also in the debate on labour law reform. Thus the labour flexibility debate that started in Europe, as well as a number of flexibility-oriented reforms, have largely been 'copied and pasted' onto the Latin American context, even though labour markets and labour costs there are far from being comparable with those of Europe. Still more important has been the influence of the International Labour Organization, as Latin America is, after Western Europe, the region that has ratified the largest number of ILO Conventions.

Political events, overall economic strategies and, above all, political ideologies played a substantial role in the early formulation and subsequent evolution of labour law in Latin America.[41] The starting point can be located in the

---

39 The exceptions are Cuba, independent from Spain in 1898, but occupied by the United States until 1902; Panama, which declared independence from Colombia in 1903, and the Dominican Republic, independent from Haiti in 1844 and then a dependency of Spain until 1865.

40 This is most noteworthy with regard to the definition of *unfair labour practices*, which appears in the laws of Argentina, Chile, the Dominican Republic and Panama. However, it would seem that provisions on unfair labour practices are very rarely used in Latin American countries.

41 See, for example, A.S. Bronstein, 'Societal change and industrial relations in Latin America: Trends and prospects', in *International Labour Review* (1995), Vol. 134, No. 2, pp.163–86; and A.S. Bronstein, 'Labour law reform in Latin America: Between state protection and flexibility', in *International Labour Review* (1997), Vol. 136, No. 1, pp. 5–26.

Table 6.1 Ratification of ILO Conventions by Latin American countries[42]

Country	ILO Conventions ratified and in force
Argentina	66
Bolivia	45
Brazil	80
Chile	50
Colombia	54
Costa Rica	48
Cuba	76
Dominican Republic	32
Ecuador	55
El Salvador	29
Guatemala	69
Honduras	22
Mexico	70
Nicaragua	54
Panama	68
Paraguay	36
Peru	67
Uruguay	78
Venezuela, Bolivarian Republic of	50

first two decades of the last century, when countries as diverse as Argentina, Colombia, Guatemala and Uruguay adopted legislation on weekly rest, hours of work, work of minors and women, and workers' compensation. To a large extent these laws coincided with an overall transformation of the economy, as urban factory work became increasingly important alongside the hitherto traditional rural and mining-based economy. The laws also reflected political change as the traditional rural and mining oligarchies started to lose political control to the bourgeoisie, who sought to make a tacit alliance with the emerging urban proletariat, and promulgated worker-friendly laws for their benefit. In 1917, for the first time ever, the Mexican Constitution made the protection of the worker a State political commitment, whereas the liberal

---

42 Source: ILOLEX database, available at: http://www.ilo.org. Data correct at 21 November 2008. The table shows only the Conventions that are in force for each country, as many Conventions that were formerly ratified have been automatically denounced as a result of the ratification of a revising Convention. The total number of ratifications is therefore higher than that of the Conventions actually in force; for example Uruguay has ratified 105 ILO Conventions, but only 78 of them are in force in the country; in Brazil, the number of ratifications is 93 but that of ILO Conventions in force is 80.

constitutions of the nineteenth century had committed the State only to protect individual rights, property rights and freedom of commerce. In 1924 Chile adopted one of the first ever laws on the contract of employment, which was followed in the 1930s by Labour Codes and comprehensive labour laws in Mexico and Chile (1931), Brazil (1934), Venezuela (1936), Ecuador (1936) and Bolivia (1939). This process was further consolidated in the 1940s, when Labour Codes were adopted in Brazil and Costa Rica (1943), Nicaragua (1945), Guatemala and Panama (1947), and in the early 1950s, with the enactment of Labour Codes in Colombia (1950) and the Dominican Republic (1951).

Economic strategies also played an important role in this process, as since the 1930s and in some cases as late as the 1980s many Latin American countries implemented industrialization programmes, mainly in the form of import-substitution strategies[43] backed by customs barriers. These policies were very largely State-driven, so that a noteworthy feature of this period was the growth of public employment in both public administration and in State-owned enterprises, which made up the backbone of the overall economy. To a large extent these policies drew inspiration from Keynesian theories, and from the early 1950s they had strong support from the UN Economic Commission for Latin America. It was in this context that the protection of the local workforce became in a sense a counterpart to the protection that the State granted to local business. Thus there was barely any need to challenge labour law on the ground that it affected industrial competitiveness, for domestic markets were closed to international competition and all local employers had to abide by the same labour laws, and bear the same or comparable labour costs.

Latin American populism was a no less important element in the development of labour law and a labour relations system, starting as early as the 1930s in Brazil under the corporatist Estado Novo (New State) of Getulio Vargas, and in Mexico during the administration of Lázaro Cárdenas (1936–40). The most well-known example of populism, however, is that of Argentina during the first period of Peronism (1946–55).[44] Some late forms of populism took place in Panama, under the leadership of Omar Torrijos (1968–81), and in Peru during the military government of Juan Velasco

---

43 Import substitution is a trade and economic policy based on the premise that a developing country should attempt to substitute products which it imports (mostly finished goods) with locally produced substitutes.

44 Actually it started in 1943, when Peron was appointed Secretary of Labour and Social Security, and was consolidated after 1946, with Peron already holding the Presidency of Argentina.

Alvarado (1968–75). With the exception perhaps of Peru, the trade unions became key stakeholders in the political coalitions that controlled the State in the systems of several Latin American countries. For example, the General Confederation of Workers, in Argentina, and the Confederation of Mexican Workers became the strongest pillars, respectively, of the Peronist Party and the Institutional Revolutionary Party (PRI), and had significant political leverage.

Nowadays, while trade unions still have a voice, they no longer enjoy the political power they had under populist regimes. But reminders of the strong ties that once existed between the State and the unions are still visible in some legislation, for example the Brazilian *Consolidação* (Recast) of Labour Laws and the Argentinian Law on Professional Associations (trade union law). Both provided for a State-imposed, top-down trade union structure,[45] which drew inspiration from the Italian Rocco law of 1925, promulgated under Mussolini's fascist regime, and both have survived the political regimes under which they were introduced. Indeed, the Brazilian State-imposed trade union structure has so far prevented Brazil from ratifying ILO Convention No. 87. Though Argentina did ratify that Convention, the ILO Committee of Experts has repeatedly made calls for the country to revise its law on professional associations as it clearly provides for a single-union monopoly and there is a bias in favour of workers' representation by sectoral-level organizations, thus making it difficult for workers to be represented by organizations of their own choosing, which is a core rule under Convention No. 87.[46]

Political populism has led in all instances to the promulgation of labour-friendly laws which the political power used to reward the working classes for their support. The Argentinian law on Contract of Employment, 1974, drafted by advocates of the General Confederation of Workers in the aftermath of Peron's return to power (1973–74), and the Labour Code of Panama, 1971, promulgated under Torrijos, provide perhaps the clearest examples of this trend.[47] It was also under the populist administration of Velasco Alvarado

---

45 In the case of Brazil, the Consolidation of the Labour Law 1943 (still in force) also determines the structure and roles of the employers' associations.

46 See the individual observations made by the CEACR on the application of that Convention by Argentina, all available on the ILO database ILOLEX at http://www.ilo.org The case of compliance by Argentina to Convention No. 87 has also been debated by the Committee on the Application of Standards of the ILO Conference (see, for example, ILO, *Report of the Committee on the Application of Standards*, Provisional Record 22, International Labour Conference, 96th Session, Geneva, 2007 and has given rise to numerous complaints before the Committee of Freedom of Association (information also available in ILOLEX).

47 While both laws have been largely revised since their enactment, the overall pro-worker orientation did not change significantly.

that Peru undertook far-reaching reforms of the organization of production, which included significant workers' participation in 'industrial communities', and even workers' self-management in 'socially owned' enterprises (Empresas de Propiedad Social), which bore considerable resemblance to Yugoslav self-management experiences during the Titoist regime. Yet today, barely anything remains of Velasco's reforms.

Last but certainly not least, political instability also played a significant role in the framing of labour laws, especially labour relations systems, in a number of countries. Argentina was alternatively ruled by elected governments and military juntas between 1930 and 1983. Brazil had military-appointed governments between 1964 and 1985. In both Uruguay and Chile, military forces snatched political power in 1973 and held it until 1985 and 1989 respectively. Similar remarks could be made with regard to many other Latin American countries, with the noteworthy exceptions of Costa Rica, Mexico and Venezuela. In all cases, military takeovers were accompanied by tough restrictions on civil and political freedoms, including, of course, freedom of association. This took the form, for example, of disbanding trade unions or the direct appointment of trade union leaders by the government, imprisonment (or worse) of trade union activists, confiscation of trade union assets, a freeze on collective bargaining and a ban on strikes. It was also under military governments that some labour flexibilization processes started to be implemented, though some years later a number of democratically elected governments also did the same.

Democracy, economic liberalization and labour law reforms

By the mid-1970s, labour laws that protected the individual worker, on the one hand, but coupled with restrictions on freedom of association on the other hand, were a common feature in the majority of Latin American countries. This situation was comparable to that of Spain under Franco's regime. However, from the 1980s on, most of the Latin American countries that were hitherto under military or dictatorial regimes came back to democratic rule. Apart from one exception, this process was completed in the early 1990s.[48] With democracy coming in, the State started to release its firm grip on the trade union movement and collective bargaining and industrial action were permitted once more.

---

48 The restoration of democracy started in Ecuador in 1979; it continued in Peru (1980), Bolivia and Honduras (1982), Argentina (1983), Brazil and Uruguay (1985), Guatemala (1986), Paraguay (1989) and Chile (1990). During this period democracy was also restored in Nicaragua, El Salvador and Panama.

Out of the democratization process new political constitutions emerged, that were adopted in many countries after 1978.[49] They almost invariably included a long list of workers' rights; for example Article 7 of the Constitution of Brazil, 1988, sets out no less than 24 guarantees for the workers, and Article 102 of that of Guatemala spells out 20 minimum social rights of the workers. Various reforms of the Labour Code, for example in the Dominican Republic in 1992, Costa Rica in 1993, Paraguay in 1993, and El Salvador in 1994,[50] followed the same trend. As the ILO collaborated in the drafting of most of these codes or amendments to them, it is unsurprising that, to a very large extent, they have drawn inspiration from the doctrine of the ILO supervisory bodies in the areas of freedom of association and collective bargaining. Most of these reforms were aimed at solving problems relating to the compatibility of national law with ILO Conventions. Eventually they earned praise from the ILO Committee of Experts, though a number of problems did remain outstanding.

At the same time the economic import-substitution and protectionist model was dying away. For most countries the 1980s were characterized by poor economic performance, decrease of per capita income, high inflation, huge foreign debt and rising unemployment – this period is commonly referred to as the lost decade of Latin America.

It was in this context that Keynesian policies started to be challenged by neo-liberal thought. Even by the late 1970s Pinochet's Chile had embarked on a full range of economic liberalization measures, including privatization of State-owned enterprises, the downsizing of the public administration, elimination of subsidies to the private sector, reduction of social expenditure, privatization of the pensions system, the opening of the internal market to international competition and the reduction of custom duties. Undoubtedly, the curtailment of fundamental rights, including basic trade union freedoms and far-reaching reform of labour law to the detriment of workers, were also part of this strategy. The social cost of the programme was very high, and there is little wonder that it could be implemented only with the brutal repression that characterized Pinochet's regime. Yet it is undisputed that, however socially unfair, the Chilean economic strategy was highly successful: economic growth returned, though growth did not benefit all Chileans.

It is perhaps because of Chile's economic success (and also because of pressure from international financial institutions) that other countries – this time

---

49 Ecuador, 1978; Peru, 1979 (replaced in 1994, under the Fujimori regime); Honduras, 1982; El Salvador, 1983; Guatemala, 1985; Nicaragua, 1986; Brazil, 1988; Colombia, 1991; Paraguay, 1992; Argentina, 1994.

50 The Organic Law of Labour 1990, of Venezuela, also shares this approach.

democratically elected – eventually formulated and implemented analogous programmes. Structural adjustment programmes were put in place in Bolivia, Costa Rica and Mexico from 1985, in Colombia in 1990, in Argentina in 1991, in Peru in 1992 and in Brazil in 1994. Bilateral or multilateral Free Trade Agreements, such as NAFTA, MERCOSUR, DR-CAFTA, were part of this strategy and greatly contributed to the opening up of so far relatively closed economies and provided a foundation for discussion of the adaptability of domestic labour markets to the needs and constraints of both internal and international competition.

It was in this context that the labour flexibility debate and reform of labour laws came to the forefront, and many countries revised their labour laws at least once, and in many cases several times, from the early 1990s on, with a view to making them more business-friendly. The Preamble to Colombian Law No. 50, of 28 December 1990, stated: 'modernization of the economy makes it necessary that our labour law be more flexible so that our production becomes more competitive, investment is promoted and employment generation is increased'. It is also worth recalling that promotion of employment was one of the declared objectives of these reforms (for example the law that introduced atypical contracts in the Argentinean reform of 1991 was to be known as the *National* Employment Law), and they all relied on the assumption, though not supported by any evidence, that employers would be encouraged to hire workers if dismissals were made easier and cheaper.

However, contrary to what one might imagine, flexibility-oriented labour reform has not been a unanimous trend throughout Latin America. Certainly, many reforms – for example in Argentina, Brazil, Panama and Peru, not to mention Chile under Pinochet – introduced greater flexibility in the contract of employment, most notably by making dismissals easier and cheaper and by facilitating the use of fixed-term and other atypical contracts of employment. Yet, other reforms, for example in the Dominican Republic, El Salvador and Venezuela, kept, and in some cases even strengthened, the already existing protections. Also, whereas more flexibility was introduced in the field of individual employment relations, more guarantees were also provided for in the area of collective labour relations, for example in Costa Rica, the Dominican Republic and El Salvador; some reforms, including constitutional reforms in countries such as Brazil, Guatemala and Peru, guaranteed freedom of association and the right to strike in the civil service, and Argentina went further by providing for collective bargaining rights for civil service organizations. In addition, many flexibility-oriented reforms were later toned down by other reforms that restored the traditional labour-protection orientation of labour law. The case of Chile provides with a clear example of this trend.

Box 6.6 Labour law reform under the dictatorship of Pinochet (1973–90) and under democratic rule (1990 onwards), Chile

The changes introduced in Chile's Labour Code under Pinochet were among the most far-reaching of the flexibility-oriented reforms. In the field of collective labour relations, trade unions and collective bargaining were allowed to exist only at the enterprise level, and even then not in all enterprises. It was made illegal for any unions to represent non-members; and unions had no exclusive bargaining rights. Thus collective agreements were only applicable to union members, and nothing prevented the employer from offering better pay and conditions of work to non-members as a means of discouraging them from joining a union. Furthermore, serious restrictions were put on the right to strike. In the field of individual labour relations, the reforms did away with a former law of the 1960s that required that dismissals to be justified on valid grounds. Instead, employers were permitted to dismiss workers on any grounds or on no grounds at all, subject to a period of notice and severance pay, which was equivalent to one month's salary for each year of service, with a ceiling of five months' pay. Also, an employer could hire a worker under a fixed-term contract of employment, for a maximum of two years, without any need to justify it objectively. In practice, the two-year limit could be bypassed by a short break between two contracts, something which was implicitly accepted by the law. Other reforms aimed at conferring greater flexibility on the organization of the working time, while other provisions excluded workers aged less than 21 years or more than 65 years from the coverage of the minimum wage.

The reforms introduced after the end of Pinochet's regime in 1990 came in several waves. One of the first measures of the new government was to give official recognition to central-level national workers' organizations (Centrales Sindicales), which had been outlawed under Pinochet.[51] A further reform increased the ceiling set by the previous legislation on the amount of dismissal compensation (from five months to 11 months' pay) and reduced to 12 months the maximum duration of a fixed-term contract of employment. It was also provided that a worker who had worked for the same employer for 12 months over a timespan of 15 continuous months, under several fixed-term contracts of employment, would be deemed to have been working under a contract of employment of unlimited duration.

---

51 Only the Central Unica de Trabajadores (CUT) was in fact created and received recognition, but the law does not rule out the establishment of other central-level national confederations.

Other measures included the 48-hour working week in commerce and tourism, minimum wage coverage for workers aged over 65 years, better protection of workers' claims in cases of insolvency of the employer, and the establishment of subsidiary liability by the principal enterprise in respect of its contractors' obligations in relation to their employees.

The 1990 reforms did not, however, end the phase of post-Pinochet reforms, and an important step was taken in 1999 with the ratification of Convention Nos. 87, 98 and 135, followed in 2000 by that of the Labour Relations (Public Service) Convention, 1978 (No. 151). New legislative reforms were adopted with a view to bringing Chilean law into conformity with these Conventions, though the ILO Committee of Experts has observed that certain questions remain outstanding.[52]

No less important were the changes introduced in 2001 by Law No. 19759, perhaps the most important reform of this period. This law has: (a) established the 45-hour working week; (b) increased the amount of severance pay and dismissal compensation; (c) provided for internal democracy in workers' organizations and modified certain provisions on collective bargaining; (d) set up a legal framework for part-time work and telework; and (e) prescribed that the exercise of management prerogatives is qualified by the exercise of the workers' constitutional rights.

Finally, Law No. 20123 of 2006 provided for the regulation of subcontracting, temporary work enterprises and the contract of employment for temporary services. It also provided for a comprehensive reform of the labour courts.

At the same time tribunals have also played a noteworthy role, and in many cases have stopped or at least have put some hurdles in the way of the increasing tendency towards subcontracting and the substitution of precarious forms of employment for the standard employment relationship. Discrimination on different grounds (religion, sex and age) has also been tackled by the tribunals, which have continued to develop a worthwhile progressive jurisprudence. No less important is the strong support that the ILO Decent Work Agenda has received from practically all Latin American countries, an overwhelming majority of which have ratified the eight fundamental Conventions.

---

52 See the observations and direct request of the Committee of Experts on the Application of Conventions and Recommendations (CEACR) addressed to Chile in respect to Conventions Nos. 87 and 98 in the ILO database at http://www.ilo.org.

Table 6.2 Ratification of ILO Conventions on fundamental human rights in Latin America*

Country	Freedom of association and collective bargaining		Elimination of forced and compulsory labour		Elimination of discrimination in respect of employment and occupation		Abolition of child labour	
	Convention No. 87	Convention No. 98	Convention No. 29	Convention No. 105	Convention No. 100	Convention No. 111	Convention No. 138	Convention No. 182
Argentina	18/01/1960	24/09/1956	14/03/1950	18/01/1960	24/09/1956	18/06/1968	11/11/1996	05/02/2001
Bolivia	04/01/1965	15/11/1973	31/05/2005	11/06/1990	15/11/1973	31/01/1977	11/06/1997	06/06/2003
Brazil	...	18/11/1952	25/04/1957	18/06/1965	25/04/1957	26/11/1965	28/06/2001	02/02/2000
Chile	01/02/1999	01/02/1999	31/05/1933	01/02/1999	20/09/1971	20/09/1971	01/02/1999	17/07/2000
Colombia	16/11/1976	16/11/1976	04/03/1969	07/06/1963	07/06/1963	04/03/1969	02/02/2001	28/01/2005
Costa Rica	02/06/1960	02/06/1960	02/06/1960	04/05/1959	02/06/1960	01/03/1962	11/06/1976	10/09/2001
Cuba	25/06/1952	29/04/1952	20/07/1953	02/06/1958	13/01/1954	26/08/1965	07/03/1975	...
Dominican Republic	05/12/1956	22/09/1953	05/12/1956	23/06/1958	22/09/1953	13/07/1964	15/06/1999	15/11/2000
Ecuador	29/05/1967	28/05/1959	06/07/1954	05/02/1962	11/03/1957	10/07/1962	19/09/2000	19/09/2000
El Salvador	06/09/2006	06/09/2006	15/06/1995	18/11/1958	12/10/2000	15/06/1995	23/01/1996	12/10/2000
Guatemala	13/02/1952	13/02/1952	13/06/1989	09/12/1959	02/08/1961	11/10/1960	27/04/1990	11/10/2001
Honduras	27/06/1956	27/06/1956	21/02/1957	04/08/1958	09/08/1956	20/06/1960	09/06/1980	25/10/2001
Mexico	01/04/1950	...	12/05/1934	01/06/1959	23/08/1952	11/09/1961	...	30/06/2000
Nicaragua	31/10/1967	31/10/1967	12/04/1934	31/10/1967	31/10/1967	31/10/1967	02/11/1981	06/11/2000
Panama	03/06/1958	16/05/1966	16/05/1966	16/05/1966	03/06/1958	16/05/1966	31/10/2000	31/10/2000
Paraguay	28/06/1962	21/03/1966	28/08/1967	16/05/1968	24/06/1964	10/07/1967	03/03/2004	07/03/2001
Peru	02/03/1960	13/03/1964	01/02/1960	06/12/1960	01/02/1960	10/08/1970	13/11/2002	10/01/2002
Uruguay	18/03/1954	18/03/1954	06/09/1995	22/11/1968	16/11/1989	16/11/1989	02/06/1977	03/08/2001
Venezuela, Bolivarian Republic of	20/09/1982	19/12/1968	20/11/1944	16/11/1964	10/08/1982	03/06/1971	15/07/1987	26/10/2005

* Dates correct as of 21 November 2008.

Thus Labour law in Latin America today faces a number of outstanding challenges that can be summarized as follows: (a) the scope of labour law has narrowed as a result of the frequent use of labour under civil and commercial law arrangements; (b) unionization rates have decreased and, apart from a few exceptions, collective bargaining has lost its strength; (c) labour inspection and law enforcement in general leaves much to be desired. Yet none of these challenges are as important as the one which arises out of the lack of application of labour law to workers in the informal economy, which is overwhelmingly present in a great majority of Latin American countries today.

Asia and the Pacific[53]

The most distinctive feature of Asia seems to be its great diversity, for the region is made up of countries very varied in their history, culture, social structure and economic development. Labour markets and industrial relations reflect this variety, resulting in a range of different labour law systems. On the one hand, there are countries such as Australia or Japan which have a longstanding industrial tradition behind them. It might be expected that these countries already have well-entrenched labour laws and industrial relations institutions. However, important changes have taken place recently in both countries. No less significant changes have taken place in New Zealand, where the institutional framework for labour relations has moved sequentially from a highly regulated labour market until 1991 to a deregulated labour market between 1991 and 2000, and then again to a (moderately) regulated market after 2000. On the other hand, there are several distinctive groups of countries and territories, namely those whose economic take-off dates from the 1970s (Malaysia, the Republic of Korea, Singapore, Taiwan (China), Thailand, and the special economic zone of Hong Kong (China)); those whose economic development is much more recent, for example India and Vietnam; and those whose economy is just taking off or is not taking off at all. China, which does not fit into any of these groups, offers a completely different panorama whose most remarkable features are its very rapid transformation, impressive growth rates and opening up to international investment, while remaining under the control of a one-party political system. Thus

---

53 The author is grateful to Sean Cooney, the author of a paper prepared for this publication, *Labour law trends in the Asia-Pacific region*, which has been used for this chapter. Sean Cooney is Associate Professor, University of Melbourne Law School and Associate Director, Asian Law Centre, University of Melbourne, Australia.

foreign-owned enterprises employed 91.7 million workers in 2000, while State-owned enterprises employed some 80 million workers.[54]

The Australian model of industrial relations

For most of the twentieth century, Australia had an industrial relations system that was almost unique in the industrialized world. Whereas most developed nations had systems that could be characterized as being based on a 'bargaining model' of industrial relations, in which outcomes were negotiated between the parties, subject to various procedural requirements and minimum standards set by State institutions, Australia operated an 'arbitral model' in which State arbitration institutions played a central role in determining outcomes where the parties were unable to agree themselves and in establishing working conditions through industrial awards applied either to particular enterprises or across particular industries.

In recent years Australia has been moving from a centralized regulatory system to a decentralized and to a large extent individualized approach. This was first initiated through the enactment of the Industrial Relations Reform Act 1993, which was followed by the Workplace Relations Act 1996. The objective of the Workplace Relations Act 1996 was to produce a shift away from the regulation of collective bargaining between unions and employers by the Australian Industrial Relations Commission, to facilitate individual or 'workplace' agreements (Australian Workplace Agreements or AWAs) between employers and employees. Apart from certain minimum requirements, the content of the AWAs was open to the parties to determine. This was further developed in 2005 by the Australian Workplace Relations Amendment (Work Choices) Act 2005 (box 6.7). A change of government has since brought about the abolition of AWAs and introduced the Fair Work Bill. The Bill provides for 10 national employment standards, modernizes the award system (without reviving compulsory arbitration, except in very limited circumstances), establishes a system of good faith bargaining, improves access to unfair dismissal remedies and restores some union rights.

---

54 See Hiromasa Suzuki, 'L'individu, le collectif et l'Etat dans les pays d'Asie du Nord-Est', in I. Dugareilh (ed.), *Mondialisation, travail et droits fondamentaux* (Paris, LGDJ, 2005), p. 140.

Box 6.7 Australia's Workplace Relations Amendment (Work Choices) Act 2005

In 2005 a far-reaching and controversial labour law reform was carried out by the Federal Government of Australia through the adoption of the Workplace Relations Amendment (Work Choices) Act 2005.[55]

Under previous reforms, industrial awards could be replaced by Australian Workplace Agreements (AWA), provided they met a no-disadvantage test, which involved a comparison between the terms of the overall agreement with the relevant award or other statutory benefits. Under the Work Choice legislation, AWAs simply needed to comply with five minimum conditions set out in the Australian Fair Pay and Conditions Standard.[56] Workplace agreements no longer needed to be certified by the Australian Industrial Relations Commission to take effect but could simply be lodged with the Office of the Employment Advocate. The new law further prohibited certain content from being included in the workplace agreement, including matters such as restricting the use of independent contractors, and clauses which confer remedies for unfair dismissal. Another important feature of the legislation consisted in the exclusion of businesses with fewer than 100 employees from the scope of unfair dismissal laws.

The law imposed a number of limitations on trade union action at the workplace level. First, union officials have been required to pass a 'fit and proper person test' in order to be permitted entry into a workplace; secondly, they must notify the employer at least 24 hours in advance that they intend to enter the workplace and must specify the reasons for the entry. Right of entry has also been limited to workplaces with 'eligible employees', who are covered by an award or collective agreement that is binding on the relevant union. Thirdly, it has become mandatory to proceed to a secret ballot in order to undertake industrial action and there is absolute prohibition on industrial action being taken during the life of a workplace agreement.

---

55 The constitutional validity of the Workplace Relations Amendment (Work Choices) Act 2005 was challenged in the High Court of Australia by the Australian states as well as by several workers' unions. A decision was handed down on 14 November 2006, with the court deciding 5–2 in favour of the validity of the legislation. In 2006, the ILC Committee on the Application of Standards held a discussion on the compatibility of the 2005 Act with Convention No. 98, amongst other reasons because the Committee of Experts had observed that the law allowed offers of employment to be made conditional on the signing of an AWA, thereby permitting workers to give up their right to collective bargaining.

56 These are four weeks' annual leave, 10 days' personal leave, parental (unpaid) leave of up to 52 weeks, maximum working time of 38 ordinary hours per week, which can be averaged over a 12-month period, plus reasonable additional hours and minimum wage rates which are determined by the Australian Fair Pay Conditions, a new body established by the Act.

Major labour law reforms in New Zealand

The case of New Zealand has drawn considerable international attention, as the country undertook far-reaching labour law reforms in the early 1990s. These reforms must be discussed in the context of the opening up of the country's economy from 1984 onwards. Until the mid-1970s, the New Zealand economy was highly protected, relying on agricultural exports to the British market, which provided it with high returns that served to protect local manufacturing and services. Unemployment was low and wages and working conditions were reasonably good; to a large extent they were determined through collective bargaining at either occupational or industry level, which covered some 50–60 per cent of all employees.[57] However, the overall economic landscape changed dramatically when the United Kingdom joined the European Community in 1973, and had to abide by the EC agricultural policy. This resulted in New Zealand's access to its most important export market being severely curtailed. The oil shocks of the 1970s, high international interest rates, and fluctuations in agricultural prices further weakened the economic position of New Zealand, which needed to make its economy more competitive in order to target more diversified markets. The Labour Government which came to power in 1984 thus initiated a far-reaching deregulation of the economy, through measures which included floating the currency, liberalizing the capital markets, suppressing subsidies and lowering custom duties. There was also considerable restructuring of the State sector.

The main area that was excluded from deregulation during this period was the labour market. But this was then addressed by the Government with the enactment of the Employment Contract Act (ECA) 1991. The ECA attracted considerable international attention when it was passed and subsequently, because it adopted a classic contractual approach to the employment relationship and was based on the assumption that employers and employees had equal bargaining powers. The overriding objective of this Act was to de-unionize workplaces and to individualize employment relationships. Under the terms of the ECA, employment contracts could be either individual or collective. Individuals, individual agents, trade unions and other organizations could negotiate both types of contract. A significant tool in achieving

---

57 New Zealand had had a system of compulsory arbitration for the settlement of industrial disputes since 1894. However, this system had all but fallen into disuse around the end of the 1970s and was abolished in 1984. Much of the supporting legal structure, however, remained in place and in particular the structures that supported the determination of wages and conditions at an industry/occupational level and usually with national coverage.

this deregulation was the policy of 'enterprise confinement' which restricted collective bargaining, and the ability to take strike action, to individual employing enterprises.

The enactment of this law was followed by a sharp decrease in the coverage of collective agreements. Trade unions in New Zealand brought a complaint against this Act before the ILO Committee on Freedom of Association, which considered that the ECA was at variance with a number of established principles on collective bargaining.[58]

The Employment Contract Act was, however, short-lived. When the Labour Government was elected in 1999, it immediately announced that the law would be repealed and replaced. This was done in 2000 with the enactment of the Employment Relations Act (ERA), which was further amended, more recently in 2004. The ERA covers the registration of unions, collective bargaining (including the obligation to bargain in good faith), strikes and lockouts and protection against unfair dismissal or other unjustified action by an employer. According to its supporters, it has the express objective of promoting collective bargaining and of implementing the principles of the Freedom of Association and Protection of the Right to Organise Convention, 1948 (No. 87), and the Right to Organise and Collective Bargaining Convention, 1949 (No. 98), in New Zealand. The ERA attempts to achieve these objectives through a variety of mechanisms but most importantly by recognizing trade unions, giving them exclusive bargaining rights, and by introducing a statutory obligation of good faith. The amendments made in 2004 were intended to strengthen the statutory objective of promoting collective bargaining and to prevent employer actions designed to undermine trade unions and collective bargaining. The amendments also included provisions intended to provide some continuity of employment where business restructuring results in work being contracted out or otherwise transferred to a new employer. This protection, however, was limited to relatively narrow groups of employees.

According to Gordon Anderson, a well-known labour law scholar in New Zealand:

> [The ERA] retained the macro level structures put in place during the 1990s but it gave greater emphasis to employee interests, both individual and collective, at the enterprise level. The major objective of the reforms was to build more positive and productive enterprise-focused employment relationships, a strategy seen as essential to economic growth. The reforms

---

58 See CFA case number 1698, Report 292 (*Official Bulletin*, Vol. LXXVII, 1994, Series B, No.1) and Report 295 (*Official Bulletin*, Vol. LXXVII, 1994, Series B, No. 3).

were also influenced by the view that employees had a right to be informed and consulted on business decisions impacting on their employment. [However] these reforms have not had a significant effect on labour market structures at the macro level. Since 2000, there has been very little growth in either trade union membership or collective bargaining coverage. The 2000 reforms have gone a considerable distance to bring New Zealand labour law back to a more central position which attempts to recognize the interests of both employers and employees. In particular it gives greater recognition to the rights of employees to bargain collectively. Following these reforms, most of the heat has gone out of the deregulation debate. Both unions and employers seem to find the current imbalance pragmatically acceptable and neither the mainstream union nor employer groups are currently seeking major changes. To the extent that debate continues, it tends to be fomented by the more extreme fringes of neoclassical economic think tanks who would seek to impose a fundamentalist neoclassical economic vision on New Zealand labour law. These views now have relatively little mainstream acceptance.[59]

Challenges to traditional labour models in Japan

Though less drastic, important changes have also taken place recently in Japan,[60] both in the field of individual and collective labour law. A major factor in the case of Japan is that the country had to face competition from other Asian countries and at the same time a serious financial crisis at the beginning of the 1990s, which led to large-scale employment adjustment and restructuring, resulting in a surge of unemployment.[61] These changes had an important bearing on both the patterns of employment and industrial relations. The long-term employment system (or, rather, the employment system that relies on the internal labour market) has been modified so as to emphasize short-term performance and the use of more mid-career recruitment. Also, the ratio of part-time and other atypical workers has grown from about 20 to 30 per cent during the decade-long economic slump. Moreover, as seen

---

59 Gordon Anderson, *Trade Liberalization and Labour Law: New Zealand National Report*, paper submitted to the XVIIIth World Congress of the International Society for Labour and Social Security Law, Paris, 2006 (Geneva, ISLSSL).

60 The author is grateful to Professor Kazuo Sugeno, who summarized these trends in his keynote speech delivered to the VIIIth Asian Regional Congress of the International Society for Labour and Social Security Law, Taipei, 2005. See also Japan Institute for Labour Policy and Training (JILPT), *Labor situation in Japan and analysis: General overview 2006/2007* (Tokyo, 2006). Available at: http://www.jil.go.jp [22 Nov. 2008].

61 Nevertheless the unemployment rate in Japan has generally been lower than the average unemployment rate in Western Europe over the same period.

in the increasing number of foreign-owned firms, a mobile employment system, relying on the external labour market, has become a distinctive model in Japan's employment systems. At the same time, the long-term/lifetime employment system[62] has become a less dominant model in Japanese industrial relations, though this would not seem to have resulted in a change in job security (this can be seen in the development of case law).[63]

No less noteworthy is the waning density and influence of trade unions. Union membership among the total workforce has been steadily decreasing over the last two decades, with the rate of those being organized into unions coming down to a little less than 20 per cent. The period after the collapse of the economic bubble is also marked by wage stagnation and even by a decrease of wages in real terms. The unions' Spring Wage Offensive (*Shunto*) has, it seems, lost its power to coordinate enterprise-based wage negotiations within and across industries.

Two further emerging developments should also be considered. First, while collective labour disputes have diminished, individual disputes are on the rise. The Japanese labour law system established after the Second World War attached the highest importance to collective bargaining disputes, and the Labour Relations Commissions played an important role in dispute-prone industrial relations until the mid 1970s. However, collective labour disputes have decreased significantly since the late 1970s as a consequence of the development of cooperative labour management relations. By contrast, since the early 1990s, the number of individual disputes in employment relations has increased sharply. For example, the number of civil litigation cases involving unpaid wages, termination of employment or alteration of working conditions has tripled. The increase in grievances can be attributed mainly to the restructuring and downsizing of enterprises, which were brought on by

---

62 Basically the life-term system (*shūshin koyō*) is a long-established Japanese practice whereby companies hire a specific number of new graduates at fixed times every year, under contract without limit of time. *Shūshin koyō* employees continue to be employed at the same company or at affiliated companies from the time they have been hired as new graduates until the time they retire, as long as there are no extraordinary circumstances. To a certain extent, *shūshin koyō* is comparable to civil service tenure.

63 Though permitted under the Labour Standards Act, since the 1970s the Supreme Court has held that an employer may not always be able to dismiss an employee. If the basis for dismissal in the specific situation concerned is remarkably unreasonable, 'or when it cannot be approved as corresponding to a socially accepted idea, the concerned expression of intention to dismiss shall be invalid as an abuse of the right of dismissal'. In 2003 the Labour Standards Act was amended so as to consolidate this doctrine. Under Article 18-2, 'A dismissal shall, where the dismissal lacks objectively reasonable grounds and is not considered to be appropriate in general societal terms, be treated as a misuse of that right and invalid.'

intensifying competition in the global market and, in particular, from other rising Asian economies. A second factor is the diversification and individualization of workers in the labour market, which has been precipitated by the needs of firms to make their workforces flexible and less costly. In light of this trend it became obvious that the collective dispute-oriented settlement system was in need of a major reform. Responding to such needs, the Ministry of Welfare and Labour established a system to provide counselling and mediation services for such disputes at the local offices of the Ministry. Since the Ministry began to offer these services in October 2001, the cases received by the offices have been increasing rapidly. Subsequently, judicial reform was undertaken to permit district courts (in Japan there is not a distinct labour court system) to deal more efficiently with labour litigation.[64] Also, since the regulation of labour issues through the judiciary's decisions has become increasingly cumbersome, the Ministry of Welfare and Labour has taken steps to enact a comprehensive law on the contract of employment, which has not existed in Japan up until now.

Secondly, another distinctive feature of Japanese society is the ageing of the population at a rate as yet unobserved elsewhere in the world. Approximately one person out of three is above 60 years of age. To maintain socioeconomic vitality, it has become vital to keep as many elderly persons as active as possible. Thus in 2004 the Elderly Persons Employment Security Act was revised, partly to ensure employment opportunities until 65 years of age and also to promote re-employment for the middle-aged and older working population.

Recent developments across Asia and the Pacific

In many of the Asian economies that are taking off, there is a radical expansion of urban and industrial areas and a large-scale movement of workers away from farming areas. Asian governments are struggling with major social problems caused by such industrialization, and are making efforts to establish labour market services to cope with frictional unemployment. They are also endeavouring to institutionalize labour law systems to secure regular

---

64 The number of consultations directed to the labour offices exceeded 907,800 in 2005, of which 176,000 related to individual legal disputes. The number of cases brought to the district courts in the same year was 2,446, which is high for Japanese standards, though very low if compared with court litigation statistics elsewhere (see Japan Institute for Labour Policy and Training, *Labor situation in Japan*, op. cit., pp. 74–5); see also K. Sugeno, 'Birth of the labor tribunal system in Japan: A synthesis of labour law reform and judicial reform', in *Comparative Labor Law and Policy Journal* (2004), Vol. 25, No. 4, pp. 519–33.

payment of wages, to establish workplace health and safety and to provide compensation for industrial accidents. In the younger economies, governments are making serious efforts to establish infrastructures for development, including some of the most basic systems for labour markets and social security (for example in Indonesia and the Philippines). On the other hand, in the mature economies, that are now threatened by global and regional competition (Australia, Japan, the Republic of Korea and Taiwan (China)), governments are making efforts to restructure their conventional economic systems in different ways: the Republic of Korea has taken an adversarial approach to industrial relations; Australia a centralizing approach; and Japan an individualizing approach. In particular, there are drives to deregulate the labour markets or to make industrial relations more cooperative in the Republic of Korea, or more decentralized in Australia.

For both developing and developed economies, the privatization of State-owned enterprises is a movement commonly being promoted (in Australia, Japan and Thailand). The increase in the number of workers in atypical employment is also a common trend in the region, with labour law reforms trying to balance protection and flexibility (as seen in the Republic of Korea and Japan). In many Asian economies, in response to the ageing of the population, efforts are being made to establish or reform pension and medical systems. Similarly, methods for utilizing and controlling immigration and emigration is a common policy issue throughout the region as workers move from less developed to more developed economies.

South Africa[65]

Labour law and industrial relations under apartheid

The Union of South Africa was established in 1910 by an Act of the British Parliament. The first decade of the new State's existence was dominated by high levels of industrial action by both black and white workers in the country's gold mining industry centred on Johannesburg. This culminated in the Rand Revolt of 1922 in which white miners staged an ultimately unsuccessful armed insurrection in support of their demand to maintain racial job reservation. In 1924 South Africa's adopted its first labour relations statute of

---

65 This entire section is a shortened version of a paper prepared for this publication; Paul Benjamin, *The challenge of labour law reform in South Africa* (2007). Paul Benjamin is a well-known labour law specialist in South Africa, and has played a substantial role in the reformulation of labour law in post-apartheid South Africa.

national application, the Industrial Conciliation Act. This Act entrenched racial separation as the dominant feature of South African labour relations for the next five and a half decades. The exclusion of black workers from the mainstream of industrial relations was accompanied by racially based job reservation which prevented African workers from obtaining key qualifications, most notably the 'blasting certificate' which was required to obtain a supervisory position in the mining industry. The combination of racially exclusive labour relations and the retention of job reservation quelled trade union militancy among white workers who benefited from the very considerable wage gap between skilled white workers and the largely black semi-skilled and unskilled workers. The right of African workers to work in urban areas was also regulated by influx control legislation, and dismissal could result in their exclusion from the area in which they had worked. While the Industrial Conciliation Act was revised in 1937 and again in 1956, its institutional architecture remained largely intact until the end of the apartheid era.

The Nationalist Party which came to power in 1948 enforced its apartheid ideology in the labour arena. In 1953 the Native Labour (Settlement of Disputes) Act established plant-based works committees as a means of under-cutting the trade unions that were organizing African workers. The 1956 Industrial Conciliation Act tightened racial separation by excluding all African workers from the statute's operation. The formation of trade unions having both white and coloured (mixed race) members, something which had previously been possible, was prohibited and existing trade unions were obliged to divide on racial grounds if a majority of either their white or coloured members voted in favour of such a restructuring. Racial job reservation was extended from the mining industry to other sectors of the economy, and the Industrial Tribunal was empowered to reserve particular job categories for white workers.

A range of other stratagems were devised to undermine independent unionism among black workers: white unions were encouraged to form apolitical 'parallel' unions for black workers in their sectors, and workplace liaison committees were promoted as an alternative to trade unions. The nominally 'independent' homelands established by the apartheid government from 1960 onwards were given the power to enact labour legislation. This exacerbated the fragmentation of labour law, and separate labour administrations bureaucracies were established in the homelands. In certain instances, these homelands prohibited South African trade unions operating within their areas.

Trade unions organizing African workers faced intense repression in the 1950s and early 1960s, an era that saw the banning of the organizations representing the political aspirations of black South Africans. Independent trade unions were all but obliterated in the early 1960s. However, a wave of strike action in 1973 foreshadowed the re-emergence of an independent trade union movement organizing African workers. The emergent union movement of the 1970s and 1980s became the core of the country's dominant trade union federation, the Congress of South African Trade Unions (COSATU), formed in 1985. The independent trade union movement fought bitter, and at times violent, battles to secure for its members basic rights, such as the deduction of trade union dues, access to employers' premises to conduct union business and the recognition of elected union shop-stewards. These rights were secured in recognition agreements concluded with employers. Many recognition agreements provided for protection against dismissal without just cause, and widespread use was made of independent arbitrators to settle these disputes.

These unions grew rapidly in their membership and by 1977 had an estimated membership of 70,000. In response, the Nationalist government appointed a Commission of Inquiry headed by Professor Nic Wiehahn to investigate labour law reform. The Commission concluded that black workers should be accorded rights of freedom of association and be entitled to participate in voluntary collective bargaining. It therefore recommended that the formal industrial relations system should be opened to all trade unions. At the same time, it proposed the creation of an industrial court with unfair labour practice powers. These changes were enacted into law in 1979 and 1980. At the same time, another Commission of Inquiry recommended the loosening of the influx control system, and its recommendations were implemented in the course of the 1980s.

During the 1980s the trade union movement continued its phenomenal growth rate. The National Union of Mineworkers, established in late 1982, was able to bring out some 350,000 members in a wage strike on 1 September 1987. This meteoric growth occurred in a period when trade unions faced intense State repression.[66]

While the Wiehahn Commission had recommended the introduction of the unfair labour practice as a means of protecting the job security of white workers in the face of the abolition of racial job reservation, the Industrial Court used its unfair labour practice powers to fashion a modern labour law for *all* employees. It articulated an unfair dismissal jurisprudence that required employers to comply with standards of procedural and substantive

---

66 In 1987, agents of the apartheid government blew up the head office of COSATU and its affiliates in Johannesburg. Many trade union officials and office-bearers were detained without trial for lengthy periods under apartheid security legislation.

fairness. This placed unprecedented curbs on the exercise of managerial prerogatives and introduced security of employment on an unprecedented level. The court also evolved the beginnings of an unfair discrimination jurisdiction. The court held that its unfair labour practice powers covered both individual and collective disputes and established rules concerning trade union recognition and the conduct of collective bargaining. The court borrowed liberally from other jurisdictions: for instance, its approach to redundancy owes much to the law in the United Kingdom; its approach to the regulation of collective bargaining drew heavily on that of the United States.[67] Throughout its existence, however, the court was understaffed, leading to lengthy delays in the resolution of disputes.

The 1980s saw extensive legislative activity in the area of labour law. In 1983 the Basic Conditions of Employment Act and Machinery Occupational Safety Act were passed. These replaced sectoral statutes such as the Factories, Machinery and Building Works Act and the Shops and Offices Act which had set minimum conditions of employment and occupational safety. The Wage Board, established under the Wage Act of 1957, continued to provide the basis for minimum wage-fixing.

The court's use of its unfair labour practice powers went beyond the limited tolerance of the Nationalist government, which in 1988 legislated to roll back some of the more progressive aspects of its jurisprudence. COSATU opposed these reforms and its affiliates embarked on a campaign of opposition, which included mass stay-aways. Trade union opposition led organized business to withdraw its earlier support for the legislation. Organized business and labour then negotiated an accord on the content of labour legislation, and in 1990 a tripartite agreement (the Laboria Minute) was concluded in which the government committed itself to withdrawing those aspects of the amendments to which organized business and labour objected. It also committed itself to extending rights of freedom of association and labour protection to groups that were excluded from the labour legislation: farm workers, domestic workers and public servants. The roots of tripartite negotiation that is such a dominant feature of contemporary South African labour relations therefore emerged in the late apartheid period.

---

67 For an informative account of the industrial court's use of comparative jurisprudence, see Clive Thompson, 'Borrowing and bending: The development of South Africa's unfair labour practice jurisprudence', in R. Blanpain and M. Weiss (eds), *The changing face of labour law and industrial relations: Liber amicorum for Clyde W. Summers* (Baden-Baden, Nomos, 1993), pp. 109–32.

Post-apartheid reforms and the Labour Relations Act

In April 1994, South Africa held its first democratic elections, bringing to an end the era of white minority rule. The new Government, headed by President Nelson Mandela of the African National Congress, faced the challenge of a labour market marked by high levels of inequality and unemployment and low levels of training and productivity. The following year, Parliament enacted the Labour Relations Act (LRA) 66 of 1995, which comprehensively restructured the legal and institutional basis of collective labour law and unfair dismissal law and created for the first time a single legal framework for labour relations applicable to all sectors of the economy. Further post-apartheid legislation included the Basic Conditions of Employment Act (BCEA) 1997, the Employment Equity Act 1998 and the Skills Development Act 1998. All these laws were subject to an intensive negotiation process between the Government, organized business and the major trade union federations, conducted under the auspices of the National Economic, Development and Labour Council (NEDLAC), which had been established in 1994. The enactment of this quartet of laws is widely regarded as one of the most substantial legislative achievements of the first years of democracy in South Africa. Both the LRA and BCEA were amended in 2002 to address unintended consequences and align the laws with changing labour market realities. Meanwhile an interim Constitution was adopted in 1993. It was followed in 1996 by the current Constitution, which established a set of constitutional labour rights, including the rights of workers to form and join trade unions, which is accompanied by the equivalent right of employers to form and join employer's organizations. The right to engage in collective bargaining is guaranteed to trade unions, employers' organizations and employers, and there is an express constitutional entrenchment of the right to strike. Unusually, the Constitution provides that 'everyone has the right to fair labour practices'.[68]

The LRA created two new institutions for dispute resolution and adjudication: a government-sponsored, though independent, Commission for Conciliation, Mediation and Arbitration (CCMA) and a specialized system of labour courts with an exclusive labour law jurisdiction. The functions of

---

68 Commentators have queried the appropriateness of including a right to fair labour practices in the Constitution. The term is open-ended and is generally used as a basis for regulating the conduct of employers and employees rather than as a basis for evaluating the constitutional sufficiency of legislation. Politically it was introduced into the interim Constitution as one of a number of provisions aimed at securing the support of the apartheid public service for the transition. (See H. Cheadle in Cheadle, Davis and Haysom, *South African constitutional law: The Bill of Rights* (Durban, Butterworths, 2002), pp. 372–6.)

CCMA include dispute resolution, dispute management, institutional building within the labour arena and the provision of education, training and information to employers and employees and their organizations. While the CCMA is under tripartite management, it is State-funded and there are no charges for referring disputes to it. All disputes about dismissals, trade union organizational rights, the interpretation of collective agreements and certain individual unfair labour practices as well as interest disputes arising from collective bargaining must be referred to conciliation.[69] Unresolved rights disputes may be referred to either arbitration or adjudication by the Labour Court. Arbitration is the route for adjudicating disputes about dismissals for a reason related to the employees' conduct or capacity, as well as disputes concerning trade union organizational rights, the interpretation of collective agreements and certain individual unfair labour practices. Arbitration may be conducted under the auspices of the CCMA, an accredited bargaining council or, by agreement, a private arbitrator appointed in terms of a collective or other agreement. The right to legal representation in arbitration is restricted, and the majority of employees who bring claims are represented by trade union officials or represent themselves. There is no appeal against the arbitrator's decisions although decisions are subject to review by the Labour Court. An arbitration award may be enforced in the same way as an order of the Labour Court. Before this can be done, the award must be certified by the Director of the CCMA. This provision was introduced to prevent fraud. An order for specific performance, such as reinstatement, must be enforced through contempt proceedings in the Labour Court; orders to pay a sum of money are enforced through the attachment and, if necessary sale, of the defaulting party's goods.

The LRA created the Labour Court as a specialist court having national jurisdiction, with the same status as a division of the High Court of South Africa. The court hears, as a court of first instance, cases about dismissals for operational requirements, strike dismissals and other cases in which the dismissal is alleged to have involved discrimination. It also hears cases concerning discrimination, whether or not these involve a dismissal. While parties may apply for more complex cases falling within the CCMA's arbitration jurisdiction to be referred to the Labour Court, this is seldom done in practice.

The review of arbitration awards issued by CCMA commissioners falls within the exclusive jurisdiction of the Labour Court, and the court is able to supervise the manner in which the CCMA fulfils its statutory dispute resolution mandate

---

69 There is a statutory obligation on the CCMA to hold a conciliation meeting within 30 days.

through the exercise of these review powers. The Labour Court has the exclusive jurisdiction to interpret the Labour Relations Act and other labour legislation. This includes an exclusive jurisdiction to interdict unofficial industrial action, as well as other unlawful conduct arising from a strike or lock-out. However, this exclusive jurisdiction of the specialist labour courts does not extend to all employment matters, and claims arising out of employment contracts may be brought in a number of different forums. Decisions of the Labour Court can be appealed before the Labour Appeal Court.

In 2003, the government published (as part of a wide-ranging enactment to restructure the courts) proposals to abolish the specialized labour courts and transfer their jurisdiction to the High Court and Supreme Court of Appeal. These proposals have proved to be highly controversial and, as of 2007, have not been enacted. However, the uncertainty concerning the future of the labour courts has resulted in a situation in which they have been staffed almost exclusively by part-time judges appointed for short terms of office.

The LRA seeks to promote orderly collective bargaining, in particular at the sectoral level. It contains neither a legally enforceable 'duty to bargain' nor a procedure to regulate employer recognition of trade unions. Rather, it seeks to promote collective bargaining by entrenching in the statute key trade union organizational rights and, at the same time, establishing a protected positive right to strike. The core components of trade union recognition are entrenched as statutory rights available to representative unions.

The LRA fosters and rewards representative unionism. In other words, it promotes inter-union cooperation and union amalgamation. Only unions that are sufficiently representative in a workplace are entitled to organizational rights. More specifically, representative unions are entitled to the following rights: collection of union dues by check-off; reasonable access by union officials to employer premises to conduct union business (including recruiting members and conducting ballots); recognition by the employer of elected trade union representatives who may represent employees in grievances and disciplinary procedures and monitor employer compliance with collective agreements and employment legislation; time off for union office-bearers for union business and training; disclosure of information for the purposes of collective bargaining, and collective bargaining rights.

Collective agreements usually concern terms and conditions of employment or any other matter of mutual interest between the parties. The only formality in respect to collective agreements is that they must be reduced to writing. Though they are legally binding on the parties to the agreement and their members, they can also be extended so as to bind non-union members if the party union has majority membership within the workplace. Collective agreements override the provisions of any inconsistent individual employment contracts.

An important feature of the LRA is the possibility of establishing sectoral-level *bargaining councils*. These are statutory bodies that registered unions and employers' organizations may voluntarily and cooperatively establish within a specific economic sector. They represent the centrepiece of the system of bargaining fostered by the LRA. The main powers and functions of bargaining councils include the making and enforcing of collective agreements; preventing and resolving labour disputes; establishing and managing a dispute resolution fund; promoting and establishing training and education schemes; establishing and managing schemes or funds to benefit its parties or members; and making and submitting proposals on policies and laws that affect a sector or area. According to unofficial data, some 50 bargaining councils have been so far established,[70] most notably in the building, clothing, knitting, leather, furniture manufacturing and motor industry sectors. There are also a number of bargaining councils operating in the public sector; these include the Education Labour Relations Council, the Public Health and Welfare Sectoral Bargaining Council and the General Public Service Sectoral Bargaining Council.

Bargaining councils are able to extend party agreements to non-parties by a process of ministerial extension. This remains one of the most controversial aspects of the LRA, particularly because of its perceived negative impact upon small employers who are covered by a bargaining council but do not participate in negotiations. Despite its prominence in labour law debates, the issue of extension of agreements affects a relatively small proportion of the workforce. On the other hand, closed shops and agency shops may be established by collective agreement.[71]

Traditionally, South African law regulated industrial action through a system of 'negative immunities' for employees who embarked on strike action after complying with statutory procedures. Employees were protected against claims of damages or interdicts for breach of contract but not against dismissal. During the 1980s, the Industrial Court granted a measure of protection against strike dismissals although its jurisprudence stressed there was a

---

70 Labour Protect, *Details for bargaining councils in South Africa*. Data published on the website, available at: http://www.labourprotect.co.za.

71 The initial draft bill provided for the operation of agency shop, but did not permit closed shop clauses on the basis that these would violate the freedom of association provisions in the Constitution. The labour movement opposed this approach and succeeded in including the right to closed shop arrangements in the Labour Relations Act as well as securing a constitutional provision stating that 'National legislation may recognize union security arrangements contained in collective agreements' (s. 23(6) of the Constitution).

threshold of tolerance beyond which employers were not required to suffer strike action. As a result, many of the major lawful strikes of the 1980s, such as the mineworkers' strike of 1987, culminated in mass dismissals. This changed, however, under the 1993 interim Constitution, which regulated the political transformation to democracy and entrenched the right of workers to strike as well as employers' recourse to lockout. The right to strike was further entrenched in s. 23 of the Constitution of 1996, as was the employers' reciprocal right to lockout. Now, under the LRA, a procedure has been established to regulate strike action which includes a conciliation period of 30 days, after which, if the dispute remains unresolved, the concerned party must give the other party 48 hours' notice of the strike or lockout.

The LRA extends strong protection to strikes and lockouts that comply with its provisions. First, it guarantees immunity from the reaches of the civil law, that is, they do not constitute an offence or a breach of contract; secondly, an employer is not obliged to remunerate an employee for services not rendered during a strike; and thirdly, employees are protected from dismissal. By contrast, participation in a strike which does not comply with the procedural requirements may constitute a valid reason for dismissal. Also, the prejudiced party can approach the Labour Court for an interdict or order restraining a strike or lockout, and the Labour Court can also order the payment of just and equitable compensation in the circumstances.

Secondary strikes are permitted if the primary strike is staged in compliance with the LRA. The Labour Court may, however, prohibit a secondary strike if the nature and the extent of the secondary strike is disproportionate in relation to its possible direct or indirect effect on the business of the primary employer. There is a right to engage in socioeconomic protest action which is likewise limited by criteria of proportionality.

Regulating working conditions

The Basic Conditions of Employment Act (BCEA) of 1997 guarantees certain minimum standards of employment, such as hours of work and leave entitlements, to all South African workers, while at the same time creating mechanisms to vary the application of these standards through a policy of 'regulated flexibility'. The conditions in the BCEA may be varied by collective and individual agreements as well as by ministerial and sectoral determinations. The Act prescribes the extent to which each of these can limit employee protections. Certain protections in the Act are classified as 'core rights', which cannot be varied by agreement: these include maternity leave and sick leave, prohibition of child labour and forced labour, and the limits on daily and weekly working hours.

The BCEA provides for a working week of 45 hours. It allows 10 hours of overtime to be worked at a premium of 50 per cent, and it contains a schedule setting out the procedures to be adopted to reduce working hours to 40 per week, which emphasizes the role of collective bargaining. The Act introduced two forms of working time flexibility, namely the averaging of hours of work over a period of up to four months and compressed work weeks. It further provides for three weeks of annual leave and an entitlement to three days of family responsibility leave for full-time workers. Maternity leave was transformed from a 12-week period, during which work was prohibited to a four-month period, after which the employee has a right to return to employment. The Act does not provide for maternity pay which is claimed under the Unemployment Insurance Act 2001. The BCEA emphasizes the linkages between conditions of work and health and safety and regulates night-work in a manner consistent with the ILO Night Work Convention, 1990 (No. 171). The Act is supplemented by two codes of good practice: one on the arrangement of working hours and one on the protection of employees during pregnancy. The Minister of Labour has issued a determination varying the application of the Act in respect of overtime, averaging of working hours and family responsibility for businesses employing less than 10 employees.

The Employment Conditions Commission (ECC), established by the BCEA, advises the Minister of Labour on making sectoral determinations to establish minimum wages and conditions of employment for sectors of the economy without widespread collective bargaining. The criteria that the ECC must take into account when advising the Minister include the ability of employers to conduct their businesses successfully, the position of small and medium-sized businesses (SMEs) and new businesses, the alleviation of poverty wage differentials and inequality.

There has been a considerable increase in the reach of minimum wage regulation. Minimum wages have been established for the first time for domestic workers, farm workers, forestry workers and in the taxi sector, increasing the coverage of minimum wages by some 2.5 million workers. Sectoral determinations, which include minimum wages, also continue in sectors such as cleaning, wholesale and retail, private security and clothing and knitting sectors in respect of which wage determinations were previously in force.

Discrimination and unfair dismissal

The Employment Equity Act 1998 seeks to remedy the heritage of racial discrimination inequality that is a defining feature of the South African labour market. The Act prohibits discrimination in the workplace while at the same time requiring larger employers to take affirmative action to ensure the equitable representation of black people, women and the disabled in all occupational categories and levels in the workforce. An employer may justify otherwise discriminatory conduct on the basis that it was required to comply with its affirmative act obligations or because it was an inherent requirement of the job. Discrimination includes harassment. The prohibition of discrimination is enforced by civil litigation instituted by an aggrieved party in the Labour Court. The Act does not criminalize unfair discrimination. The Employment Equity Act must be interpreted in compliance with the ILO Discrimination (Employment and Occupation) Convention, 1958 (No. 111).

The obligation to implement affirmative action measures requires employers to analyse employment policies, practices and procedures, and to consult with trade unions and employees to prepare and implement an employment equity plan. The affirmative action measures that an employer is required to take 'include preferential treatment and numerical goals but exclude quotas'. Compliance with the Employment Equity Act is a requirement for employers to contract with the State to furnish or supply services. The persistence of inordinately high levels of inequality has led to calls for a more stringent approach to be adapted to achieve equality.

The post-apartheid reform of unfair dismissal law sought to protect worker rights while at the same time reducing the costs of disputes and promoting industrial peace by ensuring that dismissal disputes did not trigger strikes. The protection against unfair dismissal developed during the pre-1995 regulation period by the old Industrial Court was codified, while aspects of its jurisprudence that were considered over-formalistic were removed. The Labour Relations Act's core provisions were supplemented by a 'soft law' code of good practice which sought to promote certainty while at the same time allowing for a flexible application of the law by permitting small businesses to comply with less formalized procedures. Dismissal cases must be referred within 30 days, although late referrals may be condoned. The arbitrator's power to award compensation was capped at 12 months (or 24 months if the dismissal was automatically unfair). The Labour Relations Act represented a trade-off: organized labour was attracted by the idea of quick arbitrations without the expense of lawyers and with the real possibility of reinstatement as a remedy. Employers saw their gains as the relatively short referral period, a simplification of their obligations in respect of internal disciplinary inquiries and the cap on compensation award.

Dismissal cases form the vast bulk (in excess of 80 per cent) of the CCMA's case-load, with between 80,000 and 90,000 cases being referred annually. Compared to civil courts, the CCMA has provided swift dispute resolution. On average, the first conciliation meeting is held within 26 days of the dispute being referred[72] and slightly over 50 per cent of cases are settled through conciliation. Arbitrations take an average of seven months (from the date of first referral to the CCMA) to be completed. On average, arbitrations are completed within 47 days of the referral to arbitration, which must be made within 90 days of the failure of the conciliation process. A merged conciliation-arbitration process introduced in 2002, which allows arbitration to start immediately after conciliation, has significantly reduced the period taken to resolve disputes.

Employees are successful in respect of slightly over 60 per cent of dismissal cases in which there is an arbitration award. While the Labour Relations Act provides for reinstatement as the primary remedy for workers dismissed without a valid reason, in practice financial compensation is by far the most common remedy. Only 23 per cent of employees who are found to have been unfairly dismissed receive reinstatement orders. This equates to some 3,000 employees annually. Some 10 per cent of arbitration awards are taken on judicial review in the Labour Court. This significantly delays the conclusion of matters as it takes a further 23 months from the date of the arbitration award for the Labour Court to hear the review application. In about 40 per cent of cases in which an award is made in favour of the employee, the employer does not comply voluntarily and the employee is forced to institute enforcement proceedings to obtain compensation or reinstatement.

Redefining the employment relationship

Since 1994, both unemployment and informal employment have increased significantly within the South African labour market. Figures for 2002 show that in South Africa, out of a total economically active population of 20.3 million people, 6.6 million were in full-time employment, 3.1 million were in atypical employment,[73] 2.2 million in informal work and 8.4 million were unemployed.[74] As a result, a very significant proportion of the workforce earns its livelihood through insecure and unprotected work. There has been a rise in self-employment in both the formal and the informal sector in the last 10 years. In March 2003 the unemployment rate peaked at 32 per cent (5.1

---

72 CCMA, *Annual Report 2005–2006* (Johannesburg, 2006), p. 15. Available at: http://www.ccma.org.za.

73 This includes temporary, part-time and outsourced work as well as approximately 1 million domestic workers.

74 E. Webster and K. von Holdt, 'Work restructuring and the crisis of social reproduction: A southern perspective', in E. Webster and K. von Holdt (eds), *Beyond the apartheid workplace: Studies in transition* (Durban, University of KwaZulu-Natal Press, 2005).

million people). This equates to 42.5 per cent (8.4 million people) in terms of the expanded definition of unemployment.[75] Improved economic growth has subsequently seen the unemployment rate drop to 26.2 per cent in September 2004. The rate of unemployment continues to be racially skewed, being in excess of 30 per cent for black persons and excess of 35 per cent for black women, while for whites it remains in the order of 5 per cent. Youth unemployment is particularly severe, with 70 per cent of the unemployed being under the age of 35.

Changes in the labour market have taken the form of outsourcing, with an exponential increase in the incidence of temporary employment services (TESs). There has been a significant rise in temporary work. In 2006, over 800,000 workers were engaged on temporary assignments on any given day, and the number of registered temporary employment agencies has risen from 1,076 in 2000 to 3,140 in 2006. The wages of workers in externalized employment are significantly lower than those employed in the firms whom they supply with goods or services. The LRA and BCEA regulate the placement of employees through TESs by providing that the TES is the employer and making the client jointly liable for any breaches of labour law. However, there is no temporal limit on the period for which a worker may be supplied by a TES to a client, and many firms have permanently outsourced work through arrangements of this type.

The rise of informal employment has provoked a debate as to whether the traditional definition of an employee included in all four labour statutes was adequate to ensure protection for an increasingly informalized workforce.[76] In 2002 the LRA and BCEA were amended to introduce a rebuttable presumption of employment into the principal labour statutes.[77] The presence of any one of seven factors in an employment relationship brings the presumption into operation. These factors include those traditionally used by the courts to determine the existence of a contract of employment (control, supervision) as

---

75 The official rate of unemployment is calculated on the basis of those persons who are unemployed who: (a) did not work during the seven days prior to being interviewed; (b) want to work and are available to start work within a week of the interview; (c) and have taken active steps to look for work or start some form of self-employment in the four weeks prior to the interview. The expanded definition of unemployment excludes factor (c) and therefore includes 'discouraged' work-seekers who are excluded from the narrower definition.

76 For a fuller account see Paul Benjamin, 'Beyond the boundaries: Prospects for expanding labour market regulation in South Africa', in G. Davidov and B. Langille (eds), pp. 181–204.

77 The presumption is found in s. 200A of the Labour Relations Act 66 of 1995 and s. 83A of the Basic Conditions of Employment Act 75 of 1997.

well as one ('economic dependence') which had not been part of South African law and one (being part of the employer's organization) which had previously been rejected by the courts. These amendments were justified in government policy documents on the basis that they would assist vulnerable workers to assert their rights as employees. Significantly, the presumption applies irrespective of the form of the employment relationship, emphasizing that the court must inquire into the realities of an employment relationship rather than being content to scrutinize the wording of the contract. Once the employee satisfies the presumption's relatively low hurdle of establishing that one of the factors is present, the employer must produce evidence about the nature of the employment relationship to show that the claimant is not an employee.

A model for southern Africa

South Africa's post-apartheid labour regime has begun to have a profound impact on labour law within the southern African region. The South African Development Community (SADC)[78] adopted the Charter of Fundamental Social Rights of Workers in 2003, which emphasizes the improvement and harmonization of workers' protection and rights with the region and requires member States to ratify and implement the eight ILO fundamental Conventions. A SADC Labour Relations Conference held in October 1999 in Johannesburg adopted a wide-ranging communiqué dealing with minimum standards, collective bargaining, dispute prevention and dispute resolution. The Conference noted that action should be taken at country level to improve the effectiveness of existing systems of dispute prevention and dispute resolution.

The institutional architecture of labour law in democratic South Africa's regime has had a significant impact on labour law reforms in the southern African region, particularly in the area of dispute resolution. Lesotho (2000), Swaziland (2000), Botswana (2004), the United Republic of Tanzania (2004) and Namibia (2007) have all enacted laws to establish specialist dispute resolution institutions that promote the role of mediation and arbitration as the

---

78 The South African Development Community was established in 1980 as a loose alliance of nine states in southern Africa with the main aim of coordinating development projects in order to lessen economic dependence on South Africa (then under apartheid). Its current members are Angola, Botswana, the Democratic Republic of Congo, Lesotho, Madagascar, Malawi, Mauritius, Mozambique, Namibia, South Africa, Swaziland, United Republic of Tanzania, Zambia and Zimbabwe.

primary mechanism for the prevention and settlement of labour disputes.[79] While the model of the CCMA has played a prominent role in these reform processes, the variety of institutions that have been adopted show the extent to which the South African experience has been adapted to the circumstances of the different countries within the region. Lesotho and Swaziland follow the South African model of creating independent dispute resolution bodies governed by tripartite boards. The Tanzanian Commission for Mediation and Arbitration has the status of an independent government department, and in Namibia dispute resolution is to be located under the control of the Labour Commissioner. In Botswana these functions are performed by a panel of mediators and arbitrators that is appointed by the Minister and chaired by the Commissioner. A number of these countries follow the South African approach of placing an obligation on the agency to conciliate disputes referred to it within 30 days. The arbitrator's decisions are not subject to appeal in Lesotho but may be reviewed by the Labour Court. In addition, there has been a significant move towards establishing specialist labour courts, including labour appeal courts, as the final arbiters in labour law matters.[80] Recently the new dispute resolution institutions in southern Africa have come together in a programme supported by the ILO to establish the Southern African Dispute Resolution Forum. The Forum will promote cooperation on training and technology transfer and stimulate debate on how to entrench and sustain best practice in dispute resolution in the southern African region.

South African influence can also be seen in the approach to drafting legislation. Those countries which have adopted new Labour Acts (as opposed to amending existing laws) have tended to emulate the South African approach of entrenching expressly the basic rights of employers and employees to freedom of association. This is true of both Namibia's 2007 legislation and the United Republic of Tanzania's 2004 enactment. Swaziland has followed the South African example of developing an unfair dismissal policy that draws on Convention No. 158 of 1982 and places the same caps on compensation for unfair dismissal (24 months if the dismissal is automatically unfair and 12 months in other cases) as South Africa. The South African approach of supplementing the statute with 'soft law' codes of good practice has been adopted in Lesotho, Namibia and the United Republic of Tanzania. Lesotho, for instance, published in 2003 an extensive code of good practice dealing with trade union recognition and collective bargaining. The code contains a model

---

79 Mozambique is in the process of enacting similar reforms.
80 Lesotho established a Labour Appeal Court in 2000.

recognition agreement. Significantly, none of the SADC countries have adopted the approach of eschewing a legally enforceable duty to bargain.

South Africa's legislative response to the increasing informalization of work has also begun to influence other SADC countries. The United Republic of Tanzania's Employment and Labour Relations Act 2004 contains, for example, a presumption of employment modelled on the provision introduced by South Africa in 2002.

Chapter 7

Final remarks

The quest for a fair globalization that creates opportunities for all will dominate international affairs in the next decade. Whether seen from the angle of social and political stability and security concerns or through the eyes of the many people for whom the benefits of globalization are today a mirage, real concerns about fairness and opportunities cannot be washed away.[1]

The question is how global processes can be better regulated in order to deliver both economic growth and social justice embedded in the rule of law... [R]ules and practices governing productive work are as essential as property rights for the functioning of the market economy. . . [Also], labour laws also have an important moral dimension – the idea embodied in the ILO Constitution, that 'labour is not a commodity'. They thus provide an excellent case study of the possibilities for creating a legal framework within which economic integration in a globalized market economy can be reconciled with the ideals of social justice.[2]

Every period of history entails changes, and these bring with them their quotas of promises and hopes, of risks and anxieties, of challenges and answers. The beginning of the twenty-first century is no exception. If we let ourselves be overtaken by pessimism, we cannot help but believe that in the field of labour law the quota of risks and anxieties is greater today than that of promises and hopes, and the proportion of challenges is greater than that of answers.

Nevertheless, with a vision that is not only more optimistic but also more realistic, we should also acknowledge that at the turn of the twentieth century labour law has met with some degree of success; first of all, it has gained ground for freedom of association, mainly in the old communist countries, but also in many other parts of the world where democracy has made a comeback.

---

1 ILO, *A fair globalization: The role of the ILO*, Report of the Director-General on the World Commission on the Social Dimension of Globalization, International Labour Conference, 92nd Session, Geneva, 22004.
2 Bob Hepple, *Labour laws in the context of globalization*, paper prepared for this publication, 2007.

In the same way, there has been progress on extending the scope of the employment relationship and the liability of the employer within the framework of a productive decentralization strategy. One of the most worthwhile achievements in this respect is that an increasing number of governments have taken steps to afford protection to workers who would otherwise be either left out of the scope of labour law or be legally dependent on employers who do not have decision-making authority in terms of their workers' job security and working and living conditions. This is very likely because governments now seem to have realized that beyond the social and labour issues that are at stake, fair regulation is of great importance for the overall governance of the labour market.

No less important is an acknowledgement that the relationship between international trade and labour law is today a crucial issue. We have seen in this book that this debate has begun in earnest, and there seems to be widespread recognition that global competition should not be to the detriment of workers' rights and overall living and employment conditions. We have reached the point now where we need to agree on the appropriate strategies and tools to tackle this problem rather than to discuss whether international trade and labour rights are separate issues which should not be addressed together.

If there is a field where progress has unquestionably been made, it is in the recognition of the fundamental rights of the worker at the workplace. Over many decades the common wisdom was that workers' subordination to the employer meant that they had to give up a number of fundamental rights and freedoms when these were likely to conflict with the employer's rights and prerogatives. Today this presumption has been all but completely reversed in a great number of countries, as far-reaching progress has been made in areas such as the prohibition of discrimination on an expanded number of grounds, protection of the worker's privacy and freedom of thought and of expression. Thus the rule is now that these rights are to be placed *above* management rights; while exceptions are obviously to be admitted, they must be objectively justified by a legitimate aim, and the means of achieving that aim must be appropriate and necessary.

Some years ago the eminent Brazilian labour law professor Wagner Giglio gave a lecture on the future of labour law. His message could be summarized in two ideas: first, that the future is uncertain, so that he was not able to forecast the direction labour law would take; secondly, to the extent that work is performed by human beings, there will always be a need for labour laws to exist.

There is certainly no doubt that the social, political, technological, economic and organizational contexts in which labour law was based in the past century are today undergoing deep and far-reaching mutation. Yet this fact should not lead to the conclusion that the solutions and protection that labour laws offered to workers in the twentieth century are no longer valid. Dependent work continues to exist and the vulnerability of the worker, which provided the *raison d'être* for labour law, continues to be an unchallenged fact. In short, the essence of the problems that gave birth to labour law is still there. It is simply the case that today these problems have become more complex. The question now consists in how to render labour law more effective so that it can continue to play its proper role to the benefit of all those workers who need protection.

In other words, the answer to those who argue that labour law is purely a product of the twentieth century, and is rather dated today, is that the great challenge of labour law now is to how respond to the problems of the twenty-first century in order to avoid a return to the social injustices of the nineteenth.

Bibliography

Alcock, A. 1971. *History of the International Labour Organization* (London, Macmillan).

Anderson, G. 2006. *Trade liberalization and labour law: New Zealand national report*, paper submitted to the XVIIIth World Congress of the International Society for Labour and Social Security Law, Paris, 5–8 Sept. (Geneva, International Society for Labour and Social Security Law (ISLSSL)).

Ashwin, S.; Clarke, S. 2003. *Russian trade unions and industrial relations in transition* (New York, Palgrave Macmillan).

Auer, P.; Cazes, S. 2003. *Employment stability in an age of flexibility: Evidence from industrialized countries* (Geneva, International Labour Organization (ILO)).

—; Berg, J.; Coulibaly, I. 2005. 'Is a stable workforce good for productivity?', in *International Labour Review*, Vol. 144, No. 3, pp. 319–43.

Benjamin, P. 2006. 'Beyond "lean" social democracy: Labour law and the challenge of social protection', in *Transformation: Critical Perspectives on Southern Africa*, Vol. 60, pp. 32–57.

—. 2006b. 'Beyond the boundaries: Prospects for expanding labour market regulation in South Africa', in G. Davidov and B. Langille (eds), *Boundaries and frontiers of labour law: Goals and means in the regulation of work* (Oxford, Hart Publishing), pp. 181–204.

—. 2007. *The challenge of labour law reform in South Africa*, unpublished paper prepared for this publication.

Béraud, J.-M. 2003. *Etude préalable à l'adoption d'un Acte uniforme en Droit du Travail dans le cadre de l'Organisation pour l'Harmonisation en Afrique du Droit des Affaires (OHADA)*, IFP/Dialogue Document No. 2 (Geneva, ILO).

Bronstein, A.S. 1991. 'Temporary work in Western Europe: Threat or complement to permanent employment?', in *International Labour Review*, Vol. 130, No. 3, pp. 291–310.

—. 1995. 'Societal change and industrial relations in Latin America: Trends and prospects', in *International Labour Review*, Vol. 134, No. 2, pp. 163–86.

—. 1997. 'Labour law reform in Latin America: Between state protection and flexibility', in *International Labour Review*, Vol. 136, No. 1, pp. 5–26.

di Caprio, A. 2004. 'Are labor provisions protectionist?: Evidence from nine labor-augmented US trade arrangements', in *Comparative Labor Law & Policy Journal*, Vol. 26, No. 1, pp. 1–34.

Castells, M. 1966. *The information age: Economy, society and culture: The rise of the network society*, Vol. 1 (Oxford, Blackwell Publishers).

Cheadle, H.; Davis, D.; Haysom, N. 2002. *South African constitutional law: The Bill of Rights* (Durban, Butterworths).

Commission for Conciliation, Mediation and Arbitration (CCMA). 2006. *Annual Report 2005–2006* (Johannesburg).

Compa, L. 2002. 'Pursuing international labour rights in U.S. courts: New uses for old tools', in *Relations Industrielles/Industrial Relations*, Vol. 57, No. 1, pp. 48–76.

Cooney, S. 2007. *Trends in labour law in Asia and the Pacific*, unpublished paper prepared for this publication.

Cornish, M. 2007. *Securing sustainable human rights justice for workers*, unpublished paper prepared for this publication.

—; Simand, H. 1992. 'Religious accommodation in the workplace', in *Canadian Labour Law Journal*, Vol. 1, Nos 1–2, pp. 166–85.

Department of Enterprise, Trade and Employment, Programme for Prosperity and Fairness, Employment Status Group. 2001. *Code of practice for determining employment or self-employment status of individuals* (Dublin). Available at: http://www.entemp.ie [16 Nov. 2008].

Doumbia-Henry, C.; Gravel, E. 2006. 'Free trade agreements and labour rights: Recent developments', in *International Labour Review*, Vol. 145, No. 3, pp. 185–206.

Durkheim, E. 1967. *De la division du travail social*, 8e édition (Paris, Les Presses universitaires de France). Translated as *The division of labour in society* (New York, Macmillan, 1933).

European Commission (EC). 1976. 'Council Directive 76/207/EEC of 9 February 1976 on the implementation of the principle of equal treatment for men and women as regards access to employment, vocational training and promotion, and working conditions', *Official Journal of the European Union*, L 039 (Feb.).

—. 1998. *Transformation of labour and future of labour law in Europe*, final report (Luxembourg).

—. 2000a. 'Council Directive 2000/43/EC of 29 June 2000, implementing the principle of equal treatment between persons irrespective of racial or ethnic origin', *Official Journal of the European Union*, L 180/22 (July).

—. 2000b. 'Council Directive 2000/78/EC of 27 November 2000, establishing a general framework for equal treatment in employment and occupation', *Official Journal of the European Union*, L 303/16 (Dec.).

—. 2000c. 'Charter of Fundamental Rights of the European Union', *Official Journal of the European Communities*, C 364/01.

—. 2002. *Framework agreement on telework* (Brussels). Available at: http://www.ec.europa.eu [21 Nov. 2008].

—. 2003. *User's guide to the European Union's scheme of Generalized Tariff Preferences* (Luxembourg).

—. 2004. *Framework agreement on work-related stress* (Brussels). Available at: http://www.ec.europa.eu [21 Nov. 2008].

—. 2006a. *Modernising labour law to meet the challenges of the 21st century*, Green Paper, COM (2006) 708 final (Luxembourg).

—. 2006b. *Implementing the partnership for growth and jobs: Making Europe a pole of excellence on corporate social responsibility*, Communication from the Commission, COM (2006) 0136 final (Luxembourg).

—. 2006c. 'Directive 2006/54/EC of the European Parliament and of the Council of 5 July 2006, on the implementation of the principle of equal opportunities and equal treatment of men and women in matters of employment and occupation (recast)', *Official Journal of the European Union*, L 204/23 (July).

—. 2007a. *Towards common principles of flexicurity: More and better jobs through flexibility and security*, Communication from the Commission to the European Parliament, the Council, the European Economic and Social Committee and the Committee of the Regions, COM (2007) 359 final. Available at: http://www.ec.europa.eu [21 Nov. 2008].

—. 2007b. *Framework agreement on harassment and violence at work* (Brussels). Available at: http://www.ec.europa.eu [21 Nov. 2008].

European Foundation for the Improvement of Living and Working Conditions (Eurofound). 'Economically Dependent Workers', in *European Industrial Relations Dictionary* (Dublin).

—. 2002a. ' "Economically dependent workers", employment law and industrial relations', in *European Industrial Relations Observatory (EIRO) Online* database (Dublin). Available at: http://www.eurofound.europa.eu/eiro [14 Nov. 2008].

—. 2002b. 'Industrial relations in the candidate countries', in *EIROnline* database (Dublin). Available at: http://www.eurofound.europa.eu/eiro [21 Nov. 2008].

—. 2007a. *Varieties of flexicurity: Reflections on key elements of flexibility and security*, Background paper (Dublin).

—. 2007b. *Industrial relations development in Europe 2006* (Luxembourg).

—. 'Integrazione Guadagni (CGI)', in *EMIRE* database. Available at: http://www.eurofound.eu.eu/emire [14 Nov. 2008].

Faraday, F.; Denike, M.; Stephenson, K. (eds). 2006. *Making equality rights real* (Toronto, Irwin Press).

Fourastié, J. 1979. *Les Trente Glorieuses* (Paris, les Editions Fayard).

Goldberg, M. 2001. 'Privacy of the employee as a human right', in R. Blanpain and R. Ben-Israel (eds), *Labour law, human rights and social justice* (The Hague, Kluwer Law International), pp. 163–85.

Hanami, T. 2002. 'Introductory remarks', in R. Blanpain (ed.), *On-line rights for employees in the Information Society: Use and monitoring of e-mail and internet at work*, Bulletin of Comparative Labour Relations Series No. 40 (The Hague, Kluwer Law International), pp. xv–xvii.

Hepple, B. 2005. *Labour laws and global trade* (Oxford, Hart Publishing).

—. 2007. *Labour laws in the context of globalization*, unpublished paper prepared for this publication.

Hendrickx, F. 2002. 'Belgian law', in R. Blanpain (ed.), *On-line rights for employees in the Information Society: Use and monitoring of e-mail and internet at work*, pp. 65–93

Hervey, T.K. 2002. *EC law on justifications for sex discrimination in working life*, Proceedings of the VII European Congress of Labour Law of the International Society for Labour and Social Security Law, Stockholm, 4–6 Sept. (Geneva, ISLSSL).

Hodges, J. 2004. *Guidelines on addressing HIV/AIDS in the workplace through employment and labour law*, Programme on Social Dialogue, Labour Law and Labour Administration Paper No. 3 (Geneva, ILO).

Homan, T.C.B. 2002. 'Dutch law', in R. Blanpain (ed.): *On-line rights for employees in the Information Society: Use and monitoring of e-mail and internet at work*, pp. 95–124.

IKEA. 2005. *IWAY Standard: Minimum requirements for environment, social and working conditions and wooden merchandise when purchasing home furnished products* (Leiden).

International Confederation of Free Trade Unions (ICFTU). 2005. *Comments by ICFTU/Global Unions on the World Bank's* Business in 2005: 'Hiring and Firing of Workers' (Washington, DC).

International Labour Organization (ILO). *Ratifications of the Fundamental human rights Conventions by country*, ILOLEX database (Geneva). Available at: http://www.ilo.org [21 Nov. 2008].

—. 1973. *Report of the Committee of Experts on the Application of Conventions and Recommendations*, Report III (Part 4A), International Labour Conference, 58th Session, Geneva, 1973 (Geneva).

—. 1974. *Report of the Committee of Experts on the Application of Conventions and Recommendations*, Report III (Part 4A), International Labour Conference, 59th Session, Geneva, 1974 (Geneva).

—. 1976. *Report of the Committee of Experts on the Application of Conventions and Recommendations*, Report III (Part 4A), International Labour Conference, 61st Session, Geneva, 1976 (Geneva).

—. 1986. *Equal remuneration, General Survey of the Committee of Experts on the Application of Conventions and Recommendations on the Equal Pay Convention, 1951 (No. 100) and Recommendation, 1951 (No. 90)*, Report III (Part 6B), International Labour Conference, 72nd Session, Geneva, 1986 (Geneva).

—. 1991. *The dilemma of the informal sector*, Report of the Director-General, International Labour Conference, 78th Session, Geneva, 1991 (Geneva).

—. 1993. *Workers with family responsibilities, General Survey of the Committee of Experts on Convention (No. 156) and Recommendation (No. 165)*, Report III (Part 4B), International Labour Conference, 80th Session, Geneva, 1993 (Geneva).

—. 1994. *Defending values, promoting change: Social justice in a global economy*, Report of the Director-General (Part 1), International Labour Conference, 81st Session, Geneva, 1994 (Geneva).

—. 1996a. *The strengthening of the ILO's supervisory system*, Governing Body, 267th Session, Geneva, Nov. (Geneva), GB.267/LILS/5.

—. 1996b. *Reports of the Committee on Legal Issues and International Labour Standards*, Governing Body, 267th Session, Geneva, Nov. (Geneva), GB.267/9/2.

—. 1996c. *Equality in employment and occupation, General Survey by the Committee of Experts on the Application of Conventions and Recommendations*, Report III (Part 4B), International Labour Conference, 83rd Session, Geneva, 1996 (Geneva).

—. 1997. *ILO standard setting and globalization*, Report of the Director-General, International Labour Conference, 85th Session, Geneva, 1997 (Geneva).

—. 1998. *Report of the Committee on the Declaration of Principles*, International Labour Conference, 86th Session, Geneva, 1998 (Geneva).

—. 2000a. *The employment relationship: Scope*, Basic technical document, Meeting of Experts on Workers in Situation Needing Protection, Geneva, 15–19 May (Geneva).

—. 2000b. *Termination of Employment Digest* (Geneva).

—. 2001a. *Night work of women in industry: General Survey of the Committee of Experts on the Application of Conventions and Recommendations on Conventions Nos 4, 41, 89 (and its protocol No. 98)*, Report III (Part 4B), International Labour Conference, 89th Session, Geneva, 2001 (Geneva).

—. 2001b. *HIV/AIDS and the world of work: ILO code of practice on* (Geneva).

—. 2002a. *Decent work and the informal economy*, Report VI, International Labour Conference, 90th Session, Geneva, 2002 (Geneva).

—. 2002b. *Promoting gender equality: A resource kit for trade unions, Booklet 3: The issues and guidelines for gender equality bargaining* (Geneva).

—. 2003a. *Report of the Committee on the Employment Relationship*, Provisional Record No. 21, International Labour Conference, 91st Session, Geneva, 2003 (Geneva).

—. 2003b. *The scope of employment relationship*, Report V, International Labour Conference, 91st Session, Geneva, 2003 (Geneva).

—. 2004a. *Labour overview of Latin America and the Caribbean, 2004* (Lima).

—. 2004b. *Achieving equal employment opportunities for people with disabilities through legislation: Guidelines* (Geneva).

—. 2004c. *A fair globalization: The role of the ILO*, Report of the Director-General on the World Commission on the Social Dimension of Globalization, International Labour Conference, 92nd Session, Geneva, 2004 (Geneva).

—. 2006a. *The employment relationship*, Report V (Part 1), International Labour Conference, 95th Session, Geneva, 2006 (Geneva).

—. 2006b. *Seventeenth synthesis report on working conditions in Cambodia's garment sector*, Better Factories Cambodia Synthesis Report (Phnom Penh).

—. 2007a. *The United Nations and reform: Developments in the multilateral system*, Governing Body, 300th Session, Geneva, Nov. (Geneva), GB.300/4/1.

—. 2007b. *Equality at work: Tackling the challenges: Global Report under the follow-up to the ILO Declaration on Fundamental Principles and Rights at Work*, Report of the Director-General, International Labour Conference, 96th Session, Geneva, 2007 (Geneva).

—. 2007c. *Report of the Committee on the Application of Standards*, Provisional Record No. 22, International Labour Conference, 96th Session, Geneva, 2007 (Geneva).

Japan Institute for Labour Policy and Training (JILPT). 2006. *Labor situation in Japan and analysis: General overview 2006/2007* (Tokyo). Available at: http://www.jil.go.jp [22 Nov. 2008].

Kollonay Lehoczky, C. 'Ways and effects of deconstructing protection in the post-socialist new Member States – Based on Hungarian experience', in G. Davidov and B. Langille (eds), pp. 221–224.

Labour Protect. *Details for bargaining councils in South Africa*, published on the website. Available at: http://www.labourprotect.co.za [22 Nov. 2008].

Locke, R.; Kochan, T.; Romis, M.; Qin, F. 2007. 'Beyond corporate codes of conduct: Work organization and labour standards at Nike's suppliers', in *International Labour Review*, Vol. 146, No. 1–2, pp. 21–40.

de Luca Tamajo, R.; Perulli, A. 2006. *Labour law (in its individual and collective dimensions) and productive decentralization (outsourcing of work and contracting of labour)*, Report to the XVIII World Congress of the International Society for Labour and Social Security Law, Paris, 5–8 Sept. (Geneva, ISLSSL).

Maldonado, C. 1995. 'The informal sector: Legalization or laissez-faire?' in *International Labour Review*, Vol. 134, No. 6, pp. 705–728.

Mandeville, B. 1924. *The fable of the bees: Or private vices, publick benefits* (Oxford, Clarendon).

McCann, D. 2005. *Sexual harassment at work: National and international responses*, Conditions of Work and Employment Series No. 2 (Geneva, ILO).

Murcia, J.G. 'The European Commission's Green Paper on labour law', in *International Labour Review*, Vol. 146, No. 1–2, pp. 109–14.

Organisation for Economic Co-operation and Development (OECD). 1990. *Employment Outlook 1990* (Paris).

—. 2004. *Employment Outlook 2004* (Paris).

—. 2005. *Economic survey of Australia 2004*, Policy brief (Paris). Available at: http://www.oecd.org [14 Nov. 2008].

Parsons, T. 1937. *The structure of social action* (New York, McGraw-Hill).

Poggi, G. 1978. *La vicenda dello stato moderno, profilo sociologico* (Bologna, Il Mulino).

Rivero Lamas, J.; de Val Tena, A.L. (eds). 2003. *Descentralización productiva y responsabilidades de la empresa: el 'outsourcing'* (Navarra, Aranzadi).

Robinson, D.; Guy, S.; Tucker, C. 2006. *Trade liberalization and labour law: Australian national report*, paper submitted to the XVIIIth World Congress of the International Society for Labour and Social Security Law, Paris, 5–8 Sept. (Geneva, ISLSSL).

Rosenvallon, P. 1981. *Crise de l'Etat providence* (Paris, Editions du Seuil).

Samson, K. 2004. 'The "Berufsverbot" problem revisited – Views from Geneva and Strasbourg', in J.-C. Javillier and B. Gernigon (eds), *Les normes internationales du travail: un patrimoine pour l'avenir, mélanges en l'honneur de Nicolas Valticos* (Geneva, ILO), pp. 21–46.

Seifert, A.; Funken-Hötzel, E. 2004. 'Wrongful dismissals in the Federal Republic of Germany', in *Comparative Labor Law and Policy Journal*, Vol. 25, No. 4, pp. 487–517.

Sennett, R. 2006. *The culture of the new capitalism* (New Haven, CO, Yale University Press).

Servais, J.-M. 1994. 'Secteur informel: un avenir pour le droit du travail', in *Revue de la faculté de droit de Liège*, Vol. 3, pp. 661–86.

—. 2005. *International labour law* (The Hague, Kluwer Law International).

Spain, Govt. of, Ministry of Labour. 2000. 'Descentralización productiva y nuevas formas organizativas del trabajo', in *Proceedings of the Tenth National Congress of the Spanish Society of Labour Law* (Madrid).

Stone, K.V.W. 2006a. 'Rethinking labour law: Employment protection for boundaryless workers', in G. Davidov and B. Langille (eds), pp. 155–80.

—. 2006b. *Legal protections for workers in atypical employment relationships in the United States*, Report to the XVIIIth World Congress of the International Society for Labour and Social Security Law, Paris, 5–8 Sept. (Geneva, ISLSSL).

Sugeno, K. 2004. 'Birth of the labor tribunal system in Japan: A synthesis of labour law reform and judicial reform', in *Comparative Labor Law and Policy Journal*, Vol. 25, No. 4, pp. 519–33.

Supiot, A. 2005. 'Le droit du travail bradé dans le "marché des normes"', in *Droit Social*, No. 12, pp. 1087–96.

Suzuki, H. 2005. 'L'individu, le collectif et l'Etat dans les pays d'Asie du Nord-Est', in I. Dugareilh (ed.), *Mondialisation, travail et droits fondamentaux* (Paris, LGDJ), pp. 139–52.

Tajgman, D. 1995. *Employment relations and labour law in the Dar-es-Salaam informal sector*, unpublished paper (Harare, ILO).

Taylor, F.W. 2004a. *Shop management* (Whitefish, MT, Kessinger Publishing).

—. 2004b. *The principles of scientific management* (Whitefish, MT, Kessinger Publishing).

Thompson, C. 1993. 'Borrowing and bending: The development of South Africa's unfair labour practice jurisprudence', in R. Blanpain and M. Weiss (eds), *The changing face of labour law and industrial relations: Liber amicorum for Clyde W. Summers* (Baden-Baden, Nomos), pp. 109–32.

Trebilcock, A. 2006. 'Using development approaches to address the challenge of the informal economy for labour law', in G. Davidov and B. Langille (eds), pp. 63–86.

Tucker, E. 'Great expectations defeated?: The trajectory of collective bargaining regimes in Canada and the United States post-NAFTA', in *Comparative Labor Law & Policy Journal*, Vol. 26, No. 1, pp. 97–150.

U.S., Govt. of, Dept. of Labor. 2008. *The Employee Polygraph Protection Act (EPPA)* (Washington, D.C.). Available at: http://www.dol.gov [20 Nov. 2008].

—, Equal Employment Opportunity Commission (EEOC). 2007. 'Caesar's Palace to pay $850,000 for sexual harassment and retaliation', Press Release, 20 Aug. Available at: http://www.eeoc.gov [20 Nov. 2008].

—, —. 2008. 'Lockheed Martin to pay $2.5 million to settle racial harassment lawsuit', Press release. Jan. 2. Available at: http://www.eeoc.gov [20 Nov. 2008].

Valdés Dal-Ré, F. 2003. *Fundamental rights of the worker*, General Report submitted to the XVII World Congress of the International Society for Labour and Social Security Law, Montevideo, 2–5 Sept. (Geneva, ISLSSL).

Valticos, N. 1983. *Droit international du travail*, Vol. 8 of G.H. Camerlynck (ed.), *Traité de droit du travail* (Paris, Dalloz).

Vega Ruiz, M. 2004. *Legal considerations on labor regulations in free trade agreements in the Americas* (Lima, Cuadernos de Integración Andina).

Weber, A. 2006. *Rethinking corporate social responsibility: Bridging the divide between labour and trade law*, unpublished paper (Toronto, Osgoode Hall Law School).

Weber, M. 1905. *Die protestantische Ethik und der 'Geist' des Kapitalismus* (Gutersloh); English translation: Parsons, T. 1930. *The protestant ethic and the spirit of capitalism* (London, Allen & Unwin).

Webster, E.; von Holdt, K. 2005. 'Work restructuring and the crisis of social reproduction: A southern perspective', in E. Webster and K. von Holdt (eds), *Beyond the apartheid workplace: Studies in transition* (Durban, University of KwaZulu-Natal Press), pp. 3–38.

Weiss, M. 2005. 'The interface between constitution and labour law in Germany', in *Comparative Labor Law and Policy Journal*, Vol. 26, No. 2, p. 181–98.

Index

Lightning Source UK Ltd.
Milton Keynes UK
UKOW06f0806291117
313516UK00004B/12/P